Writing and Language Handbook

Table of Contents

Introducing Benchmark Advance
Common Core Writing and Language Handbook

The Common Core Writing and Language Handbook in Benchmark Advance ensures that teachers have explicit instruction to address all of the writing and language standards outlined in the Common Core ELA State Standards. Within this volume, you will find:

• A complete opinion writing unit of study with five weeks of process writing mini-lessons;

• Explicit writing to sources mini-lessons covering opinion, informative/explanatory, and narrative writing; and

• Language mini-lessons for every Grade 4 language standard.

Opinion Unit of Study

Appendix A of the Common Core ELA State Standards outlines three key text types that students should be able to write proficiently. At Grades K–5, the standards call upon students to write well-formulated opinion texts (W.1), informative/explanatory texts (W.2), and narrative texts (W.3). The opinion writing standard prepares students for the argumentative writing they will be required to do beginning in Grade 6. The opinion unit in this volume provides step-by-step mini-lessons students need to state clear opinions and support them with thoughtful reasons and evidence. The instruction reflects the Common Core's emphasis on argument writing as opposed to persuasion. As stated in Appendix A:

> When writing to persuade, writers employ a variety of persuasive strategies. One common strategy is an appeal to the credibility, character, or authority of the writer (or speaker). When writers establish that they are knowledgeable and trustworthy, audiences are more likely to believe what they say. Another is an appeal to the audience's self-interest, sense of identity, or emotions, any of which can sway an audience. A logical argument, on the other hand, convinces the audience because of the perceived merit and reasonableness of the claims and proofs offered rather than either the emotions the writing evokes in the audience or the character or credentials of the writer. The standards place special emphasis on writing logical arguments as a particularly important form of college- and career-ready writing.

In this unit, students read source texts, formulate opinions based on a prompt, state reasons for their opinion, and support their reasons with evidence directly from the text. They do not use techniques of persuasive writing. A mentor opinion writing text for this unit supports students with models of how opinions should be structured. Multiple copies allow collaborative groups to analyze these texts during the mini-lessons.

Writing to Sources

Writing standard W.4.8 in the Common Core states:

> Recall relevant information from experiences or gather relevant information from print and digital sources; take notes and categorize information, and provide a list of sources.

The mini-lessons in this section break down the process of writing to sources so that students have the opportunity to internalize the steps and practice the type of writing that they will be assessed on. The mini-lessons model and guide students to:

• Analyze a writing to source prompt;

• Read one or more source texts to find and annotate textual evidence;

• Draft a well-crafted response to the prompt; and

• Revise and edit the response.

Students have opportunities to write to opinion, narrative, informative/explanatory, and procedural texts. In addition, they receive explicit modeling and practice to write to multiple sources.

Language Mini-Lessons

The Common Core ELA State Standards include very specific language objectives at each grade level. Within the Benchmark Advance Teacher's Resource System, the "Build Language" section within the writing mini-lessons ensures that explicit language instruction occurs in an authentic context. For students who need additional support to master language standards, this volume provides a comprehensive bank of mini-lessons to support all of the Common Core Language standards for Grade 4 (conventions of standard English, knowledge of language, and vocabulary acquisition and use).

Based on your observations of students' independent writing and collaborative conversations, you may draw on these lessons during whole-group, small-group, or intervention time to target the specific language skills your students need to develop. Use these explicit mini-lessons during any of the Benchmark Advance units. For each language mini-lesson, there is a reproducible activity that can serve as independent practice or can be used for assessment.

Students practice the skill collaboratively.

Students apply the skill with their independent writing.

Teachers explicitly model each language skill.

Practice pages provide reinforcement for students who need it.

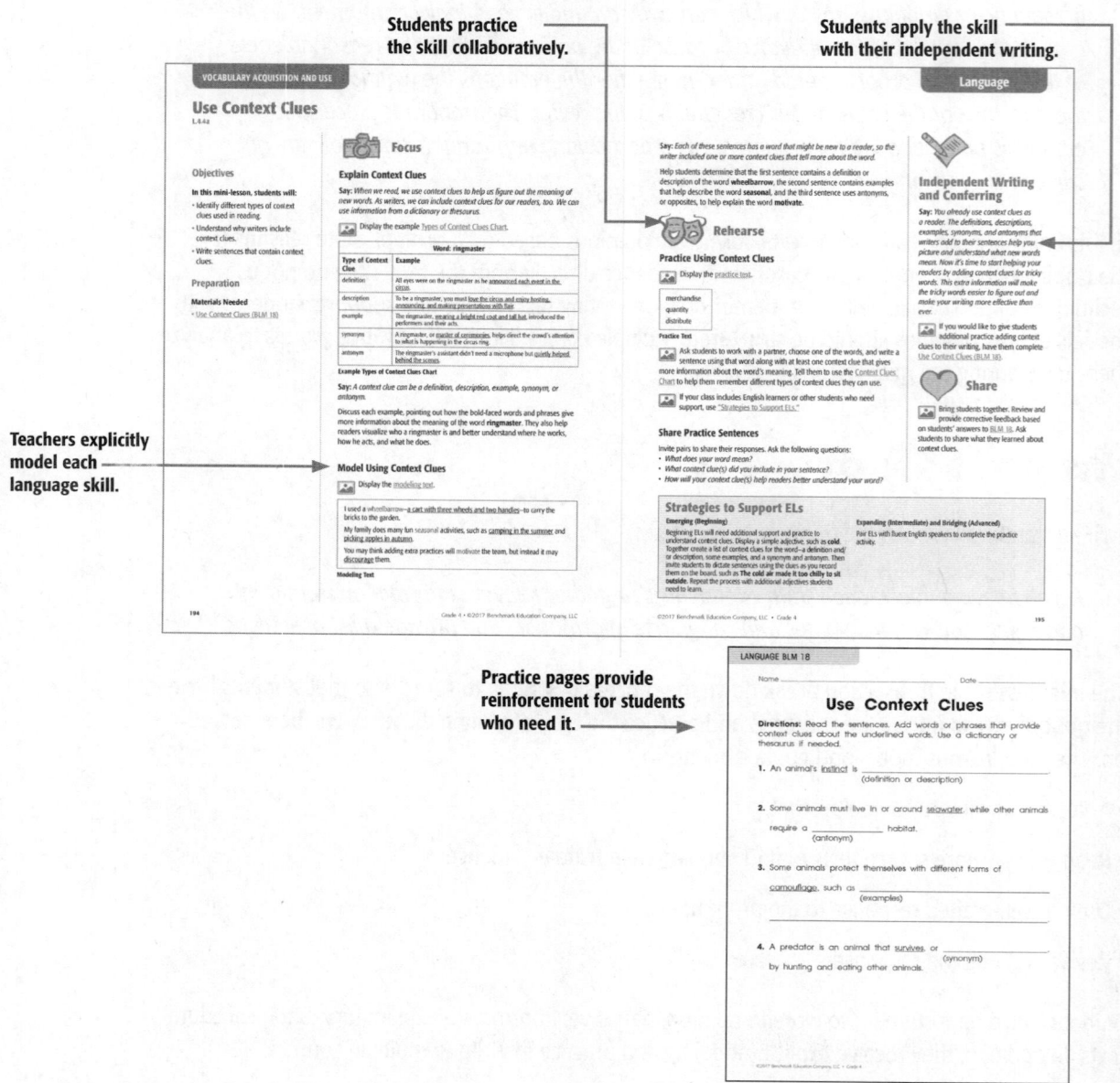

Grade 4 Opinion Mini-Lessons at a Glance

MINI-LESSON MENU		PAGE	BLM
Opinion Unit Pacing Guide		2	
Introduce Opinion Writing	Introduce the Genre	4	
Read Aloud a Source Text to Understand Key Ideas 1	Introduce the Genre	6	A
Read Aloud a Source Text to Understand Key Ideas 2	Introduce the Genre	8	A
Read and Analyze an Opinion Prompt	Model Analytical Thinking	10	B
Read to Identify the Features of an Opinion Text	Introduce the Genre	12	C
Read and Evaluate an Opinion Text 1	Model Analytical Thinking	14	D
Read and Evaluate an Opinion Text 2	Model Analytical Thinking	16	D
Analyze the Text to Formulate an Opinion	Model Analytical Thinking	18	E
Organize an Opinion Using a Planning Chart	Model the Writing Process	20	F
State Your Opinion and Reasons Clearly	Model the Writing Process	22	
Support Reasons with Facts and Evidence	Model the Writing Process	24	
Use Linking Words and Phrases	Author's Craft	26	
Use Different Ways to Introduce Source Evidence	Author's Craft	28	
Write a Conclusion that Supports an Opinion	Model the Writing Process	30	
Use a Variety of Sentence Structures	Author's Craft	32	
Avoid the First Person When Stating an Opinion	Author's Craft	34	
Revise Your Opinion to Link Reasons and Evidence	Model the Writing Process	36	
Use a Checklist to Edit a Draft	Model the Writing Process	38	
Use Keyboarding Skills to Publish an Opinion	Model the Writing Process	40	

MANAGEMENT & ASSESSMENT TOOLS	PAGE
Opinion Checklist	48
Opinion Student Self-Reflection Sheet	49
Home Connection Letter (English)	50
Home Connection Letter (Spanish)	51
Opinion Unit Class Status Sheet	52
Opinion Teacher Rubric	53

Opinion Writing Unit of Study
6-Week Suggested Mini-Lesson Pacing Guide

This flexible pacing guide includes all of the mini-lessons for the unit of study and allows time for you to include additional mini-lessons of your own choosing. Feel free to adjust the order and pace of the mini-lessons to meet the needs of your class.

	DAY 1	DAY 2
1	Introduce the Genre: Introduce Opinion Writing	Introduce the Genre: Read Aloud a Source Text to Understand Key Ideas 1
2	Model Analytical Thinking: Read and Evaluate an Opinion Text 1	Model Analytical Thinking: Read and Evaluate an Opinion Text 2
3	Model the Writing Process: State Your Opinion and Reasons Clearly	Teacher-Selected Mini-Lesson* See options below
4	Author's Craft: Use Different Ways to Introduce Source Evidence	Teacher-Selected Mini-Lesson* See options below
5	Author's Craft: Avoid the First Person When Stating an Opinion	Teacher-Selected Mini-Lesson* See options below
6	Model Writing to Sources Analyze a Source Text and Draft an Opinion Text 1	Model Writing to Sources: Revise and Edit a Response 1

*Teacher-selected mini-lesson options based on your observations of students needs.

Teacher-Selected Mini-Lesson Options	Recommended Conventions of English Lessons to Support Opinion Writing
• review a Writer's Workshop routine (see *Making Sense of the Writing Workshop*); • conduct a Language mini-lesson to support Conventions of Standard English or Vocabulary Acquisition and Use (see the Language Mini-Lessons); • conduct additional opinion read-alouds using the suggested trade book recommendations; • repeat a mini-lesson for additional practice; or • create your own mini-lesson.	The following language convention lessons are particularly meaningful within the context of writing an opinion: • L.4.2a Use Correct Capitalization, p. 180 • L.4.2b Use Commas and Quotation Marks, p. 182 • L.4.2c Use Commas in Compound Sentences, p. 184 • L.4.3a, L.4.6 Use Precise Words and Phrases, p. 188 • L.4.3b Use Punctuation for Effect, p. 190

Daily Timetables for Writer's Workshop

LESSON COMPONENT	45 MIN	60 MIN
Mini-Lesson *(Focus and Rehearse)*	15	15
Independent Writing and Conferring	20	35
Share	10	10

DAY 3	DAY 4	DAY 5
Introduce the Genre: Read Aloud a Source Text to Understand Key Ideas 2	Model Analytical Thinking: Read and Analyze an Opinion Prompt	Introduce the Genre: Read to Identify the Features of an Opinion Text
Model Analytical Thinking: Analyze the Text to Formulate an Opinion	Teacher-Selected Mini-Lesson* See options below	Model the Writing Process: Organize an Opinion Using a Planning Chart
Model the Writing Process: Support Reasons with Facts and Evidence	Teacher-Selected Mini-Lesson* See options below	Author's Craft: Use Linking Words and Phrases
Model the Writing Process: Write a Conclusion that Supports the Opinion	Teacher-Selected Mini-Lesson* See options below	Author's Craft: Use a Variety of Sentence Structures
Model the Writing Process: Revise Your Opinion to Link Reasons and Evidence	Model the Writing Process: Use a Checklist to Edit a Draft	Model the Writing Process: Use Keyboarding Skills to Publish an Opinion
Teacher-Selected Mini-Lesson* See options below	Model Writing to Sources: Analyze a Source Text and Draft an Opinion Text 2	Model Writing to Sources: Revise and Edit a Response 2

Recommended Trade Book Read-Alouds to Support Opinion Writing

• *March On! The Day My Brother Martin Changed the World*, Christine King Farris

• *I, Too, Am America*, Langston Hughes

Introduce Opinion Writing

W.4.1a, W.4.1b, W.4.4, W.4.10, SL.4.1a, SL.4.1b, SL.4.1c, SL.4.1d, SL.4.3

Objectives

In this mini-lesson, teachers will:

• Launch the opinion-writing unit of study.

• Establish themselves as an opinion-writing mentor by sharing their opinions based on evidence from a fine art image.

• Model how writers think about how to support opinions based on evidence.

Students will:

• Discuss their opinions of a fine art image.

• Talk about opinions based on evidence.

Preparation

Materials Needed

• Images of _Sunflowers, 1889_ and _The Starry Night_ by Vincent van Gogh

• Conferring Prompts

Focus

Introduce Opinion Writing

Engage students in an activity to help them understand that people form opinions in response to a source–something they have heard, seen, read, or experienced. The activity below uses the painting _Sunflowers_, 1889 by Vincent van Gogh as a source. You may wish to use this activity or base yours on a different source, such as a movie or a book your class is familiar with.

 Display an image of _Sunflowers, 1889_ and use the sample think-aloud below as a model for offering an opinion based on evidence that you see.

Say: _This is one of my favorite paintings for several reasons. I like how the painter makes the flowers appear full of energy and movement. I also like the flowers' bright colors and that they are all the same kind of flower, yet each one looks different from the rest. It's as if the painter is showing me how every sunflower is a unique individual, as is each human being._

Point out that you just offered your opinion about a source. You supported your opinion with evidence from the source (the painting). Acknowledge that students may have different opinions, or they may have the same opinion for different reasons.

Introduce the Purpose and Audience for Opinion Writing

Ask: _Why does anyone care what I think about_ Sunflowers? _Why is my opinion important?_

Allow responses, and guide students to understand that our opinions are important because they reflect what we think about something. When we give an opinion, we are not trying to persuade others to agree with us. We simply want to offer what we think and why. Point out that people offer their opinions every day. They tell people why they like to play certain sports or listen to certain music or eat certain foods.

Rehearse

Practice Telling Opinions Orally

 Invite students to look at a second fine art image with a partner and offer their opinions about it. You may wish to display Vincent van Gogh's _The Starry Night_. Remind students to offer one or two pieces of evidence from the painting to support their opinions. Tell students that they will share their opinions with the class.

Explain that the partner who is listening to an opinion should be prepared to ask questions to help his or her partner clarify ideas and reach a thoughtful answer. As needed, review your class rules for discussion. You may wish to use the Guidelines for Collaborative Conversations on page viii.

 If your class includes English learners or other students who need support, use "Strategies to Support ELs."

Share Opinions with the Class

 Invite volunteer pairs to share their opinions with the class. Ask other students who are listening to identify the evidence that the volunteers give for their opinions. Record opinions and evidence on an Opinions and Evidence Chart. Discuss the importance of using evidence to support opinions. Use one or more of the following discussion questions to facilitate student understanding:
• *What do you notice about the opinions? Are they all the same?*
• *What do you notice about the evidence?*

Opinions	Evidence that Support Opinions
1. I like the way the painter shows the difference between the land and sky at night. 2. I like the way the stars and moon look like they are glowing and moving. 3. This painting makes me think how much bigger the universe is than our human world.	1. The tree, church, and house roofs have sharp points; the stars and moon are round shapes. 2. The painter makes bright dashed lines around the center of the stars and moon that create a sense of energy and motion. 3. The moon and stars take up a lot more space in the painting and are much brighter than the little lights in the village below.

Sample Opinions and Evidence Chart

Independent Writing and Conferring

Say: *Today we learned how to offer our opinions and support them with evidence. We learned that evidence strengthens our opinions and makes them believable. In the next several weeks, we will be looking at opinion writing and will write opinions of our own.*

Encourage students to take turns offering opinions and supportive evidence about a sport they have played or watched. During student conferences, reinforce students' use of this and other strategies using the prompts on the conferring flip chart.

 **Share**

Bring students together. Invite volunteers to share their opinions and supportive evidence about a sport they like to play or watch. Provide time for students to ask clarifying questions that facilitate their understanding of the exercise.

Strategies to Support ELs

Emerging (Beginning)

 While other students complete the partner activity (or during independent writing time), encourage ELs to share their opinions about the paintings they looked at in class. Provide sentence frames to help them, for example:

I like this painting because _____.
I do not like this painting because _____.

Expanding (Intermediate) and Bridging (Advanced)

Pair ELs with fluent English speakers during the partner activity. Provide prompts such as the following to help students discuss their opinions of the art:

I like/do not like this painting because _____.
This painting makes me think of _____ because _____.
I like how the artist _____.

All Levels

 If you have ELs whose first language is Spanish, share these English/Spanish cognates: **color/el color; opinion/la opinión**.

Read Aloud a Source Text to Understand Key Ideas 1

RI.4.1, RI.4.2, W.4.1a, W.4.1b, W.4.4, W.4.10, SL.4.1a, SL.4.1b, SL.4.1c, SL.4.1d, SL.4.2

Mentor Text

Objectives

In this mini-lesson, students will:

- Listen to a source text read aloud.
- Develop a deep understanding of the source text using a main idea chart.
- Share personal opinions about the source text.

Preparation

Materials Needed

- Source text: "A Brief History of Zoos" and "Baby Panda Goes on Exhibit" from *Opinions About Modern Zoos*
- Main Idea Chart (BLM A)
- Conferring Prompts

 **Focus**

Introduce a Source Text

Say: *We know that opinions are based on what we read and experience. In our last lesson, we shared our opinions about a painting. The painting was a source. We formed our opinions in response to the source. Today, we will read a nonfiction news story. This news story is our source today. We will form opinions about the ideas we read in the news story. First, however, we need to understand the text well. Understanding takes time, so we will read the news story more than once and use a main idea chart to identify the important ideas.*

 If your class includes English learners or other students who would benefit from vocabulary and oral language development to comprehend the narrative, use "Make the Source Text Comprehensible for ELs."

Display *Opinions About Modern Zoos.* Tell students that the book includes a brief history of zoos, two news stories, and three opinion pieces.

Say: *Today we will review the introduction and focus on the first news story, which is about successful modern zoo breeding programs.*

Display and read aloud "A Brief History of Zoos" on pages 2–3. Use the following discussion questions to facilitate student understanding:
- *What does the introduction say about why people started keeping zoos?*
- *What is the difference between the first zoos and modern zoos?*

Read Aloud the Source Text

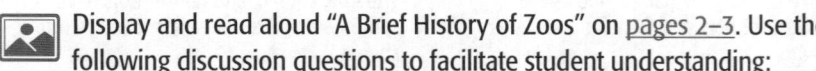 Display and read aloud "Baby Panda Goes on Exhibit." Model finding a main idea and details that support it in order to fill in the Main Idea Chart (BLM A). Students will complete the chart in the Rehearse section of the lesson.

After first paragraph on page 5. Say: *As I read, I'm thinking about the main ideas of the text to make sure I understand it. An important idea might be "Zoos around the world are working together to try to save pandas from extinction." One detail that supports this is the birth of Xiao Liwu in San Diego.*

Respond Orally to the Source Text

Engage students in a text-dependent discussion about the main ideas in the news story using some or all of the following questions.
- *Why is the birth of Xiao Liwu important?*
- *Why do zoos have breeding programs?*
- *Besides breeding programs, what else does the text say zoos do for animals?*
- *What are the main reasons animals raised in zoos are not returned to the wild?*
- *What happened when Xiao Liwu was born? Why is this important?*

Rehearse

Analyze the Source Text

Independent Writing and Conferring

Distribute copies of BLM A. Invite students to work with a partner to complete the chart for "Baby Panda Goes on Exhibit." Tell them to look for main ideas and supporting details.

Main Ideas	Key Details
A number of zoos around the country are working together to try to save animals from extinction by breeding them in captivity.	Debut of panda cub Xiao Liwu on January 10, 2013, at the San Diego Zoo in California Pandas are endangered Zoos have breeding programs for more than 300 kinds of animals Columbus Zoo—two male tiger cubs St. Paul, Minnesota—arctic foxes
Animals born in zoos attract attention.	Hundreds of people came out on a stormy day to see Xiao Liwu Every day, people wait in long lines Live "panda cam" on zoo website Standing-room-only lecture on breeding program followed birth of Xiao Liwu
Zoos sometimes help animals born in the wild.	Snow leopard cub in Bronx Zoo from Pakistan, in 2006

Sample Main Idea Chart (BLM A)

Share Ideas

Invite volunteers to share examples of main ideas and details they found in the text.

Say: *We just read a news story about a panda born in a modern zoo. What do you think about the birth of Xiao Liwu? In a short paragraph of three to four sentences, offer your opinion and support it with at least two reasons from the text.*

Share

Bring students together. Invite volunteers to read aloud their paragraphs. Provide time for students to ask clarifying questions to better understand the paragraphs being shared. Remind students to use complete sentences when asking questions.

Make the Source Text Comprehensible for ELs

Emerging (Beginning)

While other students complete the partner activity (or during independent writing time), use the pictures in the text to name the animals. Point to a picture and say its name. Have students repeat, using the following sentence frame:

This animal is a _____.

Expanding (Intermediate) and Bridging (Advanced)

Pair ELs with fluent English speakers during the partner activity. Display simple sentence frames and model how students can use them to talk about main ideas. For example:

A main idea of this text is _____.
A detail to support the main idea is _____.

All Levels

If you have ELs whose first language is Spanish, share these English/Spanish cognates: **animal/el animal; baby/el bebé; panda/el panda; leopard/el leopardo; zoo/el zoo; extinct/extinto.**

Read Aloud a Source Text to Understand Key Ideas 2

RI.4.1, RI.4.2, W.4.1a, W.4.1b, W.4.4, W.4.10, SL.4.1a, SL.4.1b, SL.4.1c, SL.4.1d, SL.4.2

Mentor Text

Objectives

In this mini-lesson, students will:

• Listen as a source text is read aloud.

• Develop a deep understanding of the source text using a main idea chart.

• Share personal opinions about the source text.

Preparation

Materials Needed

• Source text: "Elderly Sea Otter Becomes Basketball Sensation" from *Opinions About Modern Zoos*

• Main Idea Chart (BLM A)

• Conferring Prompts

 **Focus**

Introduce a Source Text

Say: *In our last session, we read a nonfiction news article about modern zoos and completed a main idea chart as a way to analyze the most important information in the article. Today, we will read a second nonfiction news article about modern zoos. To form opinions about what we read, we need to understand this text well. We will read the story more than once and complete a main idea chart to identify the important concepts and information.*

If your class includes English learners or other students who would benefit from vocabulary and oral language development to comprehend the narrative, use "Make the Source Text Comprehensible for ELs."

Display the article "Elderly Sea Otter Becomes Basketball Sensation." Read aloud the title. Explain to students that this article tells about a second type of program created to keep animals healthy at modern zoos.

Read Aloud the Source Text

Read aloud "Elderly Sea Otter Becomes Basketball Sensation." Stop at the place indicated (or at other points you choose) to model finding a main idea and details that support it, in order to fill in the Main Idea Chart (BLM A). Students will complete BLM A in the Rehearse section of the lesson.

Bottom of page 13. Say: *The first part of the article tells about Eddie and how he gets his exercise. I think the reason why Eddie plays basketball is the main idea of this section. On page 12, the text says that zookeepers have come up with ways to keep zoo animals healthy by providing a choice of activities for them. I think that is an important idea in this article. One detail that supports this is that zookeepers at the Oregon Zoo gave Eddie a toy basketball and a hoop. Another detail is that the exercise helps keep Eddie healthy by providing a way to exercise his arms.*

Respond Orally to the Source Text

Engage students in a text-dependent discussion about the most important information introduced in the article.

• *What are some of the behavioral enrichment activities mentioned in the article?*

• *Why did zookeepers and zoo veterinarians invent these activities?*

• *How can these activities improve life for animals in captivity?*

Rehearse

Analyze the Source Text

 Distribute copies of BLM A. Invite students to work with a partner to complete the chart. Tell them to look for main ideas and supporting details.

Remind students that as they work with their partners, they need to listen to their partner with care, take turns talking, speak in complete sentences, and limit their conversation to the topic of main ideas and supporting details.

Main Ideas	Key Details
Zookeepers have come up with ways to keep zoo animals healthy by providing a choice of activities for them.	Eddie the sea otter at the Oregon Zoo plays basketball for physical therapy to exercise his arms and elbows. Dead prey is hidden in a Komodo dragon's enclosure. Tigers and lions use large plastic balls. Fruit is hidden in bird enclosures. Some seals, primates, and elephants create paintings.
Some of these activities are designed to promote physical health, others promote mental health.	Basketball helps Eddie with the stiffness of arthritis, an effect of aging. Painting, with the help of zookeepers, exercises muscles and may help to prevent boredom.
These activities are designed to imitate movement and activities animals would experience in the wild.	The Komodo dragon is exercising its instinct to hunt when it looks for hidden prey. Lions and tigers using the big balls practice the natural physical actions of hunting. Birds searching for hidden fruit are practicing their natural instinct to forage.

Sample Main Idea Chart (BLM A)

Share Ideas

Invite volunteers to share examples of main ideas and details they found.

Independent Writing and Conferring

Ask students to write a paragraph that summarizes the news article. Remind them that a summary only describes key events in a text.

Share

Bring students together. Invite volunteers to read aloud their paragraphs. Provide time for students to ask clarifying questions about the summaries. Remind students to use complete sentences when asking and answering questions.

Make the Source Text Comprehensible for ELs

Emerging (Beginning)

While other students complete the partner activity (or during independent writing time), use the pictures in the text to name the animals. Point to a picture and say its name. Have students repeat, using the following sentence frame:

This animal is a _____.

Expanding (Intermediate) and Bridging (Advanced)

Pair ELs with fluent English speakers during the partner activity. Display simple sentence frames and model how students can use them to talk about main ideas. For example:

An important idea in the text is _____.
A detail to support the main idea is _____.

All Levels

If you have ELs whose first language is Spanish, share these English/Spanish cognates: **animal/el animal; exercise/ el ejercicio; zoo/el zoo; instinct/instinto; tiger/el tigre; lion/ el león; reptile/el reptil.**

Read and Analyze an Opinion Prompt

W.4.4, W.4.10, SL.4.1a, SL.4.1b, SL.4.1c, SL.4.1d, SL.4.2, SL.4.3

Objectives

In this mini-lesson, students will:

• Read and analyze an opinion prompt.

• Discuss how to apply this strategy to their independent writing in response to a source.

Preparation

Materials Needed

• Analyze an Opinion Prompt (BLM B)

• Conferring Prompts

 **Focus**

Explain Reading and Analyzing an Opinion Prompt

Explain to students that a prompt is just another way to ask a question. For example, an opinion prompt will ask students to develop their own opinions about a text. Students will then explain and defend their opinions in an essay. Explain that, to answer a prompt, students must first read it carefully. As writers, they need to analyze the prompt to make sure they understand what it is asking, so that they can thoroughly and thoughtfully respond.

Say: *Today I'll show you how to read and analyze an opinion prompt.*

Model Reading and Analyzing an Opinion Prompt

 Display and read aloud the <u>modeling opinion prompt</u>.

> Zoos began as places where animals were confined strictly for human entertainment. Now they are places of science and education that still try to entertain visitors. In your opinion, what is the most important reason to have modern zoos? State a clear opinion, and give supporting reasons <u>based on evidence from the introduction and news articles</u>.

Modeling Opinion Prompt

Reread sentence 1. Explain that this sentence summarizes information given in one or more of the source texts, which are named in the final line of the prompt: the introduction and the news articles.

Reread sentence 2. Explain that the linking word **now** is a clue that links the information in the first sentence with the information in the second sentence. The second sentence also summarizes information from the source texts.

Reread sentence 3. Explain that this sentence poses a question to the writer. Point out that this prompt is asking writers to express an opinion about the information stated in the sources.

Reread sentence 4. Underline the words "based on evidence from the introduction and news articles." Explain that in order to respond thoroughly to this prompt, the writer not only needs to state an opinion but they also need to provide clear reasons using evidence from the three sources. The writer must state his or her opinion about the most important reason to have modern zoos. Then, the writer needs to support that opinion by referring to the information in the introduction and news stories.

Rehearse

Practice Reading and Analyzing an Opinion Prompt

 Display and read aloud the practice opinion prompt.

> Based on your reading of the introduction and two news articles in *Opinions About Modern Zoos*, evaluate the following statement: Modern zoos do a better job of keeping animals happy and healthy than zoos did long ago. Cite evidence from the text to defend your response.

Practice Opinion Prompt

Ask students to work with a partner to read and analyze the prompt. Explain that **evaluate** means they need to think carefully before making a judgment or forming an opinion. Have partners write down what the prompt is asking and how they would need to respond to answer the prompt. Students should be prepared to read their analysis to the class and be ready to explain each part of the prompt in their own words.

 If your class includes English learners or other students who need support, use "Strategies to Support ELs."

Share and Discuss

Invite partners to read aloud their analysis. Ask students what question they need to answer, or what they need to form an opinion about. Discuss how students would properly respond to the prompt. Encourage students to ask and answer questions to check their understanding of the concept of a writing prompt and to link their comments to the remarks of others.

Independent Writing and Conferring

Say: *We learned that reading and analyzing an opinion prompt requires us to break the prompt into parts to more easily understand what the prompt is asking. We need to make sure we understand the prompt so we can respond to it properly. Remember that a well-written response to an opinion prompt is backed up by reasons, or evidence, from the text.*

 Distribute Analyze an Opinion Prompt (BLM B). Ask students to break down the prompt into its parts and then write what each part is asking them to do.

 # Share

Bring students together. Invite volunteers to share their analysis of the prompt.

Strategies to Support ELs

Emerging (Beginning)

 While other students complete the partner activity (or during independent writing time), encourage ELs to talk about their opinions about various things using words and/or gestures. Provide sentence frames to support them as they talk:

I like _____ because _____.
I do not like _____ because _____.

Expanding (Intermediate) and Bridging (Advanced)

Provide sentence frames to help students talk about the prompt with a partner:

The first part of the prompt asks me to _____.
The second part of the prompt asks me to _____.
The third part of the prompt asks me to _____.

All Levels

If you have ELs whose first language is Spanish, share these English/Spanish cognates: **opinion/la opinión; exercise/el ejercicio; therapy/la terapia; arthritis/la artritis.**

Read to Identify the Features of an Opinion Text

RI.4.2, RI.4.3, W.4.1a, W.4.1b, W.4.1c, W.4.1d, W.4.4, W.4.10, SL.4.1a, SL.4.1b, SL.4.1c, SL.4.1d, SL.4.2, SL.4.3

Mentor Text

Objectives

In this mini-lesson, students will:

• Identify features of an opinion text.

• Use text evidence to analyze an opinion.

Preparation

Materials Needed

• Mentor text: "Zoos Are a Learning Environment" from *Opinions About Modern Zoos*

• Opinion Features Chart (BLM C)

• Conferring Prompts

 **Focus**

Introduce the Mentor Opinion Text

Display and read aloud the opinion writing prompt on page 15 of *Opinions About Modern Zoos*. Remind students that they read and analyzed this prompt in their last mini-lesson. Tell students that they are going to read an opinion piece based on this prompt and they will learn the features of a strong opinion text.

Read Aloud the Mentor Opinion Text

Say: *As I read, listen carefully to identify the writer's opinion and how he or she supports it. Then we'll read again to analyze the key features.*

Display and read aloud "Zoos Are a Learning Environment." Then display and distribute copies of the Opinion Features Chart (BLM C). Reread the text, stopping to discuss how the mentor text reflects the key features of a well-constructed opinion text. Use the prompts below as needed to discuss the mentor text with students.

Opinion Features	Examples from the Text
A clearly stated opinion	1st paragraph: "education is the most important function of a modern zoo."
Reasons for the opinion	1st paragraph: "Modern zoos offer the public a unique opportunity to connect with the natural world." "They provide entertaining experiences." "Zoos also inspire people to want to learn more about animals."
Evidence to support the reasons	2nd paragraph: people flock to zoos when they hear about animals like the panda cub Xiao Liwu and Eddie the sea otter playing basketball 3rd paragraph: ". . . signs at the Komodo dragon exhibit mentioned in the 'Elderly Sea Otter' article, tell about where the animal can be found in the wild. They tell what the dragon eats, and more."
Linking words and phrases that connect reasons and evidence	"therefore," "once there," "likewise," "for example," "sometimes," "in summary"
A conclusion	"If people learn about animals, they will want to help them even more."

Sample Opinion Features Chart (BLM C)

First paragraph. Say: *The author's first sentence asks a challenging question to hook the reader. The author answers the question in the second sentence. The question and answer both introduce the idea that people are interested in seeing animals from around the world. Then, the author states three reasons that zoos satisfy the needs of visitors. The author links these reasons together with the word* **therefore.** *The paragraph ends with the author's opinion: "education is the most important function of a modern zoo."*

Second and third paragraphs. Say: *Notice how the writer supports his reasons with details from the two news stories. In the second paragraph, he names the panda cub from the first article and the basketball-playing otter from the second article and says that breeding programs and special activities designed for animals attract visitors to zoos. In the third paragraph, he uses more evidence from both articles to support his opinion about the importance of education.*

Underlined throughout the text. Say: *These are called linking words and phrases. They make an opinion strong because they connect the opinion with the reason.*

Fourth paragraph. Say: *The author uses the phrase "in summary" to connect all of the evidence back to the reasons for his opinion. In the conclusion the author pushes his opening idea further when he says that, when people become educated about animals at zoos, they will do even more to help animals.*

 ## Rehearse

Analyze the Opinion Mentor Text

 Divide students into small groups and ask them to complete the second column of BLM C. Tell students to explain their thinking clearly and be prepared to answer questions that clarify their ideas for others.

 If your class includes English learners or other students who need support, use "Strategies to Support ELs."

Share Examples

Invite volunteers to share examples from the text of where the author includes features of an opinion.

 # Independent Writing and Conferring

Say: *Remember that when you write an opinion piece, you base your opinion on what you read. You look in the text for reasons and evidence that supports your opinion.*

Encourage students to work with a partner to answer the following question:
• *Do you agree or disagree with this author's opinion?*

Have students jot down a list of reasons why they agree or disagree. During student conferences, reinforce students' thinking and writing using the prompts on the conferring flip chart.

 ## Share

Bring students together. Invite volunteers to read aloud their lists of reasons. Provide time for students to ask clarifying questions that facilitate their understanding of the exercise.

Strategies to Support ELs

Emerging (Beginning)

 While other students complete the small-group activity (or during independent writing time), work with ELs to provide more practice in stating opinions and reasons. Show students something you have in the classroom such as a book, a picture, or something representing a color such as a red block. For example, **say:** *I like red because it makes me feel happy.* Have students point to something in the classroom and offer their opinion about it, and a reason. Provide simple sentence frames to help them talk about their opinions:

I like _____ because _____.
I do not like _____ because _____.

Expanding (Intermediate) and Bridging (Advanced)

 Provide sentence frames to support EL students as they discuss the features of the opinion in their groups:

This opinion includes _____.
The opinion does not include _____.

All Levels

 If you have ELs whose first language is Spanish, share these English/Spanish cognates: **introduction/la introducción; conclusion/la conclusión; evidence/la evidencia; opinion/la opinión; reason/la razón.**

Read and Evaluate an Opinion Text 1
RI.4.2, RI.4.3, W.4.1a, W.4.1b, W.4.1c, W.4.1d, W.4.4, W.4.10, SL.4.1a, SL.4.1b, SL.4.1c, SL.4.1d, SL.4.2, SL.4.3

 **Focus**

Mentor Text

Objectives

In this mini-lesson, students will:

• Read and analyze an opinion text.

• Use a rubric to evaluate an opinion text.

• Apply the mini-lesson to their independent writing.

Preparation

Materials Needed

• Mentor text: "Zoos Preserve Animal Species" from *Opinions About Modern Zoos*

• Opinion Evaluation Rubric (BLM D)

• Conferring Prompts

Introduce the Mini-Lesson

Remind students that they have learned what a source text is, how to read and analyze an opinion writing prompt, and specific features to include in a well-constructed opinion text. Tell them that today they will read another opinion text about modern zoos and evaluate the text using a rubric.

Reread the opinion writing prompt on page 15 of *Opinions About Modern Zoos*. Explain that you are going to read a second opinion text responding to this prompt. Ask students to listen carefully to the writer's opinion and how she supports it with reasons and evidence from the source texts.

Read Aloud the Mentor Opinion Text

Display the Opinion Evaluation Rubric (BLM D) and distribute copies to students. Review the key features of an opinion as needed. Display and read aloud "Zoos Preserve Animal Species." Ask students to tell you what this writer's opinion is.

Criteria	Text Examples
The writer clearly states his/her opinion.	Preserving animal species is the most important job for a zoo today.
The writer gives clear reasons for the opinion.	". . . according to the International Union for Conservation of Nature (IUCN), more than 4,000 species are on the critically endangered list. That means they face a high risk of extinction in the wild." "Zoos give endangered species a healthy home where they can flourish."
The writer's reasons are supported by evidence (examples, quotations, or restatements) from the text.	"According to the 'Baby Panda' article, 325 pandas live in captivity. That may not seem like a lot, but it is about one-sixth the total number of pandas in the world. "The San Diego Zoo's pandas have already added six cubs." As the "Elderly Sea Otter" article explained, zoos also have behavioral enrichment programs.
The writer connects reasons to evidence using linking words and phrases.	That means they face a high risk of extinction . . . But we do know that without zoos . . . That may not seem like a lot, but it is about one-sixth the total . . . Of course, modern zoos do more . . . In conclusion, wild places are shrinking.
The writer provides a concluding statement or section that sums up the opinion.	In conclusion, wild places are shrinking. . . . Zoos offer a place where animals can be happy, healthy, and even increase in number.

Sample Opinion Evaluation Rubric (BLM D)

Model completing the first row of the rubric. Students will complete the rest of the rubric during the Rehearse section of the lesson.

Say: *The first row of the rubric asks me to evaluate whether the author clearly states her opinion. She does. The third sentence is the strongest statement of her opinion. Her opinion is that the most important job of a modern zoo is to preserve animal species.*

Rehearse

Analyze the Mentor Opinion Text

 Ask students to work in small groups to complete BLM D. They should analyze the opinion text using copies of the book and the rubric. If necessary, review the Guidelines for Collaborative Conversations on page viii before groups begin. Stress that you expect students to focus the discussion on the task at hand, to listen with care to each other, and build on each other's ideas in a respectful, cooperative way. Groups should be prepared to present their analysis and respond to questions from their peers.

 If your class includes English learners or other students who need support, use "Strategies to Support ELs."

Share Ideas

Have students share their evaluation of the opinion text. Students may not agree with the evaluations of other students. Encourage them to challenge the ideas of others thoughtfully and be prepared to support their ideas with reasons.

Independent Writing and Conferring

Ask students to respond to the opinion text "Zoos Preserve Animal Species" in writing. Have them state whether they think the author did a good job clearly expressing her opinion and giving the reasons and evidence or if the text could be improved. Have them use evidence to support their thinking.

Share

Invite volunteers to share their thoughts about the opinion essay. Encourage listeners to ask questions to clarify the speaker's point of view and any ideas they don't understand. Guide students to discuss different points of view in a positive and supportive way.

Strategies to Support ELs

Emerging (Beginning)

 While other students complete the small-group activity (or during independent writing time), continue working with students to practice making opinions. Show students pictures of animals such as pandas, monkeys, bears, birds, and fish. Provide sentence frames for them to share their responses.

I like _____ because _____.
I do not like _____ because _____.

Expanding (Intermediate) and Bridging (Advanced)

 Provide sentence frames to support ELs as they discuss the writer's opinion in their groups:

The writer's opinion is _____.
The writer's reason is _____.
The evidence is _____.

All Levels

 If you have ELs whose first language is Spanish, share these English/Spanish cognates: **opinion/la opinión; evidence/la evidencia; reason/la razón.**

Read and Evaluate an Opinion Text 2

RI.4.2, RI.4.3, W.4.1a, W.4.1b, W.4.1c, W.4.1d, W.4.4, W.4.10, SL.4.1a, SL.4.1b, SL.4.1c, SL.4.1d, SL.4.2, SL.4.3

Mentor Text

Objectives

In this mini-lesson, students will:

• Read and analyze an opinion text.

• Use a rubric to evaluate an opinion text.

• Apply the mini-lesson to their independent writing.

Preparation

Materials Needed

• Mentor text: "Keeping Animals Healthy Is a Zoo's Most Important Business" from *Opinions About Modern Zoos*

• Opinion Evaluation Rubric (BLM D)

• Conferring Prompts

 **Focus**

Introduce the Mini-Lesson

Remind students that they have already evaluated one opinion text based on the news articles about modern zoos. Today they will evaluate another opinion text. They should use what they learned in the previous mini-lesson to help them be even more critical readers today. Remind students that each writer's opinion is different, but all opinions are valid if the writer can support them using the text.

Read Aloud the Mentor Opinion Text

Display a blank Opinion Evaluation Rubric (BLM D) and distribute copies to students. Display and read aloud "Keeping Animals Healthy Is a Zoo's Most Important Business." Ask students to tell what the writer's opinion is. If necessary, read the opinion text aloud a second time.

Model completing the first row of the rubric. Students will complete the rest of the rubric during the Rehearse section of the lesson.

Say: *The first row of the rubric asks me to evaluate whether or not the author states her opinion clearly. She does that in the first sentence of her essay. She says a modern zoo's most important job is to keep its animals healthy.*

Criteria	Text Examples
The writer clearly states his/her opinion.	"Keeping animals healthy is the most important job for a modern zoo."
The writer gives clear reasons for the opinion.	It preserves species. It is good for the zoo's business.
The writer's reasons are supported by evidence (examples, quotations, or restatements) from the text.	Zookeepers make sure animals have more than their basic needs of food and shelter. Behavioral-enrichment programs help animals live longer. Behavioral-enrichment programs are crowd pleasers. Xiao Liwu has attracted hundreds of people. Providing balls encourages lions and tigers to use their instincts. "Zoo breeding programs also keep animal populations healthy. In the 'Baby Panda' article, zoologist Nora Johnson noted that more than eighty snow leopards have been born in the Bronx Zoo."
The writer connects reasons to evidence using linking words and phrases.	**Not only does this** preserve species . . . **For example,** as the article on Eddie the otter explained . . . **Let's not forget** that modern zoos are . . . **But** his online videos . . .
The writer provides a concluding statement or section that sums up the opinion.	"Zoos have always been a place for entertainment, from the menageries of ancient Egypt to the first modern zoo in France 200 years ago. . . . Keeping animals healthy keeps zoos in business."

Sample Opinion Evaluation Rubric (BLM D)

 ## Rehearse

Analyze the Mentor Text

 Ask students to work in small groups to complete <u>BLM D</u>. They should analyze the opinion text using the rubric. If necessary, review the <u>Guidelines for Collaborative Conversations</u> on page viii before groups begin. Remind students to focus the discussion on the task at hand and to express their ideas to each other by speaking in complete sentences. Groups should be prepared to present their analysis and respond to questions from their peers.

If your class includes English learners or other students who need support, use <u>"Strategies to Support ELs."</u>

Share Ideas

Have students share their evaluation of the opinion text. Students may not agree with all the evaluations of other students. Encourage students to challenge the ideas of others in a thoughtful way and be prepared to support their ideas with reasons.

 ## Independent Writing and Conferring

Ask students to respond to the opinion in writing. Ask them to state whether they think the author did a good job clearly expressing her opinion and giving reasons and evidence, or if the text could be improved. Have them use evidence to support their thinking.

 ## Share

Invite volunteers to share their thinking about the opinion text "Keeping Animals Healthy Is a Zoo's Most Important Business." Encourage listeners to ask questions if there is something they don't understand about the speakers' ideas. Prompt students to discuss different points of view in a positive and supportive way.

Strategies to Support ELs

Emerging (Beginning)

While other students complete the small-group activity (or during independent writing time), work with students on using linking words. Use concrete objects to model connecting an opinion with examples, for example, use pieces of fruit, two or three books, or different colored pens. Point to the pens. **Say:** *I like pens. For example, I like red pens.* Ask students to repeat as you point to the pens and then a different color pen. Provide the following <u>sentence frames</u> to help students respond:

I like _____.
For example, I like _____.

Expanding (Intermediate) and Bridging (Advanced)

Pair students with fluent English speakers to complete the small-group activity. Provide <u>sentence frames</u> to support EL students as they discuss the writer's opinion:

I think the writer's text is _____.
My reason(s) is/are _____.
The writer has not included _____.
I like that the writer _____.

All Levels

If you have ELs whose first language is Spanish, share these <u>English/Spanish cognates</u>: **important/importante**; **opinion/la opinión**.

Analyze the Text to Formulate an Opinion

RI.4.2, RI.4.3, W.4.1a, W.4.1b, W.4.1c, W.4.1d, W.4.4, W.4.10, SL.4.1a, SL.4.1b, SL.4.1c, SL.4.1d, SL.4.2, SL.4.3

Mentor Text

Objectives

In this mini-lesson, students will:

- Understand how to form an opinion in response to a prompt.
- Find evidence to support an opinion.
- Apply the mini-lesson during independent writing.

Preparation

Materials Needed

- Source text: "Baby Panda Goes on Exhibit" from *Opinions About Modern Zoos*
- Opinion Prompts (BLM E)
- Conferring Prompts

 **Focus**

Introduce the Mini-Lesson

Explain to students that when they write an opinion essay in response to a specific prompt, they must formulate an opinion that they can support with evidence from the text.

Model Formulating an Opinion

 Display and read aloud the modeling opinion prompt. Model taking notes on a simple T-chart with the headings "Good Idea" and "Bad Idea."

> In the article "Baby Panda Goes on Exhibit," the author states that most animals born in zoo breeding programs will live their entire lives in zoos. In your opinion, is it a good idea to continue breeding programs for animals that may never have the chance to experience life in their natural habitats? State your opinion and support it with evidence from the article.

Modeling Opinion Prompt

Say: *The prompt asks me to state my opinion about zoo breeding programs. My first inclination is to say that these programs are a good idea because, without them, many species of animals might become extinct. But before I decide on my opinion for sure, I'm going to look back at the news article to see if the evidence supports this opinion, or whether it supports a different opinion. I'm going to take notes about the evidence I find on a simple chart to help me keep track.*

 Display page 4 from the source text, "Baby Panda Goes on Exhibit."

Say: *On this page, I see evidence to support my opinion. Pandas are on a list of "critically endangered species" and only 1,600 may live in the wild. I'll write these facts under the "Good idea" side of my opinion notes.* Model writing the notes.

 Display page 5.

Say: *Here, I see evidence to support both sides of the question. A pair of pandas at the San Diego Zoo has had six cubs born successfully. This pair has helped to keep pandas from going extinct. That supports my opinion. On the other hand, a zoo spokesperson is quoted as saying that pandas, in general, do not breed well in captivity. This suggests that if pandas can live in the wild, it is easier for them to breed. I'll write that down in the second column.*

Continue to model how to review the text to search for evidence and take notes until you decide which opinion the text best supports.

Say: *Based on my analysis, I have decided that although it would be wonderful if endangered animals like pandas and snow leopards born in zoos could later live in the wild, the space for those animals to live in is decreasing. Thus, I think that breeding programs are a good idea.*

Rehearse

Practice Formulating an Opinion

 Display and read aloud the practice opinion prompt.

> You have read about the behavioral-enrichment programs at many zoos. What do you think is the most important reason for these programs: to provide animals with activities that reinforce their natural behaviors or to provide entertainment for people who go to the zoo? Support your opinion with evidence from the text.

Practice Opinion Prompt

Ask students to work in small groups to evaluate the evidence in the text before they formulate an opinion. Have them take notes on a simple chart with the headings "Reinforce Natural Behaviors" and "Provide Entertainment for Zoo Visitors." After completing the chart, groups should weigh the evidence and write down a statement of their opinion. Students should be prepared to read their opinion statement to the class and explain why they formulated that opinion.

 If your class includes English learners or other students who need support, use "Strategies to Support ELs."

Share and Discuss

Invite groups to read aloud their opinion statements. Ask students what evidence they have to support their opinions. Encourage students to ask and answer questions to check their understanding and to link their comments to the remarks of others.

Independent Writing and Conferring

 Opinion Prompts (BLM E) contains prompts for students to work with. Note that three differentiated prompts are provided. Based on your observation of students, cut out and assign the appropriate prompt to each student.

Assign prompt 1 (the practice prompt) to struggling writers. This prompt only requires students to analyze one source.

Assign prompt 2 (an unseen prompt based on one source) to students who need some scaffolding to write independently.

Assign prompt 3 (an unseen prompt based on two sources) to students who need little guidance and support for independent writing.

 Share

Invite two or three volunteers to read aloud the opinions they've formulated based on the prompt they addressed. Ask them to share the analysis they conducted to arrive at their opinion.

Strategies to Support ELs

Emerging (Beginning) and Expanding (Intermediate)

Beginning and intermediate ELs may have difficulty unpacking the prompt and making an opinion. While other students collaborate on the small-group activity or write independently, meet one on one with students to support developmentally appropriate comprehension and writing skills based on their independent writing and language levels.

All Levels

If you have ELs whose first language is Spanish, share these English/Spanish cognates: **opinion/la opinión; reason/la razón**.

Organize an Opinion Using a Planning Chart

W.4.1a, W.4.1b, W.4.1c, W.4.1d, W.4.4, W.4.8, W.4.10, SL.4.1a, SL.4.1b, SL.4.1c, SL.4.1d, SL.4.2, SL.4.3

Mentor Text

Objectives

In this mini-lesson, students will:

• Learn the role of reasons and evidence in an opinion text.

• Organize evidence to support reasons using a planning chart.

• Work collaboratively in a small group.

• Share ideas during whole-group discussion.

• Apply the mini-lesson to their independent opinion text planning.

Preparation

Materials Needed

• Source text: "Zoos Preserve Animal Species" and "Baby Panda Goes on Exhibit" from *Opinions About Modern Zoos*

• Opinion Text Planning Chart (BLM F)

• Conferring Prompts

 **Focus**

Introduce the Mini-Lesson

Explain to students that once writers have formed their opinions, they need to develop their ideas. To develop ideas for an opinion text, writers think about how to support an opinion with reasons and evidence. Tell students that today you'll show them how to use a planning chart to organize reasons and evidence to support an opinion.

Model Organizing Your Ideas

 Display and reread the opinion writing prompt on page 15 and "Zoos Preserve Animal Species" from *Opinions About Modern Zoos.*

 Display a blank Opinion Text Planning Chart (BLM F). Explain that you will model organizing ideas, as if you are the writer of the opinion essay "Zoos Preserve Animal Species." Use the sample think-alouds as you gather evidence from the source text and display the entries on the planning chart.

Opinion: The most important reason to have modern zoos is to preserve animal species.	
Reasons	**Evidence/Source**
Some animals face a high risk of extinction in the wild.	According to IUCN, more than 4,000 species are on the critically endangered list. (page 4, "Baby Panda Goes on Exhibit")
Zoos give endangered animals a safe and healthy home.	The Bronx Zoo took in abandoned snow leopard cub who is now part of the breeding program for endangered snow leopards. (page 7, "Baby Panda Goes on Exhibit") "Most male sea otters live for about twelve years in the wild. Eddie is almost sixteen years old." (page 11, "Elderly Sea Otter Becomes Basketball Sensation")
Zoo programs allow endangered animal populations to grow.	There are 325 pandas living in captivity; zoos have developed a successful plan to breed pandas. (page 5, "Baby Panda Goes on Exhibit") More than eighty snow leopard cubs have been born at the Bronx Zoo. (page 7, "Baby Panda Goes on Exhibit")

Conclusion:
Zoos make sure that the widest variety of animal species is preserved. The number of endangered species is growing. Animals that live in the wild have less space. Zoos offer a safe and healthy place for animals to live where endangered animal populations can grow.

Sample Opinion Text Planning Chart (BLM F)

Opinion. Say: *I think about the prompt and ask myself, "What is the most important reason to have modern zoos?" After rereading the source text, my opinion is that the most important job is to preserve animal species.*

Reason. Say: *Remember, it's not enough for me to state my opinion. I also need to provide clear reasons for my opinion. My reasons are that more animals are becoming endangered, and zoos give endangered species a safe and healthy home. Also, zoo programs allow animal populations to grow.*

Evidence. Say: *Now I need to support my reasons with evidence from the text. When I give strong evidence to support my reasons, it makes my opinion strong, too. It makes my opinion more solid.*

Evidence from "Baby Panda Goes on Exhibit." Say: *My opinion is that zoos are helping to save endangered animals from extinction. Remember that one of my reasons is that zoos give endangered species a safe, healthy home. Evidence from this article is that zoos have been working to successfully breed pandas. The San Diego Zoo's pandas have added six cubs. Another piece of evidence is that some zoos, such as the Bronx Zoo, help save animals born in the wild.*

 **Rehearse**

Practice Organizing Your Ideas

 Distribute copies of BLM F and display "Baby Panda Goes on Exhibit." Ask students to work in small groups to generate at least three pieces of text evidence to support the opinion that the most important reason to have modern zoos is to preserve animal species. Tell students that you will focus on how to write an effective conclusion later, but that for now students should jot ideas down during the planning stage.

If your class includes English learners or other students who need support, use "Strategies to Support ELs."

Share Ideas

Invite a spokesperson from each group to report on the evidence their group identified in the text. Make sure that students have actually used information from the text–not their own creative thinking–to support the reason. Stress the importance of citing sources when writing an opinion to a source.

Independent Writing and Conferring

Review the key points from this mini-lesson: strong opinion writers think through the reasons and the evidence that supports their opinions before they begin to draft.

Ask students to apply what they have learned as they organize their ideas for their opinion piece during independent writing time. During conferences, guide students to focus on clearly stating the reasons for their opinions and on locating the text evidence that supports their reasons.

 **Share**

Bring students together. Invite volunteers to share their opinions, reasons, and some of the text evidence they plan to use. Provide time for students to ask clarifying questions to be sure they understand how to plan writing an opinion text effectively.

Strategies to Support ELs

Emerging (Beginning) and Expanding (Intermediate)

Work with EL students one on one while other students work independently or with a partner. Help them voice a simple opinion about zoos in any way they can, and then help them find support for their opinions in the text.

Expanding (Intermediate) and Bridging (Advanced)

Pair ELs with fluent English speakers to use the planning chart as they write down reasons and evidence for their opinions.

All Levels

If you have ELs whose first language is Spanish, share these English/Spanish cognates: **preserve/preserver; species/los especies; evidence/la evidencia; idea/la idea; opinion/la opinión; reason/la razón**.

State Your Opinion and Reasons Clearly

W.4.1a, W.4.1b, W.4.4, W.4.10, SL.4.1a, SL.4.1b, SL.4.1c, SL.4.1d, SL.4.2, SL.4.3

Objectives

In this mini-lesson, students will:

- Find and analyze the opinions and reasons in an opinion text.
- Share analysis during collaborative conversations.
- Apply the mini-lesson to their own drafting.

Preparation

Materials Needed

- Conferring Prompts

Build Language and Conventions

Based on your observations of students' writing, build language conventions, knowledge, and vocabulary using the Language Mini-Lessons. See the unit pacing guide for suggested language mini-lessons to support opinion writing.

 **Focus**

Introduce the Mini-Lesson

Explain that this drafting mini-lesson will focus on how writers begin an opinion text by clearly stating their opinion and the reasons for their opinion.

Model Stating an Opinion and Reasons Clearly

 Display and read aloud the first modeling text.

> Zoos are a fun place to see lots of different animals. Many people visit zoos. Modern zoos provide a great opportunity to learn.

Modeling Text 1

Ask: *Can you tell what the author's opinion is? Can you tell what his reasons are?*

Guide students to understand that the author may have an opinion about zoos, or he may just be introducing a report on how zoos educate people. Explain that opinion writers need to clearly state their reasons and their opinion up front.

 Display and read aloud the second modeling text.

> Where would you go if you wanted to see animals from around the world? Unless you had the time and money to visit every continent, you'd go to a zoo! Modern zoos offer the public a unique opportunity to connect with the natural world. They provide entertaining experiences. Zoos also inspire people to learn more about animals. Therefore, education is the most important function of a modern zoo.

Modeling Text 2

Reread sentences 1 and 2. Explain that the writer's first sentence is a question that grabs the reader's attention. The author answers her question in the second sentence and introduces her thinking about modern zoos. Zoos are a place where people can see animals from around the world.

Reread sentences 3, 4, and 5. Point out that each of these sentences describes something that people can find at a modern zoo: a unique opportunity to connect with the natural world, entertainment, and inspiration to learn more about animals. Each sentence provides a reason for the opinion the writer states at the end of her paragraph.

 **Reread sentence 6.** Here, the writer states a clear, strong opinion that responds directly to the writing prompt. (If necessary, display and reread the opinion writing prompt on page 15 of *Opinions About Modern Zoos* to show students how the writer has directly responded to the question posed.)

Point out that the writer uses the word **therefore** to signal that the reasons she gives in the preceding sentences are what lead her to form this opinion. Explain that she emphasizes her opinion by placing it at the end of the paragraph.

Remind students that this is just one way to structure an opening paragraph. Most importantly, the opening paragraph must include both a clearly stated opinion and the reasons for that opinion.

 ## Rehearse

Practice Analyzing an Opinion and Reasons for Clarity

 Display and read aloud the practice text.

> Here's a simple fact: according to the International Union for Conservation of Nature (IUCN), more than 4,000 species are on the critically endangered list. That means they face a high risk of extinction in the wild. That also means that preserving animal species is the most important job for a zoo today. Zoos give endangered species a healthy home where they can flourish. Zoo programs help animals stay strong and repopulate.

Practice Text

Invite students to work in small groups to analyze this opening paragraph by identifying the opinion(s) and the reason(s) the writer gives for the opinion(s).

 If your class includes English learners or other students who need support, use "Strategies to Support ELs."

Share Ideas

Invite a spokesperson from each group to report on the opinions and reasons they identified in the paragraph.

 # Independent Writing and Conferring

Say: *We've just analyzed two opening paragraphs to learn how writers clearly state their opinions and reasons at the beginning of an opinion text. Writers may structure their opening paragraphs in different ways, but the most important thing to remember as you begin to draft your opinion pieces is to clearly state your opinion and your reasons for the opinion.*

During conferences, guide students so that they state opinions clearly and include reasons that they will be able to support with evidence in the text.

 ## Share

Invite volunteers to share their opening paragraphs. Ask students to listen for and identify opinions and reasons. Encourage listeners to provide supportive comments and to ask questions to clarify their understanding.

Strategies to Support ELs

Emerging (Beginning)

While other students complete the small-group activity (or during independent writing time), work one on one with beginning ELs to read the opening paragraph and identify the opinion and reasons.

Expanding (Intermediate) and Bridging (Advanced)

 Provide sentence frames that ELs can use to discuss the opening paragraph in their small groups:

My opinion is _____ because _____.
An example of a strong opinion is _____.
An example of a reason for that opinion is _____.

All Levels

If you have ELs whose first language is Spanish, share these English/Spanish cognates: **paragraph/el parrafo; support/soportar; evidence/la evidencia; opinion/la opinion; reason/la razón**.

Support Reasons with Facts and Evidence

W.4.1b, W.4.4, W.4.10, SL.4.1a, SL.4.1b, SL.4.1c, SL.4.1d, SL.4.2, SL.4.3

Mentor Text

Objectives

In this mini-lesson, students will:

- Identify facts and evidence in a text to support an opinion and reasons.

- Evaluate how well evidence supports specific reasons.

- Select text evidence during independent drafting.

Preparation

Materials Needed

- Source texts: "Zoos Are a Learning Environment," "Baby Panda Goes on Exhibit," and "Elderly Sea Otter Becomes Basketball Sensation" from *Opinions About Modern Zoos*

- Conferring Prompts

 **Focus**

Introduce the Mini-Lesson

Explain that in this drafting mini-lesson you will show students how writers cite, or include, specific facts and evidence from a text to support their opinions and reasons in the body of an opinion piece.

Model Citing Text Evidence

 Display and read "Zoos Are a Learning Environment." Ask a volunteer to restate the writer's opinion and reasons.

 Display the modeling text.

> Zoo keepers are often stationed at exhibits to answer questions. For example, the Oregon Zoo responded to the public's interest in Eddie by having keepers talk about sea otters and the science of behavioral enrichment. Sometimes, a zoo will offer special lectures. They even fly in expert zoologists to speak on a variety of topics, as happened at the San Diego Zoo.

Modeling Text

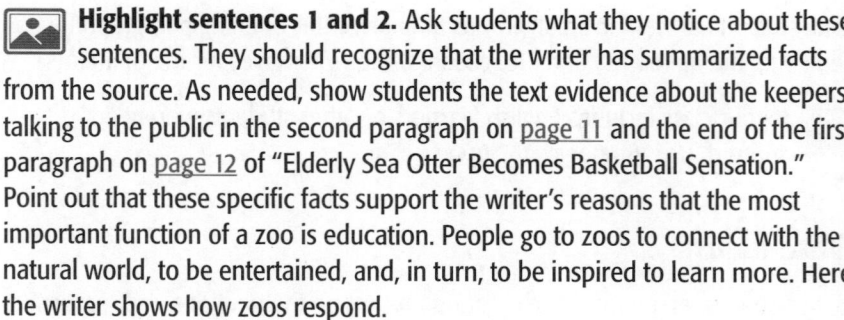 **Highlight sentences 1 and 2.** Ask students what they notice about these sentences. They should recognize that the writer has summarized facts from the source. As needed, show students the text evidence about the keepers talking to the public in the second paragraph on page 11 and the end of the first paragraph on page 12 of "Elderly Sea Otter Becomes Basketball Sensation." Point out that these specific facts support the writer's reasons that the most important function of a zoo is education. People go to zoos to connect with the natural world, to be entertained, and, in turn, to be inspired to learn more. Here the writer shows how zoos respond.

Highlight sentences 3 and 4. Ask students what they notice about these sentences. They should recognize that the writer summarizes details from a different source text to support her reasons and opinion. Review the text evidence on page 6 of "Baby Panda Goes on Exhibit."

Say: *These sentences summarize text evidence that supports the author's opinion that zoos serve to provide education. Notice also that the evidence supports the reasons the author gives for her opinion—zoos offer people a chance to connect with the natural world and that connection inspires people to want to learn more about animals.*

Emphasize that when writers look for text evidence to support their opinions and reasons, they must make sure they include specific facts and details that come directly from the source. And they must make sure the evidence directly supports their reasons and opinions.

Rehearse

Practice Supporting Reasons with Evidence

 Display the practice text and read it with students.

> Of course, modern zoos do more than put endangered animals on display. As the "Elderly Sea Otter" article explained, zoos also have behavioral-enrichment programs. These programs help animals stay strong by offering them opportunities to do what they would do in the wild.

Practice Text

Ask students to work in small groups to analyze the text to determine if the writer has supported her opinion and reason with solid evidence. Students should be prepared to identify the type of evidence in the passage—whether it is a direct quotation or a summary—where the evidence came from, and why (or why not) it is strong evidence.

 If your class includes English learners or other students who need support, use "Strategies to Support ELs."

Share Ideas

Invite volunteers to share evidence that supports the writer's opinion and reason. Students should note whether the writer is quoting directly or summarizing the text. Discuss how choosing the best text evidence makes an opinion piece stronger. Encourage students to explain their own ideas and understanding about citing text evidence in support of reasons and opinions.

Independent Writing and Conferring

Say: *We've learned that it is important to select strong evidence from a text to support your opinions and reasons. As you draft your opinion piece, remember to choose evidence that matches your opinion and the reasons you formed that opinion. If you can't find any strong evidence, then you may need to rethink your opinion.*

Share

Invite volunteers to share the text evidence they select during independent writing. Provide time for students to ask clarifying questions that facilitate their understanding of the mini-lesson.

Strategies to Support ELs

Emerging (Beginning)

While other students complete the small-group activity (or during independent writing time), work one on one with beginning ELs to practice sharing opinions and stating evidence. State an opinion and give a piece of evidence. For example, **say:** *I like soccer. Soccer is fast.*

Provide sentence frames to help students provide opinions about sports. If necessary, show students pictures of different sports to demonstrate.

I like _____.
_____ is _____.

Write students opinions as they use the sentence frames. Point out the opinion sentence and the reason sentence.

Expanding (Intermediate) and Bridging (Advanced)

Pair ELs with fluent English speakers during the small-group activity.

All Levels

If you have ELs whose first language is Spanish, share these English/Spanish cognates: **cite/citar; summarize/resumir; paragraph/el parrafo; support/soportar; evidence/la evidencia; opinion/la opinión; reason/la razón.**

Use Linking Words and Phrases

W.4.1b, W.4.1c, W.4.4, W.4.10, SL.4.1a, SL.4.1b, SL.4.1c, SL.4.1d, SL.4.2, SL.4.3

 **Focus**

Objectives

In this mini-lesson, students will:

• Understand and identify linking words and phrases in an opinion text.

• Add linking words and phrases to connect opinions and reasons.

• Apply the mini-lesson to their independent writing.

Preparation

Materials Needed

• Conferring Prompts

Build Language and Conventions

Based on your observations of students' writing, build language conventions, knowledge, and vocabulary using the Language Mini-Lessons. See the unit pacing guide for suggested language mini-lessons to support opinion writing.

Introduce the Mini-Lesson

Explain to students that when stating an opinion, it's important to give the reasons *why* you have that opinion. Writers use linking words and phrases, such as **because**, **then**, and **likewise**, to connect their opinions and their reasons. In this mini-lesson, students will learn how to use linking words and phrases to connect their opinions and their reasons.

Model Using Linking Words and Phrases

 Display and read aloud the modeling text.

When the public finds out about a new baby animal, it flocks to the zoo. Once there, people have many opportunities to learn about these and dozens of other types of animals.

Likewise, exhibit signs give the public good information. For example, signs at the Komodo dragon exhibit mentioned in the "Elderly Sea Otter" article tell about where the animal can be found in the wild.

Modeling Text

Reread paragraph 1. Explain that the author uses the phrase "once there" to link her reasons—people go to the zoo to be entertained and to connect with the natural world—with evidence from the text to support her opinion—zoos provide learning opportunities for people.

Reread paragraph 2. Point out the linking word **likewise**. Explain that the writer uses this word to introduce more evidence to support her opinion. Then she uses the linking phrase "for example" to cite the specific evidence.

Rehearse

Practice Using Linking Words and Phrases

 Display and read aloud the practice text.

> Zoos should provide behavioral-enrichment programs for animals. These activities reinforce their natural behaviors. Animals in zoos need to keep their minds and their bodies healthy.

Practice Text

Ask students to work with a partner to complete the following:
- identify the writer's opinion;
- identify the writer's reason;
- identify evidence; and
- add linking words and/or phrases to connect the reason to the opinion and/or to the evidence.

 If your class includes English learners or other students who need support, use "Strategies to Support ELs."

Share Practice Sentences

 Call on students to point out the writer's opinion and reasons. Ask other students to read their text revision incorporating the linking words and phrases. Encourage students to share a variety of revisions. If necessary, display the example text.

> Zoos should provide behavioral-enrichment programs for animals because these activities reinforce their natural behaviors. Also, animals in zoos need to keep their minds and their bodies healthy.

Example Text

Independent Writing and Conferring

Remind students that linking words and phrases help writers make the clear connection between their opinions and the reasons for their opinions. Writers also use linking words and phrases to make connections between reasons for an opinion and evidence from the text.

Encourage students to use linking words and phrases in their opinion drafts during independent writing time.

Share

Bring students together. Invite volunteers who have effectively used linking words and phrases in their opinion pieces to read aloud from their work.

Strategies to Support ELs

Emerging (Beginning)

 While other students complete the partner activity (or during independent writing time), work with small groups of ELs to connect opinions with reasons. Model the process by stating an opinion linked by a reason. Show students an apple. Pantomime eating an apple. **Say:** *I like apples because they are crunchy.* Provide a sentence frame and have students state things they like and why. For example:

I like _____ because _____.

Expanding (Intermediate) and Bridging (Advanced)

Pair ELs with fluent English speakers during the partner activity.

All Levels

 If you have ELs whose first language is Spanish, share these English/Spanish cognates: **evidence/la evidencia; opinion/la opinión; reason/la razón**.

Use Different Ways to Introduce Source Evidence

W.4.1b, W.4.1c, W.4.4, W.4.10, SL.4.1a, SL.4.1b, SL.4.1c, SL.4.1d, SL.4.2, SL.4.3

Objectives

In this mini-lesson, students will:

• Understand and identify ways to introduce source evidence in an opinion text.

• Use different approaches to referencing source text evidence.

• Apply the mini-lesson to their independent writing.

Preparation

Materials Needed

• Conferring Prompts

 **Focus**

Introduce the Mini-Lesson

Explain to students that when writing an opinion piece, there are different ways to introduce evidence from a source text. Writers can introduce evidence by identifying the source, either by its title or by a description. When quoting directly from a source, writers use quotation marks and attribute the quote. Writers can introduce evidence by paraphrasing—or restating in their own words—either specific examples from a source text or general information gathered from one or more sources. In this mini-lesson, students will learn different ways to introduce evidence from a source text to support their reasons and opinions.

Model Using Different Ways to Introduce Source Evidence

 Display the modeling text.

1. Zookeepers today make sure animals have more than their basic needs of food and shelter met. They give their animals activities to keep their natural skills sharp. For example, as the article on Eddie the otter explained, the National Zoo in Washington, D.C., hides prey for its Komodo dragon to hunt.

2. To quote zoologist Jed Cotona: "Animals that live in the wild now are having trouble finding enough space."

3. For example, signs at the Komodo dragon exhibit mentioned in the "Elderly Sea Otter" article tell about where the animal can be found in the wild.

Modeling Text

Read example 1. In this example, the writer introduces evidence by paraphrasing it from the source. The source itself is introduced by the linking phrase "for example," but instead of using the title of the source text, the writer describes it as "the article on Eddie the otter."

Read example 2. Here the author introduces a direct quotation from a source by stating that she's about to quote someone and then naming him: "To quote zoologist Jed Cotona."

Read example 3. To introduce this source, the author first states the evidence (signs at the Komodo dragon exhibit), and then tells where this evidence comes from by giving the title of the article ("mentioned in the 'Elderly Sea Otter' article").

Rehearse

Practice Using Different Ways to Introduce Source Evidence

 Display and read aloud the practice text.

1. According to the "Baby Panda" article, 325 pandas live in captivity.

2. The San Diego Zoo's pandas have already added six cubs. "This is clearly a success story. Pandas, in general, do not breed well in captivity," said a San Diego Zoo spokesperson.

Practice Text

Ask students to work with a partner to brainstorm different ways to introduce source evidence in these sentences. For example 1, students may use the complete title of the article ("Baby Panda Goes on Exhibit"). They may try different words and phrases, such as "As the 'Baby Panda' article states" or "the article says that . . ." For example 2, students may use a phrase such as "According to a San Diego Zoo spokesperson," or they may paraphrase the comments. Have students write their revised sentences and be prepared to share them with the class.

 If your class includes English learners or other students who need support, use "Strategies to Support ELs."

Share Practice Sentences

Ask volunteers to share their revised sentences. Have students share some of the words and phrases they brainstormed. Record their ideas on a list that students can refer to as they draft their opinion pieces.

Independent Writing and Conferring

Remind students that writers introduce source text evidence in many different ways. Explain that, depending on the evidence available in the source text, a writer may want to use some or all of the ways you have discussed. Encourage students to use two or three ways to introduce evidence in their opinion drafts during independent writing time.

Share

Bring students together. Invite volunteers who have introduced evidence in different ways in their opinion pieces to read aloud from their work.

Strategies to Support ELs

Emerging (Beginning)

While other students complete the partner activity (or during independent writing time), work with students to orally practice sentences using the pronouns **he**, **she**, **I**, and using proper nouns. For example, **say:** *He sits there. John sits there. I sit at the desk. Mr. Jones sits at the desk.*

Expanding (Intermediate) and Bridging (Advanced)

Pair ELs with fluent English speakers during the partner activity.

All Levels

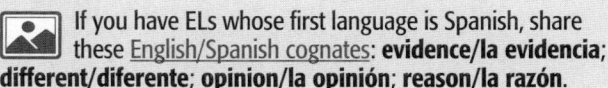 If you have ELs whose first language is Spanish, share these English/Spanish cognates: **evidence/la evidencia; different/diferente; opinion/la opinión; reason/la razón.**

Write a Conclusion that Supports the Opinion

W.4.1d, W.4.4, W.4.10, SL.4.1a, SL.4.1b, SL.4.1c, SL.4.1d, SL.4.2, SL.4.3

Objectives

In this mini-lesson, students will:

• Understand that conclusions restate the opinions and reasons expressed in an introduction.

• Evaluate source introductions and conclusions.

• Apply the mini-lesson to their independent writing.

Preparation

Materials Needed

• Conferring Prompts

Build Language and Conventions

Based on your observations of students' writing, build language conventions, knowledge, and vocabulary using the Language Mini-Lessons. See the unit pacing guide for suggested language mini-lessons to support opinion writing.

 Focus

Introduce the Mini-Lesson

Explain that this mini-lesson will focus on how to write a strong conclusion to an opinion text.

Model Writing a Conclusion

 Display and read aloud the introduction and conclusion from "Zoos Are a Learning Environment."

Introduction

Where would you go if you wanted to see animals from around the world? Unless you had the time and money to visit every continent, you'd go to a zoo! Modern zoos offer the public a unique opportunity to connect with the natural world. They provide entertaining experiences. Zoos also inspire people to want to learn more about animals. Therefore, education is the most important function of a modern zoo.

Conclusion

In summary, when people learn that animals such as pandas and snow leopards are endangered, they care more about them. When people learn that sea otters, like human beings, can get arthritis, they feel closer to our planet's cohabitants. Zoos make people feel connected to animals from every part of the globe. This is good for people. It is even better for the animals. If people learn about animals, they will want to help them even more.

Modeling Text

Say: *The conclusion uses different words, but the message is the same. When people learn about animals, they will care more about them and they'll feel more connected to them. Zoos provide the learning that helps people feel connected. The last sentence also adds a new thought, the idea that learning about animals will make people want to help them more, too.*

 Rehearse

Evaluate an Introduction and Conclusion

Invite students to work in pairs to evaluate another introduction and conclusion. Students should be prepared to answer the following questions:

• *Does the conclusion restate the opinion the writer stated in the introduction?*

• *Does the conclusion restate the reasons for the writer's opinion?*

• *How did the writer vary her language in the introduction and conclusion?*

Display and read aloud the practice text.

Introduction

Here's a simple fact: according to the International Union for Conservation of Nature (IUCN), more than 4,000 species are on the critically endangered list. That means they face a high risk of extinction in the wild. That also means that preserving animal species is the most important job for a zoo today. Zoos give endangered species a healthy home where they can flourish. Zoo programs help animals stay strong and repopulate.

Conclusion

In conclusion, wild places are shrinking. The number of endangered species is growing. To quote zoologist Jed Cotona: "Animals that live in the wild now are having trouble finding enough space." Zoos offer a place where animals can be happy, healthy, and even increase in number.

Practice Text

 If your class includes English learners or other students who need support, use "Strategies to Support ELs."

Share Ideas

Call on students to answer specific questions related to the practice text.

Independent Writing and Conferring

Say: *We've learned that the conclusion is the author's last chance to summarize his or her opinion and reasons and leave the reader with something to think about. Remember to write strong conclusions for your opinion texts.*

Encourage students to apply this mini-lesson as they write conclusions to their opinion texts during independent writing time. During conferences, reinforce students' use of this and other strategies using the prompts on your conferring flip chart.

 **Share**

Ask two or three students to share the introductions and conclusions they have drafted during independent writing. Ask others to listen for how the conclusions support the introductions.

Strategies to Support ELs

Emerging (Beginning)

Pair beginning ELs with fluent English speakers to answer the questions about the practice text. Keep in mind that they may not be able to contribute many ideas orally. Work with ELs individually to reinforce concepts while other students write independently.

Expanding (Intermediate) and Bridging (Advanced)

 Provide simple sentence frames to help ELs talk about the practice text:

The opinion in the introduction is _____.
The opinion in the conclusion is _____.
The reasons in the introduction are _____.
The reasons in the conclusion are _____.

All Levels

If you have ELs whose first language is Spanish, share these English/Spanish cognates: **paragraph/el parrafo**; **conclusion/la conclusión**; **evidence/la evidencia**; **opinion/la opinion**; **reason/la razón**.

Use a Variety of Sentence Structures

W.4.4, W.4.5, W.4.10, SL.4.1a, SL.4.1b, SL.4.1c, SL.4.1d, SL.4.2, SL.4.3

 **Focus**

Objectives

In this mini-lesson, students will:

- Understand and identify different sentence structures in an opinion text.

- Practice writing an opinion text using a variety of sentence structures.

- Apply this mini-lesson to their independent writing.

Preparation

Materials Needed

- Conferring Prompts

Build Language and Conventions

Based on your observations of students' writing, build language conventions, knowledge, and vocabulary using the Language Mini-Lessons. See the unit pacing guide for suggested language mini-lessons to support opinion writing.

Introduce the Mini-Lesson

Explain to students that, as writers, they will want to create interesting sentences to engage the readers of their opinion texts. One way to write well and engage readers is to use varied sentence structures. In this mini-lesson, you are going to show students how to use a variety of sentence structures in their opinion texts.

Model Using a Variety of Sentence Structures

 Display and read aloud the modeling text.

> Where would you go if you wanted to see animals from around the world? Unless you had the time and money to visit every continent, you'd go to a zoo! Modern zoos offer the public a unique opportunity to connect with the natural world. They provide entertaining experiences. Zoos also inspire people to want to learn more about animals. Therefore, education is the most important function of a modern zoo.

Modeling Text

Reread the first two sentences. Point out that the writer uses two different sentence structures to hook the reader's interest. Sentence 1 is a question. Explain that questions help drive the text forward. Sentence 2 not only answers the question, but it is also written using the dependent clause "unless you had the time and money to visit every continent." Dependent clauses and introductory phrases provide an interesting rhythm so that sentences don't all sound the same.

Reread sentences 3 and 4. Point out that sentence 3 is quite long, while sentence 4 contains only four words. This contrast of long and short is another way to vary sentence structure and to create interest.

Reread the final sentence. Point out that the writer uses the linking word **therefore** to transition to the clearly stated opinion.

Rehearse

Practice Using a Variety of Sentence Structures

 Display the practice text.

> Modern zoos help endangered animals. They give them a safe place to live. They give people information about the animals. They have behavioral-enrichment programs. The programs help animals stay strong. They give them opportunities to do what they would do in the wild.

Practice Text

Help students see that these sentences use the same or similar sentence structures. Ask students to work with a partner to rewrite the practice sentences using a variety of sentence structures. Students may revise or totally rewrite the sentences. Encourage them to experiment with asking questions, using both long and short sentences, using dependent clauses, using compound sentences, and using transitional words and phrases. Pairs should write the sentences down and be prepared to read them to the class.

 If your class includes English learners or other students who need support, use "Strategies to Support ELs."

Share Practice Sentences

Invite students to read aloud the revised or rewritten sentences. Encourage listeners to ask questions to clarify their understanding of different sentence structures.

Independent Writing and Conferring

Say: *We learned that we should vary our sentence structures when writing an opinion text. Using a variety of sentence structures will keep your readers' interest and can help you clarify your opinions and reasons. Remember to include several different sentence structures as you draft your opinion pieces.*

Encourage students to use several different sentence structures when writing about modern zoos in their opinion drafts during independent writing time. During student conferences, reinforce students' use of varied sentence structures using the prompts on your conferring flip chart.

 # Share

Bring students together. Invite volunteers who have effectively used a variety of sentence structures in their opinion pieces to read aloud from their work.

Strategies to Support ELs

Emerging (Beginning)

While other students complete the partner activity (or during independent writing time), work one on one with ELs to practice writing and saying several different sentence structures. For example, **say:** *My chair is soft. I sit and read. How long can I sit here?* Model the actions as you speak. Help students write the sentences and then reread them together. Invite students to act out each sentence.

Expanding (Intermediate) and Bridging (Advanced)

Pair ELs with fluent English speakers during the partner activity.

All Levels

If you have ELs whose first language is Spanish, share these English/Spanish cognates: **conjunction/la conjunción; phrase/la frase; opinion/la opinión; reason/la razón.**

Avoid the First Person When Stating an Opinion

W.4.4, W.4.5, W.4.10, SL.4.1a, SL.4.1b, SL.4.1c, SL.4.1d, SL.4.2, SL.4.3, L.4.3b

 **Focus**

Objectives

In this mini-lesson, students will:

- Distinguish between first and third person point of view.

- Compare and analyze opinion texts using the first and third person.

- Revise a first person opinion text into the third person.

- Apply this mini-lesson to their independent writing.

Preparation

Materials Needed

- Conferring Prompts

Introduce the Mini-Lesson

Explain to students that when writing an opinion piece, writers want readers to focus on the opinion and the evidence, not on an author's emotions and personal feelings about the topic. Therefore, they usually avoid using the first person point of view, or speaking directly to the reader.

In this mini-lesson, you will show students how to adopt a more formal tone by avoiding using first person when analyzing nonfiction informational articles for an opinion text.

Model Avoiding the First Person When Analyzing Literature

 Display and read aloud the first <u>modeling text</u>.

> I can see why it makes sense from a business standpoint for zoos to use behavioral-enrichment activities. These activities are fun to watch, so they often draw big crowds of visitors. My favorite activity is when the zookeepers give pumpkins to the elephants.

Modeling Text 1

Point out to students that the writer is using the first person, referring to himself as "I."

Say: *With the use of first person in this example, the writer puts himself into the text. As a reader, I'm not able to concentrate on the evidence that he presents because I'm too busy thinking about his personal experiences at the zoo.*

 Display and read aloud the second <u>modeling text</u>.

> Modern zoos are businesses, too. They need people to come see the animals. Behavioral-enrichment programs are important for the animals. They are also crowd-pleasers.

Modeling Text 2

Ask: *What do you notice about this text? How is it different?*

Guide students to understand that this text also conveys opinions, but it leaves out the writer's personal experiences. The reader can consider the opinion and the evidence without the writer's voice intruding.

 **Rehearse**

Practice Avoiding the First Person When Analyzing Informational Articles

 Display the practice text.

> I can't stand it when I hear the details about how few pandas and snow leopards are left in the world. I'm really worried about endangered species. When a zookeeper standing outside an exhibit explains to me how Eddie the sea otter can get arthritis, just like my grandmother, it makes me feel like so sad. When I visit a zoo, the more I learn about the animals, the more I want to help them.

Practice Text

Ask students to work with a partner to rewrite the practice sentences avoiding the first person perspective. Pairs should write their sentences and be prepared to read them to the class and explain how changing the perspective improved the opinion text.

 If your class includes English learners or other students who need support, use "Strategies to Support ELs."

Share Practice Sentences

Invite partners to read aloud their sentences. Have them explain their own ideas and understanding about why writers avoid the first person voice when they analyze text for an opinion piece.

 # Independent Writing and Conferring

Say: *We learned that it's important to avoid using the first person when writing an opinion in response to a prompt that asks us to analyze informational articles. We want the readers of our opinions to focus on the opinion and the evidence we present, not on our personal feelings. As you draft your opinion piece, remember to use the third person point of view.*

Remind students to avoid using the first person point of view when they analyze the articles from *Opinions About Modern Zoos,* or other news articles, for their opinion pieces. During student conferences, reinforce students' use of the third person in their writing.

 **Share**

Bring students together. Invite volunteers who have effectively used the third person perspective in their opinion pieces to read aloud from their work.

Strategies to Support ELs

Emerging (Beginning)

While other students complete the partner activity (or during independent writing time), work one on one with beginning ELs to practice differentiating between speaking and writing using first and third person points of view. Display sentence frames to help students form sentences.

I think _____ is fun.
[Name] thinks _____ is fun.
I like to eat _____.
[Name] likes to eat _____.

Expanding (Intermediate) and Bridging (Advanced)

Pair ELs with fluent English speakers during the partner activity.

All Levels

If you have ELs whose first language is Spanish, share these English/Spanish cognates: **animal/el animal; species/los especies; point of view/el punto de vista; opinion/la opinión; reason/la razón; person/la persona.**

Revise Your Opinion to Link Reasons and Evidence

W.4.1b, W.4.1c, W.4.4, W.4.5, W.4.10, SL.4.1a, SL.4.1b, SL.4.1c, SL.4.1d, SL.4.2, SL.4.3, L.4.3b

 **Focus**

Objectives

In this mini-lesson, students will:

• Understand how to revise an opinion text by strengthening linking words and phrases to connect reasons and evidence.

• Add stronger linking words and phrases to connect reasons and evidence.

• Apply the mini-lesson to their independent writing.

Preparation

Materials Needed

• Conferring Prompts

Build Language and Conventions

Based on your observations of students' writing, build language conventions, knowledge, and vocabulary using the Language Mini-Lessons. See the unit pacing guide for suggested language mini-lessons to support opinion writing.

Introduce the Mini-Lesson

Explain that when writers revise their work, they reread it carefully and then make changes to improve it. Remind students that when stating an opinion, it's important to give the reasons why you have that opinion. Writers use linking words and phrases, such as **likewise**, "as a result," "that is why," and **therefore**, to connect reasons with the evidence to support the opinion. In this mini-lesson, students will learn about revising to strengthen the link between reasons and evidence.

Model Revising to Link Reasons and Evidence

 Display the modeling text (without revisions). Read the sentences aloud and model how a writer revises to link reasons and evidence.

> Education is the most important function of modern zoos. That is an important reason why ~~M~~modern zoos work hard to offer entertaining experiences. Visitors might see a Komodo dragon hunt for prey in his enclosure; or ~~A~~ a sea otter playing basketball. Those kinds of enrichment activities ~~Zoos~~ inspire people. As a result, ~~V~~visitors will want to learn more about animals and how to help them. If more people care about animals, there is a better chance that endangered species will survive.

Modeling Text

Read sentence 1. Explain that this is the writer's opinion.

Read sentences 2, 3, and 4. Explain that the writer is introducing reasons and evidence to support her opinion. **Say:** *This would be a stronger statement if there was a link between the opinion and the reason and evidence. The linking phrase "that is an important reason why" makes a connection between the opinion and the evidence. Also, I can add the linking word **or** to combine into one sentence the examples of entertaining activities people experience at zoos.*

Read sentence 5. Say: *I can add more specific language to this sentence to link the evidence—the animal activities—to the reason—those activities inspire people. I'll add the summary phrase "those kinds of enrichment activities" to make this link clear.*

Read sentence 6. Say: *This sentence provides an opportunity to make a point about my opinion that education is the most important function of a zoo. Adding the linking phrase "as a result" clarifies for readers the link between seeing animals at zoos and then wanting to learn more about them.*

Rehearse

Practice Using Linking Words and Phrases

 Display and read aloud the practice text.

> The most important job for modern zoos is to preserve animal species. More than 4,000 animal species are on the critically endangered list. These animals face a high risk of extinction in the wild. Modern zoos offer them a home. They can be healthy and safe. Zoo breeding programs can help animals repopulate. Their species will not disappear.

Practice Text

Ask students to work with a partner to identify the writer's opinion, reasons, and evidence, and to add linking words and/or phrases to connect the evidence to the reasons.

Brainstorm possible linking words, such as **instead**, **but**, **and**, **because**, **now**, **so**, **likewise**, and **sometimes**. If students need support, guide them to see that the last four sentences contain evidence to support the reasons.

 If your class includes English learners or other students who need support, use "Strategies to Support ELs."

Share Practice Sentences

Call on students to point out the writer's opinion and reasons. Ask other students to identify the evidence that supports the reasons.

Independent Writing and Conferring

Say: *When you revise your opinion texts, you can strengthen the presentation of evidence by using linking words to connect the evidence to the reasons for your opinion.*

Encourage students to use linking words and phrases to make connections between reasons and evidence as they revise their opinion drafts during independent writing time.

Share

Bring students together. Invite volunteers who have effectively used linking words and phrases in their opinion pieces to read aloud from their work.

Strategies to Support ELs

Emerging (Beginning)

 While other students complete the partner activity (or during independent writing time), continue to work with students to have them connect opinions with reasons. Model the process by stating an opinion linked by a reason. For example, pantomime enjoying jumping rope and feeling strong. **Say:** *I like jumping rope because it makes me strong.* Provide a sentence frame and have students state things they like and why.

I like _____ because _____.

Expanding (Intermediate)

Build on the beginning strategy above by working with students to link evidence to reasons. Model the process by stating the evidence that links to the reason. **Ask:** *How do I know jumping rope makes me strong? Because I have strong muscles in my legs.*

Expanding (Intermediate) and Bridging (Advanced)

 Pair ELs with fluent English speakers during the partner activity. Support them as they talk with their partner by providing sentence frames.

The opinion is _____.
The reason is _____.
The evidence is _____.

All Levels

 If you have ELs whose first language is Spanish, share these English/Spanish cognates: **important/importante**; **revise/revisar**; **opinion/la opinión**; **reason/la razón**.

Use a Checklist to Edit a Draft

W.4.1a, W.4.1b, W.4.1c, W.4.1d, W.4.4, W.4.5, W.4.10, SL.4.1a, SL.4.1b, SL.4.1c, SL.4.1d, SL.4.2, SL.4.3, L.4.3b

Objectives

In this mini-lesson, students will:

• Learn to edit their opinion drafts for grammar, spelling, and punctuation errors.

• Use an editing checklist to guide the editing of opinion texts.

• Apply the mini-lesson to their independent writing.

Preparation

Materials Needed

• Opinion Checklist

• Conferring Prompts

Build Language and Conventions

Based on your observations of students' writing, build language conventions, knowledge, and vocabulary using the Language Mini-Lessons. See the unit pacing guide for suggested language mini-lessons to support opinion writing.

 **Focus**

Introduce the Mini-Lesson

Explain that an important part of writing an opinion is editing the text after you've drafted it in order to correct errors. Explain that using a checklist will help students ensure they cover the important aspects of their writing during the editing process. This mini-lesson will focus on how to use a checklist to edit a text.

Model Using a Checklist to Edit a Piece of Writing

 Display the modeling text and the "Quality Writing Checklist" section from the Opinion Checklist.

> Visitors to modern zoos can see animals from all over the globe. Some of these animals are endangered species. ~~m~~More than 4,000 species are on the critically endangered list, which means they face a high risk of extinction. Zoos give~~s~~ rare and endangered animals homes where they can live safe, ~~healthily~~ healthy lives. The zookeepers make sure of that. They also ~~supplied~~ supply behavioral-enrichment activities that help animals: and ~~A~~are fun to watch. The basketball hoop for the ~~see~~ sea otter, Eddie, at the ~~o~~Oregon ~~z~~Zoo, is a good example. Playing basketball has helped his arthritis and enabled him to live to a ripe old age.

Modeling Text

Explain that you will model editing this text as if you are the writer. You will use the checklist to help look for specific problems with your writing. Model making the revisions as you think aloud.

Sentence fragments and run-on sentences. Say: *I read my draft to look for run-on sentences and sentence fragments. A sentence should have a subject and a verb and one idea. Sentence three is a run-on sentence. I need to divide it up by placing a period after the word **species** and capitalizing the word **more**. Further on, "Are fun to watch" is not a complete sentence. The subject is missing. I can fix this by removing the period at the end of the previous sentence, and adding the conjunction **and**. And I'll have to make **are** lowercase.*

Parts of speech. Say: *Now I want to look at how I use pronouns, adjectives, prepositions, and auxiliary words. I see that I used an adverb, **healthily**. That doesn't sound right. I'll edit that to **healthy**.*

Grammar. Say: *Let me reread to check my subject-verb agreements and my verb tenses. In the fourth sentence, **zoos** is plural, but **gives** matches a singular pronoun, so I'll revise it to **give**.*

Punctuation/capitalization/spelling. Say: *Now I'll check that I have used correct punctuation, capitalization, and spelling. I see several mistakes in the final two sentences. First, I have used the homonym **see** where I need **sea**. Then, I've left out commas to set off Eddie's name, so I'll add those on either side.*

*I also forgot to capitalize the name of the zoo, "Oregon Zoo." If I'm not sure if the word **zoo** should be capitalized, I can check the source text or go to the zoo website to find out the correct title.*

 ## Rehearse

Use a Checklist to Edit a Piece of Writing

 Display the underline{practice text} (without corrections) and distribute copies of the underline{Opinion Checklist}. Have students work with a partner and use the "Quality Writing Checklist" to edit the underline{practice text}.

Modern zoos are businesses. ~~It needs~~ They need people to come see the animals. Behavioral-enrichment programs help animals stay healthy, but they are also crowd-pleasers. Some popular zoo attractions include ~~k~~Komodo dragons hunting for food and tigers and lions chasing fake pray. Without zoos, we could eventually lose these and other endangered animals, like pandas. ~~t~~There are only 1,600 pandas left in the wild.

Practice Text

 If your class includes English learners or other students who need support, use underline{"Strategies to Support ELs."}

Share Ideas

Call on partners to share their experiences as they edited the practice text. What problems did they find? How did they fix the problems? Encourage students to discuss their editing choices and make other suggestions if they can.

 ## Independent Writing and Conferring

Say: *We've learned that to complete a final draft of an opinion piece, we need to make sure our writing is complete and correct. We can use a checklist to help us edit our drafts. Then we can make any necessary changes and prepare our final drafts for publishing.*

Encourage students to apply this mini-lesson as they work on the drafts of their opinion texts during independent writing time.

 ## Share

Call on two or three students to share how they edited their writing. Encourage listeners to offer comments and suggestions on their editing choices.

Strategies to Support ELs

Emerging (Beginning)

Beginning ELs are not ready to work on this writing process skill. While other students work with partners or write independently, meet one on one with students to support developmentally appropriate writing skills based on their independent writing and language skills.

Expanding (Intermediate) and Bridging (Advanced)

 Pair ELs with fluent English speakers during the partner activity. Support oral language by providing simple sentence frames:

This sentence has/does not have _____.
I can edit this sentence by _____.
I need to change _____ because _____.

All Levels

 If you have ELs whose first language is Spanish, share these English/Spanish cognates: **edit/editar; correct/correcto; punctuation/la puntuación; opinion/la opinión.**

Use Keyboarding Skills to Publish an Opinion

W.4.4, W.4.5, W.4.6, W.4.10, SL.4.1a, SL.4.1b, SL.4.1c, SL.4.1d, SL.4.2, SL.4.3, L.4.3b

Objectives

In this mini-lesson, students will:

• Understand how to use the spacebar correctly when typing their opinion pieces.

• Understand how to check the spacing between words and sentences.

• Work collaboratively with a partner or in a small group to publish an opinion text on a computer.

• Apply the mini-lesson to their independent opinion text planning.

Preparation

Materials Needed

• Conferring Prompts

Advanced Preparation

Students will need a handwritten example of an opinion text (either one that they've written or one that has been provided for them).

 **Focus**

Introduce the Mini-Lesson

Point out to students that most of the work they do in class is written by hand. But for important papers, such as reports or opinion texts, it is better to use a computer to publish their work. Explain that using a computer makes the paper neater and easier to read. It also makes it look more official, or professional. Point out that a professional look is not achieved simply by typing the text. Students must also use correct keyboarding skills. Explain that the focus of this mini-lesson is for students to learn to use the spacebar correctly and consistently to leave one space between words and one space between sentences.

Model Using a Computer to Publish an Opinion

 Display the first modeling text.

> There is no   telling what will happen to wild animals.   But we do know that without zoos, we could eventually lose all of the pandas and   snow leopards, among other   endangered animals.   According to the   "Baby Panda" article, 325 pandas live in captivity.   That may not   seem like a lot, but it is   about one-sixth the   total number of pandas   in the world.

Modeling Text 1

Point out that the text is difficult to read. Also, the opinion itself might be taken more seriously if it was correctly typed up with consistent use of the spacebar.

Say: *The inconsistency of the spaces between the words and sentences makes the paper look a little sloppy. It makes me think that maybe the writer didn't think through his ideas very carefully either.*

 Display the second modeling text, the version of the paragraph in which the spacebar is used consistently. Read it aloud to students.

> There is no telling what will happen to wild animals. But we do know that without zoos, we could eventually lose all of the pandas and snow leopards, among other endangered animals.
>
> According to the "Baby Panda" article, 325 pandas live in captivity. That may not seem like a lot, but it is about one-sixth the total number of pandas in the world.

Modeling Text 2

Grade 4 • ©2017 Benchmark Education Company, LLC

Point out to students that the correct, consistent use of the spacebar, leaving one space between words and one space between sentences, makes this text easy to read. Remind students that they want to make it easy for people to read their work. Explain that, because this text looks professional, the writer comes across as knowing what he is doing. Thus, a reader is more likely to take his opinion seriously.

 **Rehearse**

Practice Using a Computer to Publish an Opinion

Invite students to take a handwritten piece of writing and type it out using a computer. Students may work with a partner or in a small group. As needed, students should take turns typing so that each has an opportunity to use his or her keyboarding skills. Explain how to check if the spacing between words and sentences is correct. Demonstrate by using the arrow keys to check the spacing or by showing the formatting marks in the document.

 If your class includes English learners or other students who need support, use "Strategies to Support ELs."

Share Ideas

Invite a spokesperson from each partnership or group to report on the process of using the spacebar correctly. Ask students if they have any additional questions about how to check the spacing between words and sentences.

Independent Writing and Conferring

Review the key point from this mini-lesson: using a computer to publish their work can make it look neater and more professional. However, it is not enough simply to type a text. Students must also use the spacebar correctly and consistently in order to achieve a polished, professional-looking final draft.

Ask students to apply what they have learned as they finalize and type their opinion texts during independent writing time. During conferences, support students by giving feedback on their keyboarding skills, especially their use of the spacebar to leave one space between words and one space between sentences.

 **Share**

Bring students together. Invite volunteers to share about their experiences with keyboarding and using the computer to format and finalize their opinion texts.

Strategies to Support ELs

Emerging (Beginning) and Expanding (Intermediate)

Work with students one to one while other students work independently or with a partner or small group. Help them use beginning keyboarding skills to type any words they can on the computer. Encourage students to look at the screen and review the number of spaces they have placed between words and sentences. Print out the words and sentences.

Expanding (Intermediate) and Bridging (Advanced)

Pair ELs with fluent English speakers during the Rehearse activity.

All Levels

If you have ELs whose first language is Spanish, share these English/Spanish cognates: **computer/la computadora; opinion/la opinión; publish/publicar**.

Name _____ Date _____

Main Idea Chart

Main Ideas	Key Details

Name _____   Date _____

Analyze an Opinion Prompt

Prompt: The introduction says, "A modern zoo, like the earliest zoos, is for entertainment." The article about Eddie the otter states that people can only watch him play online. Do you think it is fair that visitors to the Oregon Zoo are not allowed to stand by Eddie's pool to watch him play? State your opinion and support it with evidence from the story.

Prompt Part	Prompt Part Is Asking . . .
Sentences 1 and 2	
Sentence 3	
Sentence 4	

Name _____   Date _____

Opinion Features Chart

Opinion Features	Examples from the Text

Name _____ Date _____

Opinion Evaluation Rubric

Opinion Title _____

Criteria	Text Examples
The writer clearly states his/her opinion.	
The writer gives clear reasons for the opinion.	
The writer's reasons are supported by evidence (examples, quotations, or restatements) from the text.	
The writer connects reasons to evidence using linking words and phrases.	
The writer provides a concluding statement or section that sums up the opinion.	

Name _____ Date _____

Opinion Prompts

1. You have read about the behavioral-enrichment programs at many zoos in the news article "Elderly Sea Otter Becomes Basketball Sensation." What do you think is the most important reason for these programs: to provide animals with activities that reinforce their natural behaviors or to provide entertainment for people who go to the zoo? Support your opinion with evidence from the text.

2. Zoos have been around for thousands of years. Based on "Baby Panda Goes on Exhibit," what is your opinion about continuing to maintain zoos into the future? Support your opinion with evidence from the text.

3. Zoos have been around for thousands of years. Based on "Baby Panda Goes on Exhibit" and "Elderly Sea Otter Becomes Basketball Sensation," what is your opinion about continuing to maintain zoos into the future? Support your opinion with evidence from both texts.

Name _____   Date _____

Opinion Text Planning Chart

Opinion:	
Reasons	**Evidence/Source**
Conclusion:	

Opinion Checklist

Title _____

	Yes	No	Not Sure
1. I introduce my topic with a lead that gets my readers' attention.	—	—	—
2. I state my opinion at the beginning of my paper.	—	—	—
3. I include reasons for my opinion based on my own thoughts about the topic.	—	—	—
4. I group connected ideas together.	—	—	—
5. I use evidence from the text to support my opinion.	—	—	—
6. I use linking words and phrases to connect reasons and evidence.	—	—	—
7. I include a concluding sentence or paragraph that makes my readers think.	—	—	—
8. My opinion follows an organized structure.	—	—	—
9. I choose words that make sense and make my opinion interesting.	—	—	—
10. I do not change my opinion.	—	—	—
11. I use different types of sentences.	—	—	—
12. I use my voice to show people how much I care about my opinion.	—	—	—

Quality Writing Checklist
I looked for and corrected . . .

	Yes	No	Not Sure
sentence fragments and run-ons.	—	—	—
parts of speech (pronouns, auxiliaries, adjectives, prepositions).	—	—	—
grammar.	—	—	—
indented paragraphs.	—	—	—
punctuation.	—	—	—
capitalization.	—	—	—
spelling.	—	—	—

Opinion
Student Self-Reflection Sheet

Title of the Source Text _____

Author of the Source Text _____

1. How did analyzing the source text help you form an opinion?

_____

_____

2. What did you learn about yourself as a writer? Think about the mini-lessons taught with this genre.

_____

_____

3. If you had to write another opinion essay, what would you do differently? For example, would you organize your ideas differently, state your opinion more clearly, identify more reasons and evidence, or write a stronger conclusion?

_____

_____

4. What was easy about writing your opinion essay?

_____

_____

5. What was difficult about writing your opinion essay?

_____

_____

6. It is very important to form an opinion that you can support with evidence from a text. What did you learn about this while writing your opinion essay?

_____

_____

Dear Family Members,

Our class is about to begin a Writer's Workshop unit on Opinion Texts. To write a strong opinion piece, writers state a clear position and support it with evidence and reasons. During this unit, we will read and evaluate opinion texts, and your child will have many opportunities to state and support his or her opinion. Your child will brainstorm, draft, revise and edit, and publish many opinion pieces.

This is always an exciting unit in which students will practice reading and analyzing a text and writing an opinion about it. During this unit, you can help your child by having conversations in which you share your opinions and reasons about everyday experiences, movies, food, books, television shows, music, and art. Discuss with your child how to state an opinion and provide reasons to support it by saying, "I think _____ because _____."

You can also ask your child questions to learn about his or her progress. For example:

• *What are you forming opinions about?*

• *What is your opinion? What reasons are you giving to support it?*

• *What have you written so far?*

• *What part of opinion writing do you enjoy most?*

• *What part of opinion writing is difficult to you?*

• *Are there other texts that you'd like to write an opinion piece about?*

Thanks in advance for supporting your child's writing experiences. I look forward to sharing his or her work with you!

Sincerely,

Estimados padres de familia:

Nuestra clase está por comenzar un Taller del Escritor sobre Textos de Opinión. Los escritores de textos de opinión exponen su posición con claridad y ofrecen evidencia de apoyo. En esta unidad vamos a leer y evaluar textos de opinión. Su hijo o hija tendrá muchas oportunidades para exponer su opinión y apoyarla con evidencia. Su hijo o hija tendrá la oportunidad de realizar una lluvia de ideas y elaborar un borrador. También podrá revisar, editar y publicar sus propios textos de opinión.

Esta unidad siempre resulta fascinante. Los estudiantes practicarán cómo leer y analizar un texto y cómo escribir una opinión sobre el texto. Ustedes pueden ayudar a su hijo o hija. Platiquen con él o ella sobre sus opiniones acerca de experiencias cotidianas, películas, alimentos, libros, programas de televisión, música y arte. Recuerden dar razones para apoyar sus opiniones. Muéstrenle a su hijo o hija cómo presentar una opinión fundamentada usando la siguiente estructura: "Yo pienso _____ porque _____".

También pueden investigar acerca del progreso de su hijo o hija haciéndole preguntas. Por ejemplo:

• *¿Sobre qué vas a opinar?*

• *¿Cuál es tu opinión? ¿Cuáles son las razones por las cuales opinas eso?*

• *¿Qué has escrito hasta el momento?*

• *¿Qué aspecto de escribir textos de opinión te gusta más?*

• *¿Qué aspecto de escribir textos de opinión te parece más difícil?*

• *¿Hay alguna otra cosa sobre la cual te gustaría escribir un texto de opinión?*

Les agradezco de antemano por apoyar las experiencias de su hijo o hija en torno a la escritura. ¡Espero compartir su trabajo con ustedes!

Atentamente,

Opinion Unit Class Status Sheet

Directions: At the end of each day's Writer's Workshop, document where each student is in the writing process. Use this information to help you identify students who may need support to progress.

Key:

B = Brainstorming	FD = Final Draft
N = Narrowing the Idea	TC = Teacher Conference
O = Organizing	PC = Peer Conference
D = Drafting	GC = Group Conference
RV = Revising	SR = Self-Reflection
E = Editing	

Students	Month: ____ Dates ____ to ____					Month: ____ Dates ____ to ____					Month: ____ Dates ____ to ____				
	M	T	W	Th	F	M	T	W	Th	F	M	T	W	Th	F

Grade 4 • ©2017 Benchmark Education Company, LLC

Opinion Teacher Rubric

Score	Planning and Implementation	Evidence of Genre Characteristics	Conventions of Grammar and Usage	Conventions of Mechanics
4	(CCSS W.4.1, W.4.4, W.4.5, L.4.3) The writer's ideas are well organized and well developed. The writer: • creates and maintains a meaningful organizational structure. • effectively groups related ideas. • uses well-chosen words and phrases that add effect to the opinion piece. • clearly maintains the opinion throughout the text.	(CCSS W.4.8, W.4.9b, L.4.3a) The writer demonstrates complete understanding of the features of an opinion text. The writer: • clearly introduces the topic with a strong lead that gets readers' attention. • states an opinion that shows a complete understanding of the topic. • includes multiple reasons for the opinion based on inferences made about the topic. • includes purposefully chosen text evidence to support reasons. • uses a wide variety of linking words and phrases that connect reasons with evidence. • includes an effective concluding sentence or paragraph that makes the reader think about the writer's ideas. • has a voice that shows a strong conviction about the opinion.	(CCSS L.4.1, W.4.5) The writer correctly implements all conventions. The writer: • produces well-developed complete sentences. • efficiently revises and corrects sentence fragments and run-ons. • uses parts of speech in unique ways. • uses grammar conventions in clear and concise ways.	(CCSS W.4.5, L.4.2) The writer correctly implements all conventions. The writer: • always correctly indents paragraphs. • makes no, or few, mechanical mistakes, and they do not hinder overall meaning.
3	The writer's ideas are adequately organized and developed. The writer: • creates and maintains an organizational structure. • groups connected ideas most of the time. • uses words and phrases that add effect to the opinion piece. • maintains the opinion throughout the text.	The writer demonstrates an adequate understanding of the features of an opinion text. The writer: • introduces the topic with a lead. • states an opinion about the topic. • includes at least two reasons for the opinion. • includes text evidence that supports each reason. • uses linking words and phrases that connect reasons with evidence. • includes a concluding sentence or paragraph. • has a voice that shows conviction about the opinion.	The writer implements most conventions. The writer: • produces complete sentences. • revises and corrects sentence fragments and run-ons most of the time. • uses correct parts of speech most of the time. • uses correct grammar conventions most of the time.	The writer implements most conventions. The writer: • correctly indents paragraphs most of the time. • makes occasional mechanical mistakes, but they do not hinder overall meaning.
2	The writer's ideas are somewhat organized and developed. The writer: • attempts to create an organizational structure. Ideas are difficult to follow. • attempts to group connected ideas. • inadequately maintains the opinion throughout the text. Text suggests the writer does not understand the stated opinion. • uses few words and phrases that add effect to the opinion piece.	The writer demonstrates some understanding of the features of an opinion text. The writer: • attempts to introduce the topic. Lead is weak. • states a weak opinion about the topic. • includes one reason for the opinion. • includes some text evidence that supports the reason but evidence is weak. • uses some linking words and phrases that connect reasons with evidence. • includes a weak concluding sentence or paragraph. • has a voice that shows some conviction about the opinion.	The writer implements some conventions. The writer: • produces complete sentences some of the time. • revises and corrects sentence fragments and run-ons some of the time. • uses correct parts of speech some of the time. • uses correct grammar conventions some of the time.	The writer implements some conventions. The writer: • indents paragraphs some of the time. • makes many mechanical mistakes, and they hinder overall meaning.
1	The writer's ideas are disorganized and undeveloped. The writer: • does not attempt to create an organizational structure. • does not group connected ideas. • does not maintain the opinion throughout the text. • uses few, if any, words and phrases that add effect to the opinion piece.	The writer demonstrates little, if any, understanding of the features of an opinion. The writer: • does not introduce the topic. There is no obvious lead. • states an unclear opinion. • includes one reason for the opinion. • includes little, if any, text evidence that supports the reason. • uses few, if any, linking words and phrases that connect reasons with evidence. • does not include a concluding sentence or paragraph. • has a voice that shows little, if any, conviction about the opinion.	The writer implements few, if any, conventions. The writer: • rarely produces complete sentences. • rarely revises and corrects sentence fragments and run-ons. • rarely uses correct parts of speech. • rarely uses correct grammar conventions.	The writer implements few, if any, conventions. The writer: • does not attempt to indent paragraphs. • makes many mechanical mistakes, and they hinder overall meaning.

Grade 4 Opinion Writing to Sources Mini-Lessons at a Glance

MINI-LESSON MENU		PAGE	BLM
Analyze a Source Text and Draft an Opinion Text 1	Writing to Informational Sources	56	G, H, I
Revise and Edit a Response 1	Writing to Informational Sources	58	G, H
Analyze a Source Text and Draft an Opinion Text 2	Writing to Informational Sources	60	J, K, L
Revise and Edit a Response 2	Writing to Informational Sources	62	J, K
MANAGEMENT & ASSESSMENT TOOLS		**PAGE**	
Opinion Checklist		70	
Opinion Teacher Rubric		71	

Analyze a Source Text and Draft an Opinion Text 1

RL.4.1, RL.4.2, RL.4.3, W.4.1a, W.4.1b, W.4.1c, W.4.1d, W.4.4, W.4.10, SL.4.1a, SL.4.1b, SL.4.1c, SL.4.1d, SL.4.2, SL.4.3

 **Focus**

Objectives

In this mini-lesson, students will:

- Listen to a source text that is read aloud.
- Find key information in a source text.
- Analyze a prompt by breaking it into parts.
- Find evidence in a source text to support an opinion.
- Draft a response to a prompt.

Preparation

Materials Needed

- "President Obama's Back-to-School Event Speech, 2009" (BLMs G–H)
- Opinion Planning Guide 1 (BLM I)
- Opinion Checklist
- Conferring Prompts

Introduce the Mini-Lesson

Explain that in this unit, students will practice reading and analyzing a source informational text and writing an opinion about it.

Read and Analyze the Source Text Together

 Display the excerpt from the mini-lesson source text "President Obama's Back-to-School Event Speech, 2009" (BLMs G–H) and read it aloud.

Say: *We will be writing a response to this excerpt from President Obama's speech, but before we do, we need to make sure we understand what he is saying and what his message is.*

Model for students how to annotate a text by underlining the key details as you read. Think aloud about how you distinguish between important and unimportant details. After reading, provide your summary of the main ideas in the passage.

Engage students in a text-dependent discussion about the speech and its ideas using some or all of the following questions:
- *Who is the audience for President Obama's speech?*
- *Why does he talk about an ordinary person like Shantell Steve?*
- *According to President Obama, what controls a person's destiny?*
- *What's special about Andoni Schultz?*
- *What message does President Obama want students to take away?*

Read and Analyze the Prompt Together

Distribute the Opinion Planning Guide 1 (BLM I). Tell students that you want them to focus on the "Analyze the Prompt" portion. Guide students to unpack the prompt as they have practiced previously in the Opinion unit.

Prompt: President Obama's position is that students can make their own future by setting goals and working towards them. In your opinion, did he provide convincing reasons and evidence to support his position? Support your thinking with evidence from the text.

Analyze the Prompt

Sentence from Prompt	What the Prompt Says
Sentence 1	Gives me President Obama's position.
Sentence 2	Asks me to give an opinion about whether he provided convincing reasons and evidence to support his position.
Sentence 3	Tells me to support my opinion with evidence from the text.

Sample Opinion Planning Guide 1 (BLM I)

Grade 4 • ©2017 Benchmark Education Company, LLC

Rehearse

Practice Writing an Opinion, Reasons, and Evidence

 Distribute copies of President Obama's speech on BLMs G–H, then direct students' attention to the "Opinion, Reasons, and Evidence" portion of BLM I. Tell students to discuss their opinion and reasons with a partner. They should also provide evidence that supports their reasons.

Opinion, Reasons, and Evidence

My Opinion: President Obama does provide convincing reasons and evidence.

My Reason: Uses examples of real teenagers

Evidence: Jazmin Perez didn't speak English, parents didn't go to school, got a scholarship, and is on her way to becoming a doctor.	**Paragraph:** 4. "But she worked hard, earned good grades, got a scholarship to Brown University, and is now . . . on her way to being Dr. Jazmin Perez."
Evidence: Andoni Schultz has fought brain cancer since he was three and was heading to college.	**Paragraph:** 5. "But he never fell behind, and he's headed to college this fall."
Evidence: Shantell Steve is foster child, grew up in tough neighborhood, will graduate with honors and go on to college.	**Paragraph:** 6. ". . . she managed to get a job at a local health center; start a program to keep young people out of gangs."

Sample Opinion Planning Guide 1 (BLM I)

 Students should also have a copy of the Opinion Checklist. They may proceed to independent writing as soon as they feel ready.

 If your class includes English learners or other students who need support, use "Strategies to Support ELs."

Share Opinions and Reasons

Invite students to share the opinions and reasons they recorded on their charts.

Independent Writing and Conferring

 Have students work independently to draft a well-organized opinion of the mini-lesson source text of President Obama's speech on BLMs G–H. As they work, confer with individual students to support their development of a clear opinion statement, reasons, and supporting evidence. Tell students to save their drafts for use in future lessons.

Share

At the end of the writing session, bring students together and invite one or two volunteers to read their opinion responses. Encourage listeners to respond with helpful, positive comments. Ask several students to share what it was like to write a complete response in one sitting. What were the challenges? What did they feel they were able to do well?

Strategies to Support ELs

Emerging (Beginning)

While other students complete the partner activity (or during independent writing time), reread the speech on BLMs G–H and discuss it with ELs. Ask students to share in any way they can—through words, gestures, pantomime, sketches—their opinion of the speech and why.

Expanding (Intermediate) and Bridging (Advanced)

Pair ELs with fluent English speakers during the partner activity. Display simple sentence frames and model how students can use them to talk about the story events. For example:

My opinion is _____.
My reason is _____.
My evidence is _____.

Revise and Edit a Response 1

W.4.1a, W.4.1b, W.4.1c, W.4.4, W.4.5, W.4.10, SL.4.1a, SL.4.1b, SL.4.1c, SL.4.1d, SL.4.2, SL.4.3

Objectives

In this mini-lesson, students will:

• Understand how to revise and edit a response to a prompt.

• Apply this mini-lesson to their independent writing.

Preparation

Materials Needed

• "President Obama's Back-to-School Event Speech, 2009" (BLMs G–H)

• Opinion Checklist

• Students' saved opinion draft

• Conferring Prompts

Build Language and Conventions

Based on your observations of students' writing, build language conventions, knowledge, and vocabulary using the Language Mini-Lessons. See the unit pacing guide for suggested language mini-lessons to support opinion writing.

 **Focus**

Introduce the Mini-Lesson

Explain that you will review revising and editing an opinion draft in a short mini-lesson. Tell students they will then have time to revise and edit independently and practice their skills.

Review Revising

Display the Opinion Checklist and read each criterion in the top part of the checklist with students, asking them to explain what it means and what they should look for as they evaluate their work. Briefly discuss how they can look for ways to improve their writing.

Review Editing

Display the "Quality Writing Checklist" section of the Opinion Checklist. Based on your observations of students' independent writing, discuss specific skills students may want to address as they edit their work. For example, you might have students who often write run-on sentences or sentence fragments. Encourage them to check each sentence to make sure it is a complete sentence.

Rehearse

Practice Revising and Editing a Draft

Invite each student to exchange their draft with a peer and to provide constructive feedback to help their partner revise and edit their writing. Have them check whether the opinion is clearly stated and whether the writer has provided a reason for the opinion and evidence to support it.

 If your class includes English learners or other students who need support, use "Strategies to Support ELs."

Share and Discuss

Invite students to explain the process they used to help their partners revise and edit their writing. What did they find easy about the process? What was more difficult?

Independent Writing and Conferring

Distribute the Opinion Checklist. Have students work independently to revise and edit their own draft opinion of the mini-lesson source text "President Obama's Back-to-School Event Speech, 2009" (BLMs G–H). Explain that students should look at their work first for revision, using the top part of the checklist. After they have revised, they should reread it with a fresh eye to edit, looking for things outlined on the "Quality Writing Checklist."

 **Share**

At the end of the writing session, bring students together and invite one or two volunteers to read a section of their opinion that they revised. Ask other students to share points of grammar and convention that they were able to correct in their work.

Strategies to Support ELs

Emerging (Beginning)

Beginning ELs may not be ready to work on this writing process skill. While other students work with partners or write independently, meet one on one with students to support developmentally appropriate writing skills based on their independent writing and language skills.

Expanding (Intermediate) and Bridging (Advanced)

 Pair ELs with fluent English speakers during the partner activity. Support oral language by providing simple sentence frames. For example:

I need to revise this because _____.
I need to include evidence for _____.

All Levels

If you have ELs whose first language is Spanish, share these English/Spanish cognates: **edit/editar**; **opinion/la opinion**.

Analyze a Source Text and Draft an Opinion Text 2

RI.4.1, RI.4.2, RI.4.3, W.4.1a, W.4.1b, W.4.1c, W.4.1d, W.4.4, W.4.10, SL.4.1a, SL.4.1b, SL.4.1c, SL.4.1d, SL.4.2, SL.4.3

 **Focus**

Objectives

In this mini-lesson, students will:

• Listen to a source text that is read aloud.

• Find key information in a source text.

• Analyze a prompt by breaking it into parts.

• Find evidence in a source text to support an opinion.

• Draft a response to a prompt.

Preparation

Materials Needed

• "President Reagan's State of the Union, 1986" (BLMs J–K)

• Opinion Planning Guide 2 (BLM L)

• Opinion Checklist

• Conferring Prompts

Introduce the Mini-Lesson

Explain to students that today they will practice reading and analyzing another source text and writing an opinion about it.

Read and Analyze the Source Text Together

 Display the mini-lesson source text "President Reagan's State of the Union, 1986" (BLMs J–K) and read it aloud.

Say: *We will be writing an opinion about this speech, but before we do that, we need to make sure we clearly understand what President Reagan's message is.*

If necessary, provide background to the Challenger disaster. Make sure that students understand that the State of the Union is an annual speech given by presidents in which they can outline their agenda and national priorities.

Engage students in a text-dependent discussion about the speech and its ideas using some or all of the following questions:

• *How does President Reagan describe the crew of the Challenger?*

• *What is President Reagan's opinion on the space program?*

• *How does Reagan compare Sir Francis Drake and the Challenger crew?*

• *What is the painful part of the process of exploration and discovery that Reagan is referring to?*

Read and Analyze the Prompt Together

 Distribute the Opinion Planning Guide 2 (BLM L). Tell students that you want them to focus on the "Analyze the Prompt" portion. Guide students to unpack the prompt as they have practiced previously in the Opinion unit.

Prompt: You have just read a speech President Reagan made following the Challenger disaster. In your opinion, did Reagan provide convincing reasons and evidence to support his position that people will continue to explore new horizons despite the dangers they face? Support your thinking with evidence from the text.

Analyze the Prompt

Sentence from Prompt	What the Prompt Says
Sentence 1	The source I will refer to, President Reagan's speech.
Sentence 2	Asks me to give an opinion about whether Reagan provides convincing reasons and evidence to support his position.
Sentence 3	Tells me I must include evidence from the speech to support my opinion and reasons.

Sample Opinion Planning Guide 2 (BLM L)

Grade 4 • ©2017 Benchmark Education Company, LLC

Rehearse

Practice Writing an Opinion, Reasons, and Evidence

 Distribute copies of President Reagan's speech on BLMs J–K, then direct students' attention to the "Opinion, Reasons, and Evidence" portion of BLM L. Invite partners to discuss their opinions and reasons and provide evidence from the text to support their reasons.

Opinion, Reasons, and Evidence

My Opinion: President Reagan does provide a convincing reason for people to continue space exploration.	
My Reason: He explains that explorers lead people into the future, and we must follow.	
Evidence: Exploring the universe serves us all; exploration is the way to the future.	**Paragraph:** 1. "They had a hunger to explore the universe and discover its truths. They wished to serve, and they did. They served all of us." **Paragraph:** 2. "It's all part of taking a chance and expanding man's horizons. The future doesn't belong to the fainthearted; it belongs to the brave."
Evidence: Sir Francis Drake explored the ocean.	**Paragraph:** 6. "In his lifetime the great frontiers were the oceans . . ."

Sample Opinion Planning Guide 2 (BLM L)

 Students should also have a copy of the Opinion Checklist. They may proceed to independent writing as soon as they feel ready.

 If your class includes English learners or other students who need support, use "Strategies to Support ELs."

Share Opinions and Reasons

Invite students to share the opinions and reasons they recorded.

Independent Writing and Conferring

 Have students work independently to draft a well-organized opinion of the mini-lesson source text of President Reagan's speech on BLMs J–K. As they work, confer with individual students to support their development of a clear opinion statement, reasons, and supporting evidence. Tell students to save their drafts for use in future lessons.

Share

At the end of the writing session, bring students together and invite one or two volunteers to read their opinion responses. Encourage students who have different opinions to discuss their ideas. Remind students to respect others' points of view, and to support their thinking with evidence.

Strategies to Support ELs

Emerging (Beginning)

 While other students complete the partner activity (or during independent writing time), reread the speech on BLMs J–K and discuss it. Ask students to share through words, gestures, pantomime, or sketches their opinion of the speech and why.

Expanding (Intermediate) and Bridging (Advanced)

 Pair ELs with fluent English speakers during the partner activity. Display sentence frames and model how students can use them to talk about their opinion. For example:

My opinion is _____. My reasons are _____.
Evidence for my thinking is _____.

All Levels

 If you have ELs whose first language is Spanish, share these English/Spanish cognates: **evidence/la evidencia; opinion/la opinión; reason/la razón.**

Revise and Edit a Response 2

W.4.1a, W.4.1b, W.4.1c, W.4.1d, W.4.4, W.4.5, W.4.10, SL.4.1a, SL.4.1b, SL.4.1c, SL.4.1d, SL.4.2, SL.4.3

Focus

Objectives

In this mini-lesson, students will:

• Understand how to revise and edit a response to a prompt.

• Apply this mini-lesson to their independent writing.

Preparation

Materials Needed

• "President Reagan's State of the Union, 1986" (BLMs J–K)

• Opinion Checklist

• Students' saved opinion draft

• Conferring Prompts

Build Language and Conventions

Based on your observations of students' writing, build language conventions, knowledge, and vocabulary using the Language Mini-Lessons. See the unit pacing guide for suggested language mini-lessons to support opinion writing.

Introduce the Mini-Lesson

Explain that you will review revising and editing an opinion draft in a very short mini-lesson. Tell students they will then have time to revise and edit independently and practice their skills.

Review Revising

Display the Opinion Checklist and read each criterion in the top part of the checklist with students, asking them to explain what it means and what they should look for as they evaluate their own work. Briefly discuss how they can look for ways to improve their writing.

Review Editing

Display the "Quality Writing Checklist" section of the Opinion Checklist. Based on your observations of students' independent writing, discuss specific skills students may want to address as they edit their work. For example, you may notice that some students have difficulty providing reasons and evidence. As you confer with these students, have them underline their reasons and the evidence they provide in their writing.

Rehearse

Practice Revising and Editing a Draft

Invite each student to exchange their draft with a peer and to provide constructive feedback to help their partner revise and edit their writing. Students should be prepared to explain the process of peer revising and editing to the class.

 If your class includes English learners or other students who need support, use "Strategies to Support ELs."

Share and Discuss

Invite two or three volunteers to identify an item from the "Quality Writing Checklist" that their partner was able to help them with and to give an example from their text that might help others during independent writing time.

Independent Writing and Conferring

Distribute the Opinion Checklist. Have students work independently to revise and edit their draft opinion of the mini-lesson source text "President Reagan's State of the Union, 1986" (BLMs J–K). Explain that students should look at their work first for revision, using the top part of the checklist. After they have revised, they should reread it with a fresh eye to edit, looking for things outlined on the "Quality Writing Checklist."

 # Share

Invite one or two volunteers to read a section of their opinion that they revised. Ask other students to share points of grammar and convention that they were able to correct in their work.

Strategies to Support ELs

Emerging (Beginning)

Beginning ELs may not be ready to work on this writing process skill. While other students work with partners or write independently, meet one on one with students to support developmentally appropriate writing skills based on their independent writing and language skills.

Expanding (Intermediate) and Bridging (Advanced)

Pair ELs with fluent English speakers during the partner activity. Support oral language by providing simple sentence frames. For example:

My evidence is _____.
I can edit this sentence by _____.
I need to change _____ because _____.

All Levels

If you have ELs whose first language is Spanish, share these English/Spanish cognates: **edit/editar; evidence/la evidencia; opinion/la opinión**.

Name _____ Date _____

President Obama's Back-to-School Event Speech, 2009

Excerpt from: Prepared Remarks of President Barack Obama: Back-to-School Event

1   But at the end of the day, the circumstances of your life—what you look like, where you come from, how much money you have, what you've got going on at home—that's no excuse for neglecting your homework or having a bad attitude. That's no excuse for talking back to your teacher, or cutting class, or dropping out of school. That's no excuse for not trying.

2   Where you are right now doesn't have to determine where you'll end up. No one's written your destiny for you. Here in America, you write your own destiny. You make your own future.

3   That's what young people like you are doing every day, all across America.

4   Young people like Jazmin Perez, from Roma, Texas. Jazmin didn't speak English when she first started school. Hardly anyone in her hometown went to college, and neither of her parents had gone either. But she worked hard, earned good grades, got a scholarship to Brown University, and is now in graduate school, studying public health, on her way to being Dr. Jazmin Perez.

Name _____ Date _____

President Obama's Back-to-School Event Speech, 2009 (page 2)

5   I'm thinking about Andoni Schultz, from Los Altos, California, who's fought brain cancer since he was three. He's endured all sorts of treatments and surgeries, one of which affected his memory, so it took him much longer—hundreds of extra hours—to do his schoolwork. But he never fell behind, and he's headed to college this fall.

6   And then there's Shantell Steve, from my hometown of Chicago, Illinois. Even when bouncing from foster home to foster home in the toughest neighborhoods, she managed to get a job at a local health center; start a program to keep young people out of gangs; and she's on track to graduate high school with honors and go on to college.

7   Jazmin, Andoni, and Shantell aren't any different from any of you. They faced challenges in their lives just like you do. But they refused to give up. They chose to take responsibility for their education and set goals for themselves. And I expect all of you to do the same.

8   That's why today, I'm calling on each of you to set your own goals for your education—and to do everything you can to meet them. Whatever you resolve to do, I want you to commit to it. I want you to really work at it.

Name _____ Date _____

Opinion Planning Guide 1

Prompt: President Obama's position is that students can make their own future by setting goals and working towards them. In your opinion, did he provide convincing reasons and evidence to support his position? Support your thinking with evidence from the text.

Analyze the Prompt

Sentence from Prompt	What the Prompt Says
Sentence 1	
Sentence 2	
Sentence 3	

Opinion, Reasons, and Evidence

My Opinion:	
My Reason:	
Evidence:	**Paragraph:**
Evidence:	**Paragraph:**

Name _____   Date _____

President Reagan's State of the Union, 1986

From President Ronald Reagan's State of the Union after the shuttle Challenger disaster, 1986

1   For the families of the seven, we cannot bear, as you do, the full impact of this tragedy. But we feel the loss, and we're thinking about you so very much. Your loved ones were daring and brave, and they had that special grace, that special spirit that says, "Give me a challenge, and I'll meet it with joy." They had a hunger to explore the universe and discover its truths. They wished to serve, and they did. They served all of us.

2   And I want to say something to the schoolchildren of America who were watching the live coverage of the shuttle's takeoff. I know it's hard to understand, but sometimes painful things like this happen. It's all part of the process of exploration and discovery. It's all part of taking a chance and expanding man's horizons. The future doesn't belong to the fainthearted; it belongs to the brave. The Challenger crew was pulling us into the future, and we'll continue to follow them.

3   I've always had great faith in and respect for our space program. And what happened today does nothing to diminish it. We don't hide our space program. We don't keep secrets and cover things up. We do it all up front and in public. That's the way freedom is, and we wouldn't change it for a minute.

Name _____ Date _____

President Reagan's State of the Union, 1986 (page 2)

4   We'll continue our quest in space. There will be more shuttle flights and more shuttle crews and, yes, more volunteers, more civilians, more teachers in space. Nothing ends here; our hopes and our journeys continue.

5   I want to add that I wish I could talk to every man and woman who works for NASA, or who worked on this mission and tell them: "Your dedication and professionalism have moved and impressed us for decades. And we know of your anguish. We share it."

6   There's a coincidence today. On this day three hundred and ninety years ago, the great explorer Sir Francis Drake died aboard ship off the coast of Panama. In his lifetime the great frontiers were the oceans, and a historian later said, "He lived by the sea, died on it, and was buried in it." Well, today, we can say of the Challenger crew: Their dedication was, like Drake's, complete.

7   The crew of the space shuttle Challenger honored us by the manner in which they lived their lives. We will never forget them, nor the last time we saw them, this morning, as they prepared for their journey and waved goodbye and "slipped the surly bonds of earth" to "touch the face of God."

Name _____ Date _____

Opinion Planning Guide 2

Prompt: You have just read a speech President Reagan made following the Challenger disaster. In your opinion, did Reagan provide convincing reasons and evidence to support his position that people will continue to explore new horizons despite the dangers they face? Support your thinking with evidence from the text.

Analyze the Prompt

Sentence from Prompt	What the Prompt Says
Sentence 1	
Sentence 2	
Sentence 3	

Opinion, Reasons, and Evidence

My Opinion:	
My Reason:	
Evidence:	**Paragraph:**
Evidence:	**Paragraph:**

Opinion Checklist

Title _____

	Yes	No	Not Sure
1. I introduce my topic with a lead that gets my readers' attention.	—	—	—
2. I state my opinion at the beginning of my paper.	—	—	—
3. I include reasons for my opinion based on my own thoughts about the topic.	—	—	—
4. I group connected ideas together.	—	—	—
5. I use evidence from the text to support my opinion.	—	—	—
6. I use linking words and phrases to connect reasons and evidence.	—	—	—
7. I include a concluding sentence or paragraph that makes my readers think.	—	—	—
8. My opinion follows an organized structure.	—	—	—
9. I choose words that make sense and make my opinion interesting.	—	—	—
10. I do not change my opinion.	—	—	—
11. I use different types of sentences.	—	—	—
12. I use my voice to show people how much I care about my opinion.	—	—	—

Quality Writing Checklist
I looked for and corrected . . .

sentence fragments and run-ons.	—	—	—
parts of speech (pronouns, auxiliaries, adjectives, prepositions).	—	—	—
grammar.	—	—	—
indented paragraphs.	—	—	—
punctuation.	—	—	—
capitalization.	—	—	—
spelling.	—	—	—

Opinion Teacher Rubric

Score	Planning and Implementation	Evidence of Genre Characteristics	Conventions of Grammar and Usage	Conventions of Mechanics
4	(CCSS W.4.1, W.4.4, W.4.5, L.4.3) The writer's ideas are well organized and well developed. The writer: • creates and maintains a meaningful organizational structure. • effectively groups related ideas. • uses well-chosen words and phrases that add effect to the opinion piece. • clearly maintains the opinion throughout the text.	(CCSS W.4.8, W.4.9b, L.4.3a) The writer demonstrates complete understanding of the features of an opinion text. The writer: • clearly introduces the topic with a strong lead that gets readers' attention. • states an opinion that shows a complete understanding of the topic. • includes multiple reasons for the opinion based on inferences made about the topic. • includes purposefully chosen text evidence to support reasons. • uses a wide variety of linking words and phrases that connect reasons with evidence. • includes an effective concluding sentence or paragraph that makes the reader think about the writer's ideas. • has a voice that shows a strong conviction about the opinion.	(CCSS L.4.1, W.4.5) The writer correctly implements all conventions. The writer: • produces well-developed complete sentences. • efficiently revises and corrects sentence fragments and run-ons. • uses parts of speech in unique ways. • uses grammar conventions in clear and concise ways.	(CCSS W.4.5, L.4.2) The writer correctly implements all conventions. The writer: • always correctly indents paragraphs. • makes no, or few, mechanical mistakes, and they do not hinder overall meaning.
3	The writer's ideas are adequately organized and developed. The writer: • creates and maintains an organizational structure. • groups connected ideas most of the time. • uses words and phrases that add effect to the opinion piece. • maintains the opinion throughout the text.	The writer demonstrates an adequate understanding of the features of an opinion text. The writer: • introduces the topic with a lead. • states an opinion about the topic. • includes at least two reasons for the opinion. • includes text evidence that supports each reason. • uses linking words and phrases that connect reasons with evidence. • includes a concluding sentence or paragraph. • has a voice that shows conviction about the opinion.	The writer implements most conventions. The writer: • produces complete sentences. • revises and corrects sentence fragments and run-ons most of the time. • uses correct parts of speech most of the time. • uses correct grammar conventions most of the time.	The writer implements most conventions. The writer: • correctly indents paragraphs most of the time. • makes occasional mechanical mistakes, but they do not hinder overall meaning.
2	The writer's ideas are somewhat organized and developed. The writer: • attempts to create an organizational structure. Ideas are difficult to follow. • attempts to group connected ideas. • inadequately maintains the opinion throughout the text. Text suggests the writer does not understand the stated opinion. • uses few words and phrases that add effect to the opinion piece.	The writer demonstrates some understanding of the features of an opinion text. The writer: • attempts to introduce the topic. Lead is weak. • states a weak opinion about the topic. • includes one reason for the opinion. • includes some text evidence that supports the reason but evidence is weak. • uses some linking words and phrases that connect reasons with evidence. • includes a weak concluding sentence or paragraph. • has a voice that shows some conviction about the opinion.	The writer implements some conventions. The writer: • produces complete sentences some of the time. • revises and corrects sentence fragments and run-ons some of the time. • uses correct parts of speech some of the time. • uses correct grammar conventions some of the time.	The writer implements some conventions. The writer: • indents paragraphs some of the time. • makes many mechanical mistakes, and they hinder overall meaning.
1	The writer's ideas are disorganized and undeveloped. The writer: • does not attempt to create an organizational structure. • does not group connected ideas. • does not maintain the opinion throughout the text. • uses few, if any, words and phrases that add effect to the opinion piece.	The writer demonstrates little, if any, understanding of the features of an opinion. The writer: • does not introduce the topic. There is no obvious lead. • states an unclear opinion. • includes one reason for the opinion. • includes little, if any, text evidence that supports the reason. • uses few, if any, linking words and phrases that connect reasons with evidence. • does not include a concluding sentence or paragraph. • has a voice that shows little, if any, conviction about the opinion.	The writer implements few, if any, conventions. The writer: • rarely produces complete sentences. • rarely revises and corrects sentence fragments and run-ons. • rarely uses correct parts of speech. • rarely uses correct grammar conventions.	The writer implements few, if any, conventions. The writer: • does not attempt to indent paragraphs. • makes many mechanical mistakes, and they hinder overall meaning.

Grade 4 Narrative Writing to Sources Mini-Lessons at a Glance

MINI-LESSON MENU		PAGE	BLM
Read and Analyze a Source Text	Writing to Narrative Sources	74	A, B, C, D
Read and Analyze a Narrative Prompt	Writing to Narrative Sources	76	E, F
Read Closely to Find Details and Events	Writing to Narrative Sources	78	A, C, D, E, F
Draft a Response	Writing to Narrative Sources	80	C, D, E, F
Revise and Edit a Response	Writing to Narrative Sources	82	A, C, D, E, F
MANAGEMENT & ASSESSMENT TOOLS		PAGE	
Narrative Checklist		90	
Narrative Teacher Rubric		91	

Read and Analyze a Source Text

RL.4.1, RL.4.2, RL.4.3, W.4.5, SL.4.1a, SL.4.1b, SL.4.1c, SL.4.1d, SL.4.2, SL.4.3

Objectives

In this mini-lesson, students will:

- Listen as a source text is read aloud.

- Find key details from a source text using a chart.

- Apply the mini-lesson independently to a different source text.

Preparation

Materials Needed

- "A Salute to Cory" (BLM A)

- "Lucy" (BLMs C–D)

- Details and Events Chart (BLM B)

- Conferring Prompts

 **Focus**

Introduce the Mini-Lesson

In this unit, students will practice reading narrative sources to respond to a narrative writing prompt.

Say: *When you write to a source, you read a text and then write a response to a prompt. The prompt tells you what you are to write. The first step in creating a well-written response is to make sure you thoroughly understand the source text. Today, we'll read and analyze a source text together.*

 Display the mini-lesson source text "A Salute to Cory" (BLM A).

Say: *This narrative is about a car trip to visit Camp Pendleton. Before I write about it, I must be sure I understand the key information in the passage. Today, I'll show you how I find the key details in a source text.*

Read Aloud the Source Text

Read aloud "A Salute to Cory," stopping at some or all of the places indicated (or at other points you choose) to highlight key details and events. You may wish to model for students how you annotate a text by underlining the key details as you read. Think aloud about how you distinguish between important and unimportant events and details. After reading, provide your summary of the main ideas in the passage.

After paragraph 1. Say: *After reading this paragraph, I know that the characters are the narrator, her mom, her three sisters, and an exchange student. I know they are going to visit the narrator's brother in California, who is graduating from basic training in the Marines.*

After paragraphs 2–3. Say: *These paragraphs tell where they drove on the trip.*

After paragraphs 4–5. Say: *I find out about the base in paragraph 4, and the last paragraph tells me something about the graduation event.*

Respond Orally to the Source Text

Engage students in a text-dependent discussion about the narrative, using some or all of the following questions:
- *Who are the characters?*
- *Where does the narrative take place?*
- *What happened at Camp Pendleton?*
- *How did the writer feel about what happened?*

Rehearse

Analyze the Source Text

 Distribute "A Salute to Cory" on BLM A and the Details and Events Chart (BLM B). Invite students to work in small groups to complete the chart. Tell them to look for details and events in the narrative that answer the questions. There is more than one detail or event for some of the questions. Groups should be prepared to present their analysis and respond to questions from their peers.

Question	Details and Events
Who are the characters?	the narrator, her mom, her three sisters, her brother, and an exchange student
What do you know about the characters?	narrator is a girl; traveling with mom, three sisters, and an exchange student; brother is graduating from basic training
Where does the narrative take place?	cross-country car trip to see brother in California; Camp Pendleton
What happened in the narrative?	They drove from Kansas through Oklahoma, Texas, New Mexico, and Arizona to California, making sightseeing stops; at Camp Pendleton they went shopping and to a banquet.
How did the characters feel?	excited, having fun, proud of brother

Sample Details and Events Chart (BLM B)

 If your class includes English learners or other students who need support, use "Strategies to Support ELs."

Share Ideas

Invite volunteers to share their answers to the questions. Have them discuss connections between the characters and the details and events.

Independent Writing and Conferring

 Distribute copies of the independent writing source text "Lucy" (BLMs C–D) and a blank copy of the Details and Events Chart on BLM B. Explain to students that before they write about the narrative, they need to make sure they understand the details and events in the narrative.

Read aloud the passage with students. Then ask students to reread the narrative independently to find important details and events to complete the chart.

 ## Share

Bring students together and ask them to share the information they wrote on their details and events charts. Encourage students to ask questions to clarify information they don't understand and to provide alternative details if they have any to share.

Strategies to Support ELs

Emerging (Beginning)

While other students complete the small-group activity (or during independent writing time), work with ELs to help them reread and understand the Narrative "A Salute to Cory" on BLM A.

Expanding (Intermediate) and Bridging (Advanced)

Pair ELs with fluent English speakers during the small-group activity. Display sentence frames and model how students can use them to talk about key ideas in the text. For example:

The characters are _____.
The setting is _____.
What happens in the narrative is _____.

All Levels

If you have ELs whose first language is Spanish, share these English/Spanish cognates: **base/la base; banquet/el banquete; medicine/la medicina; event/el evento; detail/el detalle.**

Read and Analyze a Narrative Prompt

RL.4.1, W.4.5, W.4.8, SL.4.1a, SL.4.1b, SL.4.1c, SL.4.1d, SL.4.2, SL.4.3

 Focus

Objectives

In this mini-lesson, students will:

- Analyze prompts by breaking them into parts.
- Apply this mini-lesson to their independent writing to sources.

Preparation

Materials Needed

- Narrative Planning Guide 1 (BLM E)
- Narrative Planning Guide 2 (BLM F)
- Conferring Prompts

Introduce the Mini-Lesson

Explain to students that a prompt is just another way to ask a question. Students will need to respond to different prompts as part of their assignments and assessments. Explain that one of the most important things about answering a prompt is to first pay attention to the details in the prompt and what it is asking them to do.

Say: *Today I'll show you how to read and analyze a prompt.*

Model Reading and Analyzing a Narrative Prompt

 Display Narrative Planning Guide 1 (BLM E) and read aloud the prompt. Explain to students how you unpack the prompt to find out exactly what it is asking you to do.

> **Prompt:** "A Salute to Cory" is an unfinished Narrative about a road trip to visit the narrator's brother. Continue the narrative, telling what happens next. Base your writing on the details about the characters, setting, and key events provided in the original narrative.

Narrative Planning Guide 1 (BLM E)

Reread sentence 1. Say: *This sentence refers to the source that I must use to answer the prompt.*

Reread sentence 2. Say: *This sentence tells me what I am asked to do—I need to continue the narrative.*

Reread sentence 3. Say: *This sentence tells me that I must use details about the characters, setting, and key events from the original narrative as I write.*

 ## Rehearse

Practice Reading and Analyzing a Narrative Prompt

 Distribute the Narrative Planning Guide 1 on BLM E to students. Ask them to work with a partner to fill in the "Analyze the Prompt" portion of the chart. Tell students to save their partially completed planning guide for future lessons.

Analyze the Prompt	
How does the prompt apply to the narrative?	The prompt asks me to respond to the narrative "A Salute to Cory."
What does the prompt ask me to do?	I need to continue writing the narrative. I must base the characters, events, and setting on details from the original narrative.

Sample Narrative Planning Guide 1 (BLM E)

 If your class includes English learners or other students who need support, use "Strategies to Support ELs."

Share and Discuss

Invite partners to read aloud the information they supplied in the chart.

 ## Independent Writing and Conferring

 Distribute copies of the Narrative Planning Guide 2 (BLM F). Have students read the prompt they will be writing a response to and break it down by sentence to determine what it is asking. Tell them to fill in the "Analyze the Prompt" portion of the chart. Tell students to save their partially completed planning guide for future lessons.

Share

Bring students together and ask them to share the information they wrote on their charts.

Strategies to Support ELs

Emerging (Beginning)

 Work individually with beginning ELs to complete the "Analyze the Prompt" section of BLM E.

Expanding (Intermediate) and Bridging (Advanced)

 Provide the following sentence frames to help students talk about the prompt with a partner:

The first part of the prompt _____.
The second part of the prompt asks me to _____.
The third part of the prompt asks me to _____.

All Levels

 If you have ELs whose first language is Spanish, share these English/Spanish cognates: **part/la parte; event/el evento; detail/el detalle**.

Read Closely to Find Details and Events

W.4.5, W.4.8, SL.4.1a, SL.4.1b, SL.4.1c, SL.4.1d, SL.4.2, SL.4.3

Objectives

In this mini-lesson, students will:

- Understand what it means to perform a close reading of a text.

- Practice close reading to find key text information to support a response.

- Apply this mini-lesson to their independent writing to sources.

Preparation

Materials Needed

- "A Salute to Cory" (BLM A)

- "Lucy" (BLMs C–D)

- Students' saved Narrative Planning Guide 1 (BLM E) from previous lesson

- Students' saved Narrative Planning Guide 2 (BLM F) from previous lesson

- Conferring Prompts

 **Focus**

Introduce the Mini-Lesson

Say: *We have practiced breaking up a prompt into parts to make sure we understand exactly what the prompt is asking us to do. After analyzing the prompt, I know I must base my writing on the details in the narrative. Today I will show you how I use close reading to find specific information that I can use as I write what happens next.*

Model Close Reading to Find Details and Events

Display the mini-lesson source text "A Salute to Cory" (BLM A) and the sample Narrative Planning Guide 1 (BLM E). Read aloud the prompt. Tell students you will focus on the "Details and Events" portion of the planning guide.

Prompt: "A Salute to Cory" is an unfinished narrative about a road trip to visit the narrator's brother. Continue the narrative, telling what happens next. Base your writing on the details about the characters, setting, and key events provided in the original narrative.

Narrative Planning Guide 1 (BLM E)

Say: *I will reread the first paragraph of the text to make sure I know who the characters are and where the story takes place.*

Model close reading paragraph one and writing details on the chart.

Say: *I want more details about the narrator and the other characters so that I can continue the writing in the narrator's voice. I'll reread to look for details.*

Model rereading and writing details on the chart about the language the narrator uses.

 **Rehearse**

Practice Close Reading to Find Details and Events

Assign students to small groups. Distribute copies of "A Salute to Cory" on BLM A. Have students take out their partially completed Narrative Planning Guide 1 on BLM E. Ask them to complete the chart by listing key details that will support their writing of the narrative. Tell students that they will need to be prepared to explain their choices of details and events during the Share and Discuss part of the lesson. Tell students to save their completed planning guide for future lessons.

Details and Events

Who	narrator, her mom, her three sisters, exchange student, brother Cory
Where	car trip from Kansas to California Camp Pendleton in California
What	on the road: stopped for sightseeing at camp: thousands of people at ceremony for those graduating from basic training in the Marines
How	narrator likes shopping; uses informal language such as "zillion miles," "grand tour," "had a blast"
What happened next?	

Sample Narrative Planning Guide 1 (BLM E)

 If your class includes English learners or other students who need support, use "Strategies to Support ELs."

Share and Discuss

Invite groups to read aloud the evidence they recorded on the chart. Students should ask questions of other groups to clarify anything they don't understand or agree with.

Independent Writing and Conferring

 Distribute copies of the independent writing source text "Lucy" (BLMs C–D). Have students take out their partially completed Narrative Planning Guide 2 (BLM F). Tell students that they are going to reread the narrative to look for details and events that will support them in developing the narrative. They should write this information in the Details and Events section of the chart.

During student conferences, observe and support students as they read closely to find details and events. Tell students to save their planning guide for future lessons.

 **Share**

Invite volunteers to read the details and events they found in the text. Ask them to explain how these details will help them in their response to the prompt.

Strategies to Support ELs

Emerging (Beginning)

Work with ELs while other students work in small groups or independently. Reread "A Salute to Cory" on BLM A with them. Have them tell the main events in the narrative in any way they can—using gestures, sketches, pantomime, and so on.

Expanding (Intermediate) and Bridging (Advanced)

Pair ELs with fluent English speakers during the group activity. Display sentence frames and model how students can use them to talk about key ideas in the text. For example:

The characters are _____.
The problem is _____.
The narrator likes to _____.

All Levels

If you have ELs whose first language is Spanish, share these English/Spanish cognates: **base/la base**; **banquet/el banquete**; **medicine/la medicina**; **event/el evento**; **detail/el detalle**.

Draft a Response

W.4.3a, W.4.3b, W.4.3c, W.4.3d, W.4.5, W.4.8, SL.4.1a, SL.4.1b, SL.4.1c, SL.4.1d, SL.4.2, SL.4.3

Objectives

In this mini-lesson, students will:

• Use specific information from a source text to draft a response to a prompt.

• Apply the mini-lesson to their independent writing to sources.

Preparation

Materials Needed

• "Lucy" (BLMs C–D)

• Students' saved Narrative Planning Guide 2 (BLM F) from previous lesson

• Narrative Checklist

• Conferring Prompts

 **Focus**

Introduce the Mini-Lesson

Tell students that today you will show them how to use the information in the planning guide to draft a well-structured narrative response to the prompt.

 Display and read aloud the top portion of the Narrative Checklist and remind students that all well-structured narrative texts include these features.

Model Writing a Draft

 Display the sample Narrative Planning Guide 1 (BLM E), which is completed except for the "What happened next?" section.

Say: *I have gathered the details on the chart and I can refer back to the source text if I need to as I'm writing. First, I'll decide what I'm going to write about. I think I will pick up on the detail of thousands of people watching the ceremony and how exciting that would be for the narrator and her family.*

Write these details in the "What happened next?" section on the chart.

 Display and read aloud the modeling text.

We sat among those thousands, all of us in the huge crowd eagerly awaiting the moment when our special person would take the stage. Our name is at the beginning of the alphabet so my brother was one of the first to march up to a big stage. A general shook his hand and gave him a paper. He looked so serious as he accepted the paper from the general. We were all so proud that we stood up and whooped.

Afterwards, it took a long time to find Cory in the crowd, but when we did, we all hugged him—six girls if you count my mom. He was our hero.

Modeling Text

Say: *Now I'll show how I used the details and events I noted to write my response to the prompt. When you write your narrative response, remember to include specific details about the place and people involved.*

Reread sentence 1. Say: *I used the information I wrote under "What happened next?" in the chart to write the first sentence.*

Reread sentences 2–4. Say: *I used my imagination to add details about watching Cory go up on stage.*

Reread sentence 5. Say: *A narrative includes the author's thoughts and feelings about the events, so next I told how the narrator felt. Details in the passage told me about the excitement that the narrator and her family felt. I wrote that when they saw Cory on stage, they stood up and whooped.*

Reread paragraph 2. Say: *Then I wrote a concluding paragraph. I referred back to information in the narrative that told about the "all-girls trip." The title of the source text is "A Salute to Cory," so I wanted to write something about how they felt about him, so I wrote that he was their hero.*

Rehearse

Prepare for Independent Writing

 Distribute the independent writing source text "Lucy" (BLMs C–D). Have students take out their partially completed Narrative Planning Guide 2 (BLM F). Have students refer to the key information, and discuss with a partner what they will draft in response to the prompt about what will happen next with Lucy. Have them fill in the "What happened next?" section. Then have them discuss how they will link the details and events in the narrative to their paragraphs. Remind students to discuss specific details and descriptions about how the narrator felt.

 If your class includes English learners or other students who need support, use "Strategies to Support ELs."

Share and Discuss

Invite students to share their ideas for their drafts.

Independent Writing and Conferring

Tell students that they have read and analyzed a source text to make sure they understand it. They have analyzed the prompt so they know what they are supposed to write about. They have found information in the text that they will use in their writing. And they have rehearsed their ideas for their draft with a partner. They are now ready to write their drafts. Distribute the Narrative Checklist to students and remind them to refer to it as they write their drafts.

Confer with individual students or groups as needed to support their drafting efforts. Tell students to save their drafts for use in future lessons.

 ## Share

Bring students together. Invite volunteers to share their drafts. Encourage listeners to offer positive suggestions for additions or changes.

Strategies to Support ELs

Emerging (Beginning)

 Work with ELs while other students work with partners or independently. Read aloud "Lucy" on BLMs C–D with them. Have them draw a picture of what they think happens next in the narrative. Then help them write a sentence to go with their picture.

Expanding (Intermediate) and Bridging (Advanced)

Pair ELs with fluent English speakers during the partner activity.

All Levels

 If you have ELs whose first language is Spanish, share these English/Spanish cognates: **base/la base; banquet/el banquete; medicine/la medicina; event/el evento; detail/el detalle**.

Revise and Edit a Response

W.4.3a, W.4.3b, W.4.3c, W.4.3d, W.4.5, W.4.8, SL.4.1a, SL.4.1b, SL.4.1c, SL.4.1d, SL.4.2, SL.4.3, L.4.1e, L.4.3a

Objectives

In this mini-lesson, students will:

- Learn how to revise and edit a response to a prompt.
- Apply this mini-lesson to their independent writing to sources.

Preparation

Materials Needed

- "A Salute to Cory" (BLM A)
- "Lucy" (BLMs C–D)
- Students' saved Narrative Planning Guide 1 (BLM E) from previous lesson
- Students' saved Narrative Planning Guide 2 (BLM F) from previous lesson
- Students' saved response to the prompt
- Conferring Prompts

Build Language and Conventions

Based on your observations of students' writing, build language conventions, knowledge, and vocabulary using the Language Mini-Lessons. See the unit pacing guide for suggested language mini-lessons to support narrative writing.

 **Focus**

Introduce the Mini-Lesson

Tell students that once writers have written their draft, they revise and edit it to improve it. They make sure they have included enough details and information to answer the prompt. They also edit their work to check for spelling, grammar, and punctuation errors.

Say: *Today I'll show you how to revise a draft.*

Model Revising a Draft

 Display the mini-lesson source text "A Salute to Cory" (BLM A), the sample Narrative Planning Guide 1 (BLM E), and the modeling/practice text. Note that the modeling text has errors inserted into it so that you can model revising it.

We sat ~~around~~ among those thousands, all of us in the huge crowd eagerly awaiting the moment when our special person would take the stage. Our name ~~was~~ is at the beginning of the alphabet so my brother was one of the first to march up to a big stage. A general shook his hand.~~And~~ and gave him a paper. ~~He~~ My brother looked so serious as he accepted the paper from the general. We ~~are~~ were all so proud that we stood up and ~~wooped~~ whooped.

Afterwards, it took a long time to find ~~him~~ Cory in the crowd, but when we did, we all hugged him—six girls if you count my m~~Mom~~om. He was our hero.

Modeling/Practice Text

Model revising a few of the errors in the text.

Read aloud sentence 1. Say: *I don't think I used the correct word here. The narrator and her family sat in with the people, not around them. I'll delete **around** and insert the preposition **among.***

Say: *I'd also like to highlight how the narrator feels about the graduating Marines. I'm going to add the word **special** in front of **person:** "awaiting the moment when our special person would take the stage."*

Read aloud sentence 5. Say: *It isn't clear that **he** is referring to "my brother." I'll revise that.*

Model Editing a Draft

 Continue working with the modeling/practice text to edit for grammar, sentence fragments, punctuation, spelling, and so on. Model correcting one or two errors in the text. Students will finish revising and editing the text in the Rehearse section.

Read aloud sentence 2. Say: *I know that narratives are written in past tense. But the fact that their name is at the beginning of the alphabet is something that is always true. In this case, the correct verb tense is present tense.*

Rehearse

Practice Revising a Draft

 Distribute "A Salute to Cory" on BLM A, and have students take out their completed Narrative Planning Guide 1 on BLM E. Have students work with a partner to continue revising and editing the narrative.

 If your class includes English learners or other students who need support, use "Strategies to Support ELs."

Share and Discuss

Invite students to share the edits they made. Encourage students to suggest other edits they would make and explain why. Be sure to address all the errors embedded in the modeling/practice text so that students have correct information.

Independent Writing and Conferring

 Have students take out the independent writing source text "Lucy" (BLMs C–D), their completed Narrative Planning Guide 2 (BLM F), and a copy of their draft. Explain that they will now edit and revise their drafts. Tell students to check that they have used details from the source narrative to fully develop the characters, setting, and key events. They should also edit for spelling, grammar, and punctuation mistakes.

When students have revised and edited their drafts, have them create the final draft of their responses.

Share

Bring students together. Invite a few volunteers to read aloud their response to the prompt. Invite students who are listening to provide feedback and ask clarifying questions.

Strategies to Support ELs

Emerging (Beginning)

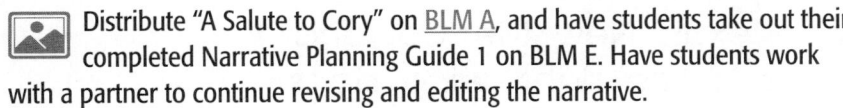 Work one on one with ELs to help them make revisions to the sentence they wrote to accompany their picture of what happened next in the narrative "Lucy" on BLMs C–D. Ask them what more they can say about the characters or the actions.

Expanding (Intermediate) and Bridging (Advanced)

Pair ELs with fluent English speakers during the partner activity.

All Levels

If you have ELs whose first language is Spanish, share these English/Spanish cognates: **base/la base; banquet/el banquete; general/el general; medicine/la medicina; event/el evento; detail/el detalle**.

Name _____ Date _____

A Salute to Cory

1   With a slam, the car door closed and we were off. My mom, my three sisters and I, and an exchange student from France were on an all-girls trip to California. We were going to see my brother Cory who was about to graduate from basic training in the Marines.

2   We left our home late in the evening. We drove from highway to highway to highway. We went from Kansas through Oklahoma, Texas, New Mexico, and Arizona. Along the way, we made sightseeing stops.

3   Four days after we left, we crossed the California border and headed to Camp Pendleton in Oceanside.

4   The base was huge, a city inside a city. The gates around it stretched a zillion miles. Cory gave us the grand tour of the training facilities. There were a lot of stores, too, so of course, we had to go shopping, and, of course, we had a blast! Afterward, Cory took us to the banquet honoring the graduates where we met his troop leader.

5   The next day was the big event. Thousands of people came to watch relatives and friends graduate.

Name _____   Date _____

Details and Events Chart

Question	Details and Events
Who are the characters?	
What do you know about the characters?	
Where does the narrative take place?	
What happened in the narrative?	
How did the characters feel?	

Name _____ Date _____

Lucy

1 It was a Thursday night, and I was doing my homework when I heard my mom on the phone.

2 "Doug, I think you should come home to say good-bye. Don't worry, I'll talk to Katie about this."

3 Then she hung up. Why would my dad need to come home from his business trip? I didn't have time to think further because my mom came and sat down on the couch next to me.

4 "Katie," she said with a worried look on her face, "we need to talk."

5 *Uh-oh,* I thought, *this doesn't sound good.*

6 "As you know, Lucy isn't in the best shape and . . . well . . . the medicine we're giving her isn't working. She's still having terrible back problems, and she hasn't gotten up in two days."

7 Lucy had been my dog for ten and a half years, and I didn't want to hear what my mom was going to say next.

Name _____ Date _____

Lucy (page 2)

8   "So, your father and I have been thinking that . . . maybe we should put her to sleep so she isn't in so much pain."

9   "No Mom, you can't do that!" I said as tears started to roll down my cheeks. Please take her to the vet and see if he can recommend anything else."

10   Mom was quiet for a moment, but then she said, "We'll take her to Dr. Smith tomorrow. We all want what's best for Lucy, so we will do whatever the vet recommends."

Name _____ Date _____

Narrative Planning Guide 1

Prompt: "A Salute to Cory" is an unfinished personal narrative about a road trip to visit the narrator's brother. Continue the narrative, telling what happens next. Base your writing on the details about the characters, setting, and key events provided in the original narrative.

Analyze the Prompt

How does the prompt apply to the narrative?	
What does the prompt ask me to do?	

Details and Events

Who	
Where	
What	
How	
What happened next?	

Name _____   Date _____

Narrative Planning Guide 2

Prompt: "Lucy" is an unfinished personal narrative about a character named Katie and her dog Lucy, who is old and unwell. Continue the narrative, telling what happens next. Base your writing on the details about the characters, setting, and key events provided in the original narrative.

Analyze the Prompt

How does the prompt apply to the narrative?	
What does the prompt ask me to do?	

Details and Events

Who	
Where	
What	
Problem	
What happened next?	

Name _____   Date _____

Narrative Checklist

Title _____

	Yes	No	Not Sure
1. My narrative has a strong lead that catches the reader's attention.	—	—	—
2. My narrative focuses on one event in my life.	—	—	—
3. I include specific details about the time, place, and people involved.	—	—	—
4. I include dialogue or express what people said.	—	—	—
5. My narrative is logically sequenced.	—	—	—
6. My narrative uses sequence words.	—	—	—
7. I include my own convictions, thoughts, and feelings.	—	—	—
8. My narrative has a strong ending.	—	—	—
9. I tell my personal narrative using kid-friendly language.	—	—	—
10. I use describing words, including adjectives and adverbs, to tell my story.	—	—	—
11. I use figurative language, including idioms, to make my personal narrative more interesting.	—	—	—
12. I broke sentence rules when necessary to make my personal narrative more interesting.	—	—	—

Quality Writing Checklist
I looked for and corrected . . .

	Yes	No	Not Sure
sentence fragments and run-ons.	—	—	—
parts of speech (pronouns, auxiliaries, adjectives, prepositions).	—	—	—
grammar.	—	—	—
indented paragraphs.	—	—	—
punctuation.	—	—	—
capitalization.	—	—	—
spelling.	—	—	—

Narrative Teacher Rubric

Score	Planning and Implementation	Evidence of Genre Characteristics	Conventions of Grammar and Usage	Conventions of Mechanics
4	(CCSS W.4.3, W.4.4, L.4.3a) The writer's ideas are well organized and well developed. The writer: • effectively orients the reader by establishing a well-elaborated situation. • recounts a well-elaborated event that is logically sequenced. • uses a variety of transition words and phrases to manage the sequence of events. • uses well-chosen concrete words and phrases and sensory details. • includes figurative language, including idioms, to make the narrative more interesting. • grabs readers' attention with a strong lead. • includes a strong ending that naturally makes the reader reflect on the narrative.	(CCSS W.4.8, L.4.3a) The writer demonstrates complete understanding of the features of a narrative. The writer: • focuses on one particular incident in the narrative. • includes specific details about the time, place, and people involved. • effectively includes dialogue or expresses what people say in a way that brings the story to life. • uses well-chosen words to describe his/her own convictions, thoughts, and feelings as well as the actual event. • makes a connection with the reader by using kid-friendly language (voice).	(CCSS L.4.1, W.4.5) The writer correctly implements all conventions. The writer: • produces well-developed complete sentences. • efficiently revises and corrects sentence fragments and run-ons. • effectively and purposefully breaks sentence structure rules to enhance meaning. • uses parts of speech in unique ways. • uses grammar conventions in clear and concise ways.	(CCSS W.4.5, L.4.2) The writer correctly implements all conventions. The writer: • always correctly indents paragraphs. • makes no, or few, mechanical mistakes, and they do not hinder overall meaning.
3	The writer's ideas are adequately organized and developed. The writer: • establishes a situation. • recounts an adequately elaborated event that is logically sequenced. • uses transition words and phrases to manage the sequence of events. • uses descriptive words and phrases and sensory details. • includes figurative language including idioms. • begins the narrative with a lead. • includes an ending.	The writer demonstrates adequate understanding of the features of a narrative. The writer: • focuses on one particular incident in the narrative. • includes details about the time, place, and people involved. • includes dialogue or expresses what people say. • describes his/her convictions, thoughts, and feelings as well as the event. • uses kid-friendly language (voice).	The writer implements most conventions. The writer: • produces complete sentences. • revises and corrects sentence fragments and run-ons most of the time. • purposefully breaks sentence structure rules to enhance meaning. • uses correct parts of speech most of the time. • uses correct grammar conventions most of the time.	The writer implements most conventions. The writer: • correctly indents paragraphs most of the time. • makes occasional mechanical mistakes, but they do not hinder overall meaning.
2	The writer's ideas are somewhat organized and developed. The writer: • attempts to establish a situation. • attempts to recount an event. Some parts are logically sequenced. • uses some transition words and phrases to manage the sequence of events. Progression of events is confusing. • inadequately describes people, places, and events. • may or may not include idioms. • begins the narrative with a weak lead. • includes a weak ending.	The writer demonstrates some understanding of the features of a narrative. The writer: • attempts to focus on one particular incident in the narrative. • includes few details about the time, place, and people involved. • includes some dialogue or attempts to express what people say. • inadequately describes his/her own convictions, thoughts, and feelings as well as the actual event. • attempts to use kid-friendly language (voice).	The writer implements some conventions. The writer: • produces complete sentences some of the time. • revises and corrects sentence fragments and run-ons some of the time. • attempts to break sentence structure rules. Meaning may or may not be enhanced. • uses correct parts of speech some of the time. • uses correct grammar conventions some of the time.	The writer implements some conventions. The writer: • indents paragraphs some of the time. • makes many mechanical mistakes, and they hinder overall meaning.
1	The writer's ideas are disorganized and undeveloped. The writer: • does not establish a situation, leaving the reader confused as to the topic. • attempts to recount an event. Event is not logically sequenced. • rarely uses transition words and phrases to manage the sequence of events. Progression of events is confusing. • does not describe people, places, and events. • does not include idioms. • does not have a lead. • does not have an ending.	The writer demonstrates little, if any, understanding of the features of a narrative. The writer: • does not focus on one particular incident in the narrative. • includes few, if any, details about the time, place, and people involved. • includes little, if any, dialogue or does not express what people say. • does not describe his/her own convictions, thoughts, and feelings as well as the actual event. • does not purposefully use kid-friendly language (voice).	The writer implements few, if any, conventions. The writer: • rarely produces complete sentences. • rarely revises and corrects sentence fragments and run-ons. • attempts to break sentence structure rules. Meaning is hindered. • rarely uses correct parts of speech. • rarely uses correct grammar conventions.	The writer implements few, if any, conventions. The writer: • does not attempt to indent paragraphs. • makes many mechanical mistakes, and they hinder overall meaning.

Grade 4 Informative/Explanatory Writing to Sources Mini-Lessons at a Glance

MINI-LESSON MENU		PAGE	BLM
Read and Analyze a Source Text	Writing to Informational Sources	94	1, 2, 3, 4, 5
Read and Analyze an Informative/Explanatory Prompt	Writing to Informational Sources	96	6, 7
Read Closely to Find Text Evidence	Writing to Informational Sources	98	1, 2, 4, 5, 6, 7
Draft a Response	Writing to Informational Sources	100	1, 2, 4, 5, 6, 7
Revise and Edit a Response	Writing to Informational Sources	102	1, 2, 4, 5, 6, 7
MANAGEMENT & ASSESSMENT TOOLS		**PAGE**	
Informative/Explanatory Checklist		111	
Informative/Explanatory Teacher Rubric		112	

Read and Analyze a Source Text

RL.4.1, RL.4.2, RL.4.3, W.4.2, SL.4.1a, SL.4.1b, SL.4.1c, SL.4.1d, SL.4.2, SL.4.3

Objectives

In this mini-lesson, students will:

- Listen and follow along as a source text is read aloud.
- Find key information from a source text using a graphic organizer.
- Apply the mini-lesson independently to a different source text.

Preparation

Materials Needed

- "Three 'Brains' in One" (BLMs 1–2)
- "Who's Who on the Soccer Field" (BLMs 4–5)
- Key Idea Web (BLM 3)
- Conferring Prompts

Focus

Introduce the Mini-Lesson

In this unit, students will read an informational source in order to respond to an informative/explanatory writing prompt. The prompt will require students to use information from the source in their written responses. Today's mini-lesson will focus on how to carefully read the source texts to find the key details.

 Display the mini-lesson source text "Three 'Brains' in One" (BLMs 1–2).

Say: *This passage is about the human brain. Before I write about it, I must be sure I understand the key ideas in the passage. Today I am going to show you how I find the key details in a source text.*

Read Aloud the Source Text

Read aloud "Three 'Brains' in One," stopping at some or all of the places indicated (or at other points you choose) to highlight key ideas. You may wish to model for students how you annotate a text by underlining the key details as you read. Think aloud about how you distinguish between important and unimportant details. After reading, provide your summary of the main ideas in the passage.

After paragraph 1. Say: *This paragraph introduces the text and gives me an idea of what the rest of the text is going to be about. From the title and the first paragraph, I predict that this text is going to be about the three main parts of the human brain and what they do.*

After paragraphs 2–4. Say: *These paragraphs describe the three sections of the brain. Each paragraph focuses on one part of the brain. The words in boldface highlight which part the author is talking about.*

After last paragraph. Say: *The last paragraph concludes the passage by briefly describing how the three parts of the brain work together.*

Respond Orally to the Source Text

Engage students in a text-dependent discussion about the informational text, using some or all of the following questions:
- *What is the main topic of this passage?*
- *How is the human brain organized?*
- *What are the main roles of each section of the brain?*

Rehearse

Analyze the Source Text

 Distribute the Key Idea Web (BLM 3). Invite students to work with a partner to complete it. Tell students to write the main topic in the center circle. They should then write a key detail on each branch, and include supporting details.

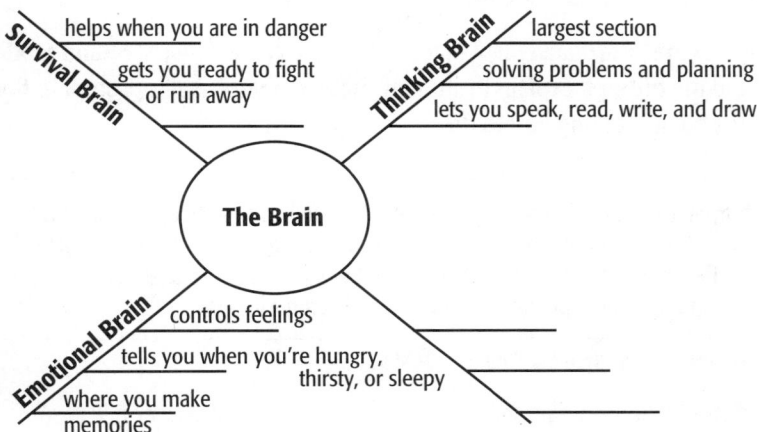

Survival Brain
helps when you are in danger
gets you ready to fight or run away

Thinking Brain
largest section
solving problems and planning
lets you speak, read, write, and draw

The Brain

Emotional Brain
controls feelings
tells you when you're hungry, thirsty, or sleepy
where you make memories

Sample Key Idea Web (BLM 3)

 If your class includes English learners or other students who need support, use "Strategies to Support ELs."

Share Ideas

Invite volunteers to show how they filled out their Key Idea Webs.

Independent Writing and Conferring

 Distribute copies of the independent writing source text "Who's Who on the Soccer Field" (BLMs 4–5) and a blank copy of the Key Idea Web on BLM 3. Explain to students that this is the passage they will write about. Before they write, they need to make sure they understand the key ideas in the passage.

Read aloud the passage with students. Then ask students to reread the passage independently to find key information and write it in the Key Idea Web.

 ## Share

Bring students together and ask them to share the information they wrote on their Key Idea Webs. Students should ask questions when they don't understand or when they disagree with the information provided by others.

Strategies to Support ELs

Emerging (Beginning)

 Reread "Three 'Brains' in One" on BLMs 1–2 with ELs. Use words, gestures, and/or sketches to show what the different parts of the brain do.

Expanding (Intermediate) and Bridging (Advanced)

 Pair ELs with fluent English speakers during the partner activity. Display simple sentence frames and model how students can use them to talk about key ideas in the text. For example:

The Survival Brain helps you _____.
The Emotional Brain helps you _____.
The Thinking Brain helps you _____.

All Levels

 If you have ELs whose first language is Spanish, share these English/Spanish cognates: **emotion/emocion**; **organize/organizer**; **defense/la defensa**.

Read and Analyze an Informative/Explanatory Prompt

W.4.5, SL.4.1a, SL.4.1b, SL.4.1c, SL.4.1d, SL.4.2, SL.4.3

 **Focus**

Objectives

In this mini-lesson, students will:

- Analyze prompts by breaking them into parts.

- Apply this mini-lesson to their independent writing to sources.

Preparation

Materials Needed

- Informative/Explanatory Planning Guide 1 (BLM 6)

- Informative/Explanatory Planning Guide 2 (BLM 7)

- Conferring Prompts

Introduce the Mini-Lesson

Remind students that in the previous mini-lesson they read an informational text source. Today, they will focus on reading and analyzing a prompt that asks them to write a response based on the information in the source.

Model Reading and Analyzing a Prompt

 Display the Informative/Explanatory Planning Guide 1 (BLM 6) and read aloud the prompt. Explain to students how you unpack the prompt to find out exactly what it is asking you to do.

Prompt: Imagine that a chef is cooking over a hot stove and accidentally spills a pot of hot water. Using only the information from "Three 'Brains' in One," explain how the different parts of the chef's brain might work to help the chef in this situation. Support your explanation with evidence from the text.

Informative/Explanatory Planning Guide 1 (BLM 6)

Reread sentence 1. Say: *This sentence is an introduction to what I will write about.*

Reread sentence 2. Say: *This sentence refers to the source that I must use to answer the prompt. It also tells me what I am asked to do—I need to explain the role of each section of the brain. That means I will write a short essay to inform or explain.*

Reread sentence 3. Say: *This sentence reminds me that I must use evidence from the passage when I write my answer.*

 ## Rehearse

Practice Reading and Analyzing a Prompt

 Distribute Informative/Explanatory Planning Guide 1 on BLM 6 to students. Ask them to work with a partner to fill in the "Analyze the Prompt" portion of the chart. Tell students to save their partially completed planning guide for future lessons.

Analyze the Prompt	
How does the prompt apply to the text?	The prompt asks me to use information from "Three 'Brains' in One."
What does the prompt ask me to do?	It asks me to explain how the different parts of the chef's brain can work to help the chef and to support the explanation with examples from the text.

Sample Informative/Explanatory Planning Guide 1 (BLM 6)

 If your class includes English learners or other students who need support, use "Strategies to Support ELs."

Share and Discuss

 Invite partners to read aloud their analysis of what the prompt is asking them to do. Invite other students to ask clarifying questions and build on the analysis of others using sentence frames such as:

- *What did you mean when you said _____?*
- *Do you mean _____?*
- *I made a similar analysis to _____. I said _____.*
- *I agree with _____. The prompt is asking me to _____.*

 ## Independent Writing and Conferring

 Distribute copies of Informative/ Explanatory Planning Guide 2 (BLM 7). Have students read the prompt they will be writing a response to and break it down to determine what it is asking. Tell them to fill in the "Analyze the Prompt" portion of the chart. Tell students to save their partially completed planning guide for future lessons.

 ## Share

Bring students together and ask them to share the information they wrote on their charts.

Strategies to Support ELs

Emerging (Beginning)

 Work individually with beginning ELs to read and discuss the article "Who's Who on the Soccer Field" on BLMs 4–5. You may want to help students draw a diagram of a soccer field and position the different players. Work with students to label the diagram.

Expanding (Intermediate) and Bridging (Advanced)

 Provide the following sentence frames to help students talk about the prompt with a partner:

The first part of the prompt asks me to _____.
The second part of the prompt asks me to _____.
The third part of the prompt asks me to _____.

All Levels

 If you have ELs whose first language is Spanish, share these English/Spanish cognates: **role/el rol**; **part/la parte**; **section/la sección.**

Read Closely to Find Text Evidence

RI.4.1, RI.4.2, RI.4.3, W.4.5, W.4.8, SL.4.1a, SL.4.1b, SL.4.1c, SL.4.1d, SL.4.2, SL.4.3

 **Focus**

Objectives

In this mini-lesson, students will:

- Understand what close reading of a text is.
- Practice close reading to find evidence to support a response.
- Identify key information in a text.
- Apply this mini-lesson to their independent writing to sources.

Preparation

Materials Needed

- "Three 'Brains' in One" (BLMs 1–2)
- "Who's Who on the Soccer Field" (BLMs 4–5)
- Students' saved Informative/ Explanatory Planning Guide 1 (BLM 6) from previous lesson
- Students' saved Informative/ Explanatory Planning Guide 2 (BLM 7) from previous lesson
- Conferring Prompts

Introduce the Mini-Lesson

Remind students that they have read a text and pulled out key details. They have also read and analyzed a prompt that asks them to explain the role of each part of the brain, using evidence from the passage to support their answer. Tell students that today they will take notes to organize their ideas for their informative/explanatory essays. And you will show them how to closely read a text to find examples to support their explanations.

Model Close Reading to Find Text Evidence

 Display the mini-lesson source text "Three 'Brains' in One" (BLMs 1–2) and the sample Informative/Explanatory Planning Guide 1 (BLM 6). Reread the prompt. Tell students you will focus on the "Key Details and Evidence" portion of the planning guide.

> **Prompt:** Imagine that a chef is cooking over a hot stove and accidentally spills a pot of hot water. Using only the information from "Three 'Brains' in One," explain how the different parts of the chef's brain might work to help the chef in this situation. Support your explanation with evidence from the text.

Informative/Explanatory Planning Guide 1 (BLM 6)

Say: *The prompt asks me to explain how different parts of the brain work to help in an emergency situation. I need to go back and search the text for evidence. I need to reread sections of the text and think about them carefully to get a better understanding of the key ideas so I will be ready to write about them later. I'll take notes on the planning guide.*

Model close reading with paragraphs one and two.

Reread paragraph 1. Say: *This paragraph identifies the three sections of the brain. In the passage, they are called the Survival Brain, the Emotional Brain, and the Thinking Brain. This information can help me organize my ideas.*

Reread paragraph 2. Say: *This paragraph tells about the section the author calls the Survival Brain. The main idea from this paragraph is that the Survival Brain's role is to help when you are threatened. It does this by helping you get ready to deal with the danger.*

Rehearse

Practice Close Reading to Find Text Evidence

 Assign students to small groups. Distribute copies of "Three 'Brains' in One" on BLMs 1–2 and have students take out their partially completed Informative/Explanatory Planning Guide 1 on BLM 6. Ask students to complete the chart by listing evidence that explains the roles of the sections of the brain. Tell students to save their completed planning guide for future lessons.

Key Details and Evidence

Details	Evidence
The "Survival Brain" helps when you are in danger. It will help the chef react quickly to the spilled water.	"It speeds up your heartbeat and breathing. It does this to make sure you have enough oxygen flowing through your body to give you the strength to act."
The "Emotional Brain" controls feelings. It will help the chef deal with the stress of the situation.	"It's also the part of your brain that signals your body to release hormones. These are special chemicals that help you cope with stress . . ."
The "Thinking Brain" controls planning. It will help the chef figure out what to do about the hot water.	"It controls your ability to figure things out . . ."

Sample Informative/Explanatory Planning Guide 1 (BLM 6)

 If your class includes English learners or other students who need support, use "Strategies to Support ELs."

Share and Discuss

 Invite groups to read aloud the evidence they recorded on the chart. Model how students can use these or other sentence frames during a collaborative conversation about their ideas. For example:

- *I'm not sure that sentence is evidence. I think _____.*
- *I agree, that is good evidence. Another piece of evidence is _____.*

Independent Writing and Conferring

 Distribute copies of the independent writing source text "Who's Who on the Soccer Field" (BLMs 4–5) and have students take out their partially completed Informative/Explanatory Planning Guide 2 (BLM 7). Tell students that they are going to reread the text to look for evidence that will support their explanation of the different roles of the players on a soccer team. They should write this information on the chart. Tell students to save their completed planning guide for future lessons.

During student conferences, observe and support students as they read closely to identify details about the different players on a soccer team that they can use in their independent informative/explanatory text.

Share

Bring students together. Invite volunteers to share the details they found in the text.

Draft a Response

W.4.2a, W.4.2b, W.4.2c, W.4.2d, W.4.2e, W.4.5, W.4.8, SL.4.1a, SL.4.1b, SL.4.1c, SL.4.1d, SL.4.2, SL.4.3

Objectives

In this mini-lesson, students will:

• Draft a response to a prompt.

• Apply the mini-lesson to their independent writing to sources.

Preparation

Materials Needed

• "Who's Who on the Soccer Field" (BLMs 4–5)

• Students' saved Informative/Explanatory Planning Guide 2 (BLM 7) from previous lesson

• Informative/Explanatory Checklist

• Conferring Prompts

Focus

Introduce the Mini-Lesson

 Display the mini-lesson source text "Three 'Brains' in One" (BLMs 1–2) and the sample Informative/Explanatory Planning Guide 1 (BLM 6). Tell students that today you will show them how to use the information in the planning guide to draft a response to the prompt.

Display and read aloud the Informative/Explanatory Checklist. Point out that when students write to a source during an assessment or in a class, they won't always have the checklist in front of them. Writers need to remember these features for future reference.

Model Writing a Draft

Display the modeling text and read it aloud.

> The human brain is a complex organ that performs many critical jobs, or functions. The brain has three distinct sections that each play a special role to help people when faced with an emergency situation, such as in the case of an accident, or when a chef spills a pot of hot water.
>
> The "Survival Brain" helps people when they face danger. It sends signals to the body to prepare it to run away, fight, or react in some way to the threat. This part of the brain would speed up the chef's heartbeat and breathing, helping him or her react immediately to the danger of the hot water.
>
> The "Emotional Brain" controls feelings. Also, this part of the brain sends signals the body to release hormones, special chemicals that help people react to stress. This part of the brain would tell the chef that he is feeling afraid, but it would also send signals to help the body deal with these feelings of stress.
>
> The biggest part of the brain is the "Thinking Brain," which helps people solve problems. This part of the brain would help the chef figure out how to deal with the spill.
>
> Each part of the brain would work to help the chef in this dangerous situation, from the first quick reaction to planning how to solve the problem.

Modeling Text

Reread paragraph 1. Say: *I took notes and gathered my evidence from the passage. I used this information to answer the prompt. First I wrote an introductory paragraph.*

Reread paragraphs 2–4. Say: *I started each paragraph with a statement explaining the role of a particular section of the brain. Then I gave specific examples from the source text to tell how that section could help the chef.*

Reread paragraph 5. Say: *Then I wrote a conclusion that summarizes my explanation.*

 **Rehearse**

Prepare for Independent Writing

 Distribute the independent writing source text "Who's Who on the Soccer Field" (BLMs 4–5), and have students take out their completed Informative/Explanatory Planning Guide 2 (BLM 7). Have students refer to their evidence and discuss with a partner what they will draft in response to the prompt about the roles of the players on a soccer team.

 If your class includes English learners or other students who need support, use "Strategies to Support ELs."

Share and Discuss

Invite students to share their ideas for their drafts.

 Encourage students to link their own ideas to those of other students using sentence frames such as:

- *I had a similar idea. I plan to _____.*
- *_____'s idea reminds me of my own. My idea is _____.*

 **Independent Writing and Conferring**

Tell students that they have read and analyzed a source text to make sure they understand it. They have analyzed the prompt so they know what they are supposed to write about. They have found evidence in the text that they will use in their writing. And they have rehearsed their ideas for their draft with a partner. They are now ready to write their drafts. Distribute the Informative/Explanatory Checklist to students and remind them to refer to it as they write their drafts.

Confer with individual students or groups as needed to support their drafting efforts. Tell students to save their drafts for use in future lessons.

 **Share**

Bring students together. Invite volunteers to share their drafts. Encourage listeners to offer positive suggestions for additions or changes.

Strategies to Support ELs

Emerging (Beginning)

 Work with ELs while other students work with partners or independently. Use the diagram of the soccer field created in a previous lesson, or ask students to work together to make one. Have them draw stick figures to show different players. Then help them write a sentence to go with their picture. Refer to "Who's Who on the Soccer Field" on BLMs 4–5.

Expanding (Intermediate) and Bridging (Advanced)

Pair ELs with fluent English speakers during the partner activity.

 For the independent activity, use the following sentence frames to help students understand the text:

The job of the goalkeeper is to _____.
The job of the defense is to _____.
The job of the midfielders is to _____.
The job of the attack is to _____.

Revise and Edit a Response

W.4.2a, W.4.2b, W.4.2c, W.4.2d, W.4.2e, W.4.5, SL.4.1a, SL.4.1b, SL.4.1c, SL.4.1d, SL.4.2, SL.4.3

 Focus

Objectives

In this mini-lesson, students will:

• Learn how to revise and edit a response to a prompt.

• Apply this mini-lesson to their independent writing to sources.

Preparation

Materials Needed

• <u>"Three 'Brains' in One"</u> (BLMs 1–2)

• <u>"Who's Who on the Soccer Field"</u> <u>(BLMs 4–5)</u>

• Students' saved Informative/ Explanatory Planning Guide 1 (BLM 6) from previous lesson

• Students' saved Informative/ Explanatory Planning Guide 2 (BLM 7) from previous lesson

• Students' saved response to the prompt

• Conferring Prompts

Build Language and Conventions

Based on your observations of students' writing, build language conventions, knowledge, and vocabulary using the <u>Language Mini-Lessons</u>. See the unit pacing guide for suggested language mini-lessons to support Informative/Explanatory writing.

Introduce the Mini-Lesson

Tell students that before preparing a final draft, writers look at their writing to revise and edit it. When they revise, they look for ways to make their writing better. They also make sure they have included not only the right information but also enough information to answer the prompt. When they edit their work, writers check for spelling, grammar, and punctuation errors.

Say: *Today I'll show you how to revise a draft.*

Model Revising a Draft

 Display the mini-lesson source text <u>"Three 'Brains' in One"</u> (BLMs 1–2), the sample <u>Informative/Explanatory Planning Guide 1 (BLM 6)</u>, and the <u>modeling/practice text</u>. Note that the modeling text has errors inserted into it so that you can model revising it.

> The human brain is a complex organ that performs many critical jobs, or functions. The brain has three distinct sections that each play a ~~distinct~~ special role to help people when faced with an ~~emergencey~~ emergency situation, such as in the case of an accident, or when a chef spills a pot of hot water.
>
> The "Survival Brain" helps people when they face danger. It sends signals to the body to prepare ~~you~~ it to run away, or fight, or react in some way to the threat. This part of the brain would help the chef's heartbeat and breathing, helping him or her react immediately to the danger of the hot water.
>
> The "Emotional Brain" controls feelings. Also, this part of the brain sends signals to the body to release hormones~~,~~; these are special chemicals that help people react to stress. This part of the brain would tell the ~~chief~~ chef that he is feeling afraid, but it would also send signals to help the body deal with these feelings of stress.
>
> The biggest part of the brain is the "Thinking Brain," which helps ~~you~~ people solve problems. This part of the brain would help the chef figure out how to deal with the hot water spill.
>
> Each part of the brain would work to help the chef in this ~~dangeros~~ dangerous situation, from the first quick reaction to planning how to solve the problem.

Modeling/Practice Text

Model revising a few of the errors in the text.

Read aloud sentence 1. Say: *In the first part of the sentence I'm missing the article **a**, "a complex organ."*

Read aloud sentence 2. Say: *I've used the word **distinct** two times in this sentence so I'll try a different word in one place. The word **special** is more specific, so I'll use that.*

Model Editing a Draft

 Continue working with the modeling/practice text to edit for grammar, spelling, and so on. Model correcting one or two errors in the text. Students will finish revising and editing the text in the Rehearse section.

Reread aloud sentence 2. Say: *I've misspelled the word* **emergency.** *The ending should be just* **y** *not* **ey.**

Rehearse

Practice Revising a Draft

 Distribute "Three 'Brains' in One" on BLMs 1–2, and have students take out their completed Informative/Explanatory Planning Guide 1 on BLM 6. Have students work with a partner to continue editing and revising the modeling text.

 If your class includes English learners or other students who need support, use "Strategies to Support ELs."

Share and Discuss

Invite students to share the edits they made. Encourage students to question edits they don't agree with in a positive way and provide alternatives. Make sure that you address all the errors embedded in the modeling/practice text so that students have correct information.

Independent Writing and Conferring

 Have students take out the independent writing source text "Who's Who on the Soccer Field" (BLMs 4–5), their completed Informative/Explanatory Planning Guide 2 (BLM 7), and a copy of their draft. Explain that they will now edit and revise their drafts. Tell students to check that they have addressed the prompt and have fully explained the roles of the players on a soccer team. They should also make sure their writing is clear and well organized. Finally, they should edit for spelling, grammar, and punctuation mistakes.

When students have revised and edited their drafts, have them create the final draft of their responses.

Share

Bring students together. Invite a few volunteers to read aloud their responses to the prompt. Invite students who are listening to provide feedback and ask clarifying questions.

Strategies to Support ELs

Emerging (Beginning)

Work with students to make corrections to the modeling/practice text. Alternatively, you could work one on one with ELs to help them edit and revise the sentences they wrote to accompany their sketches of the positions of the players on a soccer team.

Expanding (Intermediate) and Bridging (Advanced)

Pair ELs with fluent English speakers during the partner activity.

All Levels

If you have ELs whose first language is Spanish, share these English/Spanish cognates: **error/el error**; **correction/la corrección**.

Name _____ Date _____

Three "Brains" in One

1   The human brain is organized into three sections. Each section is in charge of certain body functions. In fact, these three sections act like mini-brains themselves. You might call them your Survival Brain, Emotional Brain, and Thinking Brain.

2   Your **Survival Brain** is in charge of helping you react quickly at times when you are in danger. Think about it: What does any creature do when it is threatened? It either runs away from the threat or fights to defend itself. Your Survival Brain goes into action immediately when a threat occurs. It speeds up your heartbeat and breathing. It does this to make sure you have enough oxygen flowing through your body to give you the strength to act. It also controls your body's coordination and balance. It sends signals to your muscles to help you run, jump, push, pull, and do anything else to help you deal with the danger.

Name _____ Date _____

Three "Brains" in One (page 2)

3   Your **Emotional Brain** controls your feelings and many of your body's daily functions. It tells you when you're hungry, thirsty, and sleepy. It controls your body temperature. It is also where your emotional reactions occur. It takes in new bits of information and turns them into memories you might need to recall soon afterward. If you don't use those memories right away, your Emotional Brain converts them into long-term memories you can recall months or even years later. It's also the part of your brain that signals your body to release hormones. These are special chemicals that help you cope with stress or make you feel excited about good things.

4   Your **Thinking Brain** is the largest of the three "brains." It controls your ability to figure things out and plan ahead. It is also the part that allows you to speak, read, write, draw, appreciate music, dream, predict, imagine, and do many other complex activities.

5   These three "brains" work closely together all the time, thanks to the 600 miles of neurons they contain. These neurons form between 10 trillion and 100 trillion total connections among them. That's a huge number of superhighways carrying lots of brain-signal traffic!

Name _____ Date _____

Key Idea Web

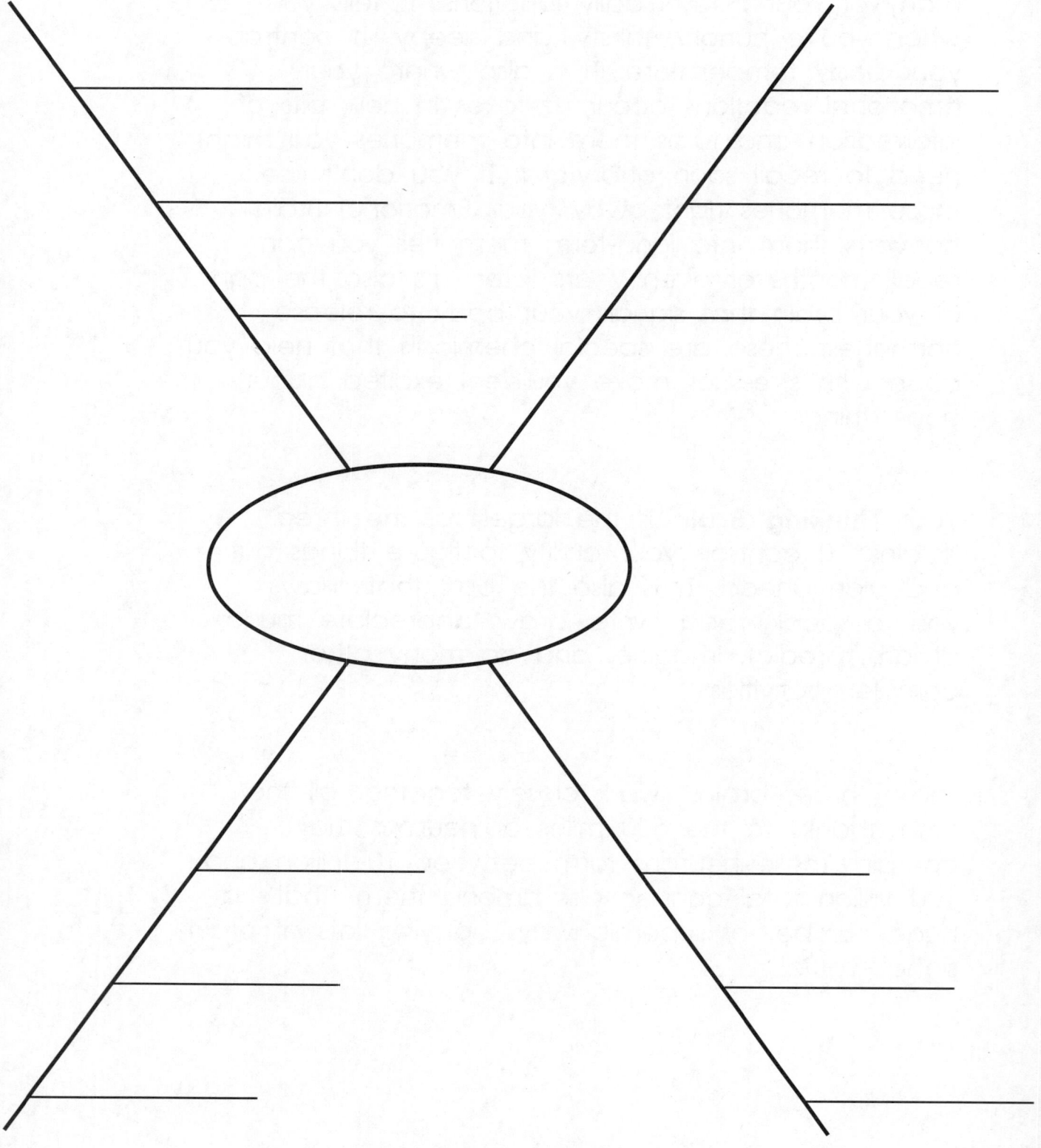

Name _____   Date _____

Who's Who on the Soccer Field

1   During a soccer game, or match, each team puts eleven players on the field. Some of the players are on offense, which means they try to score goals against the other team. Some of the players are on defense, and they try to keep the other team from scoring. Which position would you want to play?

2   The lead defender is the goalkeeper, or goalie. Good goalies are quick and fearless. The goalie is the only player on the field allowed to touch the ball with his or her hands—and only when inside the penalty box area. The other players must kick the ball or tap it with their chest, body, or head. If the ball touches the arms of any of these players, even by accident, it's a foul called a "handball."

3   Four other defenders, or backs, play in front of the goalkeeper. They are strong kickers. Sometimes, one defender is positioned behind the other back as extra protection, and this position is called sweeper.

Name _____ Date _____

Who's Who on the Soccer Field (page 2)

4   In the center of the field are three midfielders: right, left, and center. Midfielders figure out how to attack the other team and decide which attacker to pass the ball to in order to score. Sometimes midfielders, also called halfbacks, go up the field to score, and other times they go back to defend.

5   The front line is the offense. It consists of three attackers: left winger, right winger, and striker. Attackers, or forwards, are often the fastest players. On a typical score, the wingers dribble the ball down the left or right side of the field, and then pass the ball into the other team's goal area. The striker, who is near the goal, will either kick or head the ball into the goal.

Name _____   Date _____

Informative/Explanatory Planning Guide 1

Prompt: Imagine that a chef is cooking over a hot stove and accidentally spills a pot of hot water. Using only the information from "Three 'Brains' in One," explain how the different parts of the chef's brain might work to help the chef in this situation. Support your explanation with evidence from the text.

Analyze the Prompt

How does the prompt apply to the text?	
What does the prompt ask me to do?	

Key Details and Evidence

Details	Evidence

Name _____ Date _____

Informative/Explanatory Planning Guide 2

Prompt: "Who's Who on the Soccer Field" describes the jobs of the different positions on a soccer team. Using only the information in the article, explain the role of the offensive and defensive players in a soccer game. Support your explanation with specific examples of what each player does.

Analyze the Prompt

How does the prompt apply to the text?	
What does the prompt ask me to do?	

Key Details and Evidence

Details	Evidence

Name _____   Date _____

Informative/Explanatory Checklist

Title _____

	Yes	No	Not Sure
1. I researched my topic and organized my information into notes that helped me write my paper.	—	—	—
2. I introduce my topic and use words that grab my readers' attention.	—	—	—
3. I keep my paper organized by grouping information together in a way that makes sense. I use paragraphs and sections.	—	—	—
4. I use headings to organize my sections.	—	—	—
5. The information in my report is accurate.	—	—	—
6. I support my points with facts, definitions, and details.	—	—	—
7. I include graphics to support my information.	—	—	—
8. I include captions that explain each graphic.	—	—	—
9. I use linking words and phrases to connect ideas.	—	—	—
10. My report includes different viewpoints so that I do not sway my readers to think one way.	—	—	—
11. I include a strong conclusion that keeps my readers thinking.	—	—	—
12. I choose words that make my text interesting to read and easy to understand. I include words that connect to the topic.	—	—	—
13. I use at least one primary source.	—	—	—
14. I use a formal voice.	—	—	—

Quality Writing Checklist
I looked for and corrected . . .

	Yes	No	Not Sure
sentence fragments and run-ons.	—	—	—
parts of speech (pronouns, auxiliaries, adjectives, prepositions).	—	—	—
grammar.	—	—	—
indented paragraphs.	—	—	—
punctuation.	—	—	—
capitalization.	—	—	—
spelling.	—	—	—

Informative/Explanatory Teacher Rubric

Score	Planning and Implementation	Evidence of Genre Characteristics	Conventions of Grammar and Usage	Conventions of Mechanics
4	(CCSS W.4.2, W.4.4, W.4.7, W.4.8, W.4.9, L.4.3, L.4.6) The writer's ideas are well organized and well developed. The writer: • thoroughly researches the topic before writing. • includes an introduction, or lead, that grabs readers' attention. • creates and maintains a meaningful organizational structure by introducing the topic and grouping related information. • consistently varies sentence structure to facilitate clear ideas. • uses a wide variety of linking words and phrases to link ideas within categories of information. • uses well-chosen words and phrases and domain-specific vocabulary that add effect and description to the piece. • includes a strong conclusion that keeps readers thinking.	(CCSS W.4.2, W.4.7, W.4.8, W.4.9, L.4.3) The writer demonstrates complete understanding of the features of informative/explanatory writing. The writer: • thoroughly develops the topic by including facts, definitions, details, and examples. • includes unique text and graphic features (headings, charts, illustrations, etc.) that support the information. • includes thoughtfully worded captions that explain each graphic feature. • includes one or more different viewpoints so readers can draw their own conclusions. • includes carefully chosen primary sources. • consistently maintains a formal voice.	(CCSS L.4.1, W.4.5) The writer correctly implements all conventions. The writer: • produces well-developed complete sentences. • efficiently revises and corrects sentence fragments and run-ons. • uses parts of speech in unique ways. • uses grammar conventions in clear and concise ways.	(CCSS W.4.5, L.4.2) The writer correctly implements all conventions. The writer: • always correctly indents paragraphs. • makes no, or few, mechanical mistakes, and they do not hinder overall meaning.
3	The writer's ideas are adequately organized and developed. The writer: • researches the topic before writing. • includes an introduction, or lead. • creates and maintains an organizational structure and groups related information into paragraphs or sections. • varies sentence structure to facilitate clear ideas. • uses linking words and phrases to link ideas within categories of information. • uses words and phrases and domain-specific words that add effect and description to the informational piece. • includes a conclusion.	The writer demonstrates an adequate understanding of the features of informative/explanatory writing. The writer: • develops the topic by including facts, definitions, details, and examples. • includes text and graphic features (headings, charts, illustrations, etc.) that support the information. • includes captions that explain the graphics. • includes one different viewpoint. • includes primary source documents. • maintains a formal voice.	The writer implements most conventions. The writer: • produces complete sentences. • revises and corrects sentence fragments and run-ons most of the time. • uses correct parts of speech most of the time. • uses correct grammar conventions most of the time.	The writer implements most conventions. The writer: • correctly indents paragraphs most of the time. • makes occasional mechanical mistakes, but they do not hinder overall meaning.
2	The writer's ideas are somewhat organized and developed. The writer: • does some research on the project. • includes an introduction, or lead, that is weak. • attempts to create and maintain an organizational structure. Though the writer attempts to group related ideas, they are difficult to follow. • attempts to vary sentence structure. Attempt does not aid understanding. • uses some linking words and phrases to link ideas within categories of information. • uses some words and phrases that add effect and description. Domain-specific words may or may not be included. • includes a weak conclusion.	The writer demonstrates some understanding of the features of informative/explanatory writing. The writer: • somewhat develops the topic by including facts, definitions, details, etc. • includes few text and graphic features to support the information. • includes some captions that explain the graphics. Captions may or may not adequately address the graphic. • attempts to include one different viewpoint. The viewpoint does not necessarily connect to the topic. • includes one primary source document. It may or may not connect to the topic. • inconsistently maintains a formal voice.	The writer implements some conventions. The writer: • produces complete sentences some of the time. • revises and corrects sentence fragments and run-ons some of the time. • uses correct parts of speech some of the time. • uses correct grammar conventions some of the time.	The writer implements some conventions. The writer: • indents paragraphs some of the time. • makes many mechanical mistakes, and they hinder overall meaning.
1	The writer's ideas are disorganized and undeveloped. The writer: • does very little research on the topic. • does not include an introduction, or lead. • does not create or maintain an organizational structure. Ideas may be grouped, but they are difficult to follow. • does not vary sentence structure. • uses few, if any, linking words and phrases to link ideas. • uses few, if any, words and phrases that add effect and description. Writer includes few, if any, domain-specific words. • does not include a conclusion.	The writer demonstrates little, if any, understanding of the features of informative/explanatory writing. The writer: • does not develop the topic. • includes few, if any, text and graphic features to support the information. • includes few, if any, captions. Captions do not necessarily explain the graphics. • does not include different viewpoints. • does not include primary sources. • does not maintain a formal voice.	The writer implements few, if any, conventions. The writer: • rarely produces complete sentences. • rarely revises and corrects fragments and run-ons. • rarely uses correct parts of speech. • rarely uses correct grammar conventions.	The writer implements few, if any, conventions. The writer: • does not attempt to indent paragraphs. • makes many mechanical mistakes that hinder overall meaning.

Grade 4 • ©2017 Benchmark Education Company, LLC

Grade 4 Informative/Explanatory Writing to Multiple Sources Mini-Lessons at a Glance

MINI-LESSON MENU		PAGE	BLM
Read and Analyze Source Texts	Writing to Narrative Sources	114	8,9,10,11,12,13,14,15,16,17,18
Read and Analyze an Informative/Explanatory Prompt	Writing to Narrative Sources	116	19, 20
Read Closely to Find Text Evidence	Writing to Narrative Sources	118	8,9,10,11,12,14,16,17,18,19,20
Draft a Response	Writing to Narrative Sources	120	14, 16, 17, 18, 19, 20
Revise and Edit a Response	Writing to Narrative Sources	122	8,9,10,11,12,14,15,16,17,18,19,20
MANAGEMENT & ASSESSMENT TOOLS		**PAGE**	
Informative/Explanatory Checklist		137	
Informative/Explanatory Teacher Rubric		138	

Read and Analyze Source Texts

RL.4.1, RL.4.2, RL.4.3, SL.4.1a, SL.4.1b, SL.4.1c, SL.4.1d, SL.4.2, SL.4.3

Objectives

In this mini-lesson, students will:

• Listen and follow along as a source text is read aloud.

• Find key information from a source text using a story map.

• Apply the mini-lesson independently to a different source text.

Preparation

Materials Needed

• "Why Thunder Chases Lightning" (BLMs 8–9)

• "The Story of Lightning and Thunder" (BLMs 10–12)

• "How Rabbit Lost His Tail" (BLMs 14–15)

• "How Chipmunk Got Its Stripes" (BLMs 16–18)

• Story Map (BLMs 13)

• Conferring Prompts

 Focus

Introduce the Mini-Lesson

In this unit, students will read two narrative sources in order to respond to an informative/explanatory writing prompt. The prompt will require them to use information from both sources in their written responses. Today's mini-lesson will focus on how to carefully read the source texts to find the key details.

 Display the mini-lesson source texts "Why Thunder Chases Lightning" (BLMs 8–9) and "The Story of Lightning and Thunder" (BLMs 10–12).

Say: *You may be able to tell from the titles of these two stories that they are both about thunder and lightning. I'm going to answer a prompt about these texts, but before I write about them, I must be sure I understand the key ideas in each passage. Today I am going to show you how I find the key details in a source text.*

Read Aloud the Source Texts

Read aloud "Why Thunder Chases Lightning" and "The Story of Lightning and Thunder." Stop at some or all of the places indicated (or at other points you choose) to highlight key ideas. You may wish to model for students how you annotate a text by underlining the key details as you read. Think aloud about how you distinguish between important and unimportant details. After reading, provide your summary of the main ideas in each passage.

After "Why Thunder Chases Lightning." Say: *This story explains that Thunder and Lightning were a mother sheep and her son. They caused so much trouble on Earth that they were sent to live in the sky.*

After "The Story of Lightning and Thunder." Say: *This story says that Lightning and Thunder were a brother and sister. They were left behind when their village moved away, and the stars wished to take care of them in the sky. Brother made loud footsteps and Sister could make fire with a flint.*

Respond Orally to the Source Texts

Engage students in a text-dependent discussion about the fiction texts, using some or all of the following questions.
• *What did Lightning do when he got angry?*
• *What happened when Thunder chased Lightning?*
• *What happened after Brother and Sister were left behind?*
• *What magical powers did Brother and Sister have?*
• *How are these stories alike?*
• *How are they different?*

 **Rehearse**

Analyze the Source Texts

 Distribute the Story Map (BLMs 13). Invite students to work in small groups to complete it. Tell them to look for key details from each story, including the names of the characters, the setting, the problem in each story, and the main events.

Why Thunder Chases Lightning	The Story of Lightning and Thunder
Beginning: Thunder was a mother sheep and Lightning was her son. They lived among people in a village. The mother and son caused trouble and were told to live at the end of the village, away from people.	**Beginning:** Villagers were hit with a difficult snowfall, so they moved south. They accidentally left Brother and Sister behind.
Middle: Lightning continued to set fires and cause trouble, and Thunder chased him, yelling after him loudly.	**Middle:** To care for themselves, Sister started a fire with a flint and Brother used his boots to loudly plow through the snow.
End: The king banished Thunder and Lightning to the sky so they would cause less damage and not scare people as much.	**End:** Brother and Sister showed their skills to the stars. The stars then let the children live with them in the sky as thunder and lightning.

Sample Story Map (BLMs 13)

 If your class includes English learners or other students who need support, use "Strategies to Support ELs."

Share Ideas

Invite volunteers to share examples of key details they found in the text.

 # Independent Writing and Conferring

 Distribute copies of the independent writing source texts "How Rabbit Lost His Tail" (BLMs 14–15) and "How Chipmunk Got Its Stripes" (BLMs 16–18). Also give students a blank copy of the Story Map on BLMs 13. Tell students that they will be writing about the passages. But before they write, they need to make sure they understand the key details in each passage.

Read aloud the passages with students. Then ask students to reread the passages independently to find the key details for their story maps.

 **Share**

Bring students together and ask them to share the information they wrote on their story maps. Encourage students to ask questions about anything in the story they don't understand, or if they do not know the meaning of a word.

Strategies to Support ELs

Emerging (Beginning)

 While other students complete the small-group activity (or during independent writing time), reread and discuss the story "Why Thunder Chases Lightning" on BLMs 8–9 with students. Help them retell the story in any way they can, using gestures, pantomime, words, sketches, and so on. **Ask:** *What happened first? What happened next?*

Expanding (Intermediate) and Bridging (Advanced)

 Pair ELs with fluent English speakers during the small-group activity. Display simple sentence frames and model how students can use them to talk about key ideas in the text. For example:

Lightning is _____.
Thunder is _____.
Thunder chased Lightning because _____.

Read and Analyze an Informative/Explanatory Prompt

RL.4.1, RL.4.2, RL.4.3, SL.4.1a, SL.4.1b, SL.4.1c, SL.4.1d, SL.4.2, SL.4.3

 **Focus**

Objectives

In this mini-lesson, students will:

• Analyze prompts by breaking them into parts.

• Apply this mini-lesson to their independent writing to sources.

Preparation

Materials Needed

• Informative/Explanatory Planning Guide 1 (BLM 19)

• Informative/Explanatory Planning Guide 2 (BLM 20)

• Conferring Prompts

Introduce the Mini-Lesson

Remind students that in the previous mini-lesson they read two fictional text sources. Today, they will focus on reading and analyzing a prompt that asks them to write a response based on information from both of those texts.

Say: *Today we will read and analyze a prompt together. Then you will read and analyze a different prompt during independent writing time.*

Model Reading and Analyzing a Prompt

 Display Informative/Explanatory Planning Guide 1 (BLM 19) and read aloud the prompt. Explain to students how you unpack the prompt to find out exactly what it is asking you to do.

Prompt: Pourquoi tales all share certain features. They have a problem and solution that explains why things in nature are a certain way. The setting is usually important to the story. The characters are usually animals or objects in nature. How do the tales "Why Thunder Chases Lightning" and "The Story of Lightning and Thunder" reflect these features? Write a short text that answers this question. Provide examples from the two tales.

Informative/Explanatory Planning Guide 1 (BLM 19)

Reread sentences 1–4. Say: *These sentences explain that all pourquoi tales have features in common and what those features are.*

Reread sentence 5. Say: *This sentence tells me the question I need to answer—how the two stories reflect the features of a pourquoi tale.*

Reread sentences 6 and 7. Say: *These sentences tell me that I need to write a short text and use examples from the two tales in my explanation.*

Rehearse

Practice Reading and Analyzing a Prompt

 Distribute the Informative/Explanatory Planning Guide 1 on BLM 19 to students. Ask them to work with a partner to complete the chart. Tell students to save their partially completed planning guide for future lessons.

Analyze the Prompt

How does the prompt apply to the sources?	It explains that both passages are pourquoi tales, which are tales that explain events in nature.
What does the prompt ask me to do?	The prompt asks me to explain the features of a pourquoi tale using examples from the two tales.

Sample Informative/Explanatory Planning Guide 1 (BLM 19)

 If your class includes English learners or other students who need support, use "Strategies to Support ELs."

Share and Discuss

Invite partners to read aloud the information they supplied in the chart.

Independent Writing and Conferring

 Distribute copies of Informative/Explanatory Planning Guide 2 (BLM 20). Have students read the prompt they will be writing a response to and break it down to determine what it is asking. Tell them to fill in the "Analyze the Prompt" portion of the chart. Tell students to save their partially completed planning guide for future lessons.

Share

Bring students together and ask them to share the information they wrote on their charts.

Strategies to Support ELs

Emerging (Beginning)

 Work individually with beginning ELs to reread and discuss the stories about Rabbit and Chipmunk on BLMs 14–15 and BLMs 16–18. Ask students to retell the stories using words, gestures, pantomime, or sketches. **Ask:** *What happened first? What happened next?*

Expanding (Intermediate) and Bridging (Advanced)

 Provide sentence frames to help ELs talk about the prompt on BLM 20 with a partner:

The first part of the prompt asks me to _____.
The second part of the prompt asks me to _____.
The third part of the prompt asks me to _____.

All Levels

If you have ELs whose first language is Spanish, share these English/Spanish cognates: **compare/comparar**; **contrast/contraste**.

Read Closely to Find Text Evidence

RL.4.1, RL.4.2, RL.4.3, W.4.2, W.4.8, SL.4.1a, SL.4.1b, SL.4.1c, SL.4.1d, SL.4.2, SL.4.3

Objectives

In this mini-lesson, students will:

- Understand what close reading of a text is.

- Practice close reading to find evidence to support a response.

- Compare and contrast characters.

- Apply this mini-lesson to their independent writing to sources.

Preparation

Materials Needed

- "Why Thunder Chases Lightning" (BLMs 8–9)

- "The Story of Lightning and Thunder" (BLMs 10–12)

- "How Rabbit Lost His Tail" (BLMs 14–15)

- "How Chipmunk Got Its Stripes" (BLMs 16–18)

- Students' saved Informative/ Explanatory Planning Guide 1 (BLM 19) from previous lesson

- Students' saved Informative/ Explanatory Planning Guide 2 (BLM 20) from previous lesson

- Conferring Prompts

 **Focus**

Introduce the Mini-Lesson

Remind students that they have now read two pourquoi tales and pulled out the key details. They have also read and analyzed a prompt that asks them to look at both of these tales in order to identify and explain the features that all pourquoi tales share. Today you will show students how to closely read a text to find evidence to support a response.

Model Close Reading to Find Text Evidence

Display the mini-lesson source texts "Why Thunder Chases Lightning" (BLMs 8–9) and "The Story of Lightning and Thunder" (BLMs 10–12). Also display the sample Informative/Explanatory Planning Guide 1 (BLM 19). Read aloud the prompt.

> **Prompt:** Pourquoi tales all share certain features. They have a problem and solution that explains why things in nature are a certain way. The setting is usually important to the story. The characters are usually animals or objects in nature. How do the tales "Why Thunder Chases Lightning" and "The Story of Lightning and Thunder" reflect these features? Write a short text that answers this question. Provide examples from the two tales.

Informative/Explanatory Planning Guide 1 (BLM 19)

Say: *In order to respond to this prompt, I am going to have to look back at each story and see how they reflect the features mentioned in the prompt. First I'll look back to find out how each tale has a problem and solution that explains something in nature.*

Reread "Why Thunder Chases Lightning." Say: *The problem in this tale is that Lightning, the ram, causes so much trouble in the village that the king sends him away. The solution is that they are sent to the sky, and this explains why thunder and lightning are in the sky.*

Reread "The Story of Lightning and Thunder." Say: *The problem in this story is that a brother and sister are abandoned when the villagers suddenly pack up and move away because they must go where they can find food. The solution is that they find a new home in the sky and become lightning and thunder. This problem and solution also explains why thunder and lightning are in the sky.*

 **Rehearse**

Practice Close Reading to Find Text Evidence

 Assign students to small groups. Distribute copies of "Why Thunder Chases Lightning" on BLMs 8–9 and "The Story of Lightning and Thunder" on BLMs 10–12. Have students take out their partially completed Informative/Explanatory Planning Guide 1 on BLM 19. Ask them to complete the chart by listing text evidence that shows how each tale addresses a feature of the pourquoi genre. Tell students to save their planning guide for future lessons.

Evidence from the Text

Pourquoi Tale Feature	Why Thunder Chases Lightning	The Story of Lightning and Thunder
Problem	Thunder is a mother sheep and Lightning is her son, the ram, who causes trouble in the village.	A brother and sister are left behind when the villagers move away.
Solution that explains things in nature	They are sent to live in the sky. This explains how thunder and lightning came to be.	They find a home in the sky. This also explains how thunder and lightning came to be.
A setting important to the story	A village, where the people get tired of the sheep and ram causing trouble.	A village during winter. The children cannot survive alone when the people leave.
Characters are usually animals or objects in nature.	The characters are a sheep and a ram that become thunder and lightning.	The characters are children who turn into lightning and thunder.

Sample Informative/Explanatory Planning Guide 1 (BLM 19)

 If your class includes English learners or other students who need support, use "Strategies to Support ELs."

Share and Discuss

Invite groups to read aloud the evidence they recorded on the chart.

Independent Writing and Conferring

 Distribute copies of the independent writing source texts "How Rabbit Lost His Tail" (BLMs 14–15) and "How Chipmunk Got Its Stripes" (BLMs 16–18). Have students take out their partially completed Informative/ Explanatory Planning Guide 2 (BLM 20). Tell students that they are going to reread the texts to look for evidence that will help them respond to the writing prompt.

 Share

Bring students together. Invite volunteers to read the facts and details they found in the text.

Strategies to Support ELs

Emerging (Beginning)

While other students work in small groups or on independent writing, work with ELs to retell the stories "Why Thunder Chases Lightning" on BLMs 8–9 and "The Story of Lightning and Thunder" on BLMs 10–12. Create a T-Chart, and use sketches and words to list pourquoi tale features and evidence from the two stories.

Expanding (Intermediate) and Bridging (Advanced)

Pair ELs with fluent English speakers during the group activity. Display sentence frames and model how students can use them to talk about the text evidence. For example:

_____ is an example of a pourquoi tale feature because _____.

All Levels

If you have ELs whose first language is Spanish, share this English/Spanish cognate: **evidence/la evidencia**.

Draft a Response

W.4.2a, W.4.2b, W.4.2c, W.4.2d, W.4.2e, W.4.4, W.4.10, SL.4.1a, SL.4.1b, SL.4.1c, SL.4.1d, SL.4.2, SL.4.3

 **Focus**

Objectives

In this mini-lesson, students will:

- Use evidence from a source text to draft a response to a prompt.

- Apply the mini-lesson to their independent writing to sources.

Preparation

Materials Needed

- "How Rabbit Lost His Tail" (BLMs 14–15)

- "How Chipmunk Got Its Stripes" (BLMs 16–18)

- Students' saved Informative/ Explanatory Planning Guide 2 (BLM 20) from previous lesson

- Informative/Explanatory Checklist

- Conferring Prompts

Introduce the Mini-Lesson

 Display the sample Informative/Explanatory Planning Guide 1 (BLM 19) and tell students that today you will show them how to use the information in the planning guide to draft a well-structured response to the prompt.

Display and read aloud the Informative/Explanatory Checklist. Remind students that well-structured informational texts include these features. Point out that when they write to a source during an assessment or in class, they won't always have the checklist in front of them. Writers need to remember these features for future reference.

Model Writing a Draft

Display the modeling text and read it aloud.

"Why Thunder Chases Lightning" and "The Story of Lightning and Thunder" both reflect three features of pourquoi tales. They include a problem and solution that explains something in nature. They both have settings that are critical to the story, and they both have characters who are animals or objects in nature.

The problem and solution in these tales explains how lightning and thunder came to be. In "Why Thunder Chases Lightning," a young ram causes trouble in the village. The king's solution is to send the ram and his mother into the sky where they become lightning and thunder. In "The Story of Lightning and Thunder," a brother and sister are abandoned by the other villagers. Happily, they find a new home in the sky.

Both tales have important settings. The sheep live in a small village where they cause trouble and the people complain, so the king sends the sheep away. In "The Story of Lightning and Thunder," the children live in a village in the far north. The cold drives the villagers away to find food and the children can't survive on their own. Both settings are important to the story problem.

Finally, both tales include characters who are animals or objects in nature. The characters in "Why Thunder Chases Lightning" are sheep. The children in "The Story of Lightning and Thunder" turn into objects in nature.

Both of these tales reflect the important features of the pourquoi genre.

Modeling Text

Say: *I gathered my evidence about how both stories reflect the features of pourquoi tales. Then I used the text evidence I collected to respond to the prompt. First I gave the titles of the two stories and stated that both reflect three features of pourquoi tales.*

Point out that next, you summarized which features of pourquoi tales the stories reflect. Then, in each of the next three paragraphs, you gave evidence from the text to support your response.

Rehearse

Prepare for Independent Writing

 Distribute the independent writing source texts "How Rabbit Lost His Tail" (BLMs 14–15) and "How Chipmunk Got Its Stripes" (BLMs 16–18). Have students take out their completed Informative/Explanatory Planning Guide 2 (BLM 20). Have students refer to their evidence and discuss with a partner what they will draft in response to the prompt about the animal stories.

 If your class includes English learners or other students who need support, use "Strategies to Support ELs."

Share and Discuss

Invite students to share their ideas for their drafts while following the rules for participating in discussions. Encourage them to build on others' talk in conversations by linking their comments to the remarks of others.

Independent Writing and Conferring

Tell students that they have read and analyzed a source text to make sure they understand it. They have analyzed the prompt so they know what they are supposed to write about. They have found evidence in the texts that will support the ideas in their writing. And they have discussed their ideas for their draft with a partner. They are now ready to write their drafts. Distribute the Informative/Explanatory Checklist to students and remind them to refer to it as they write their drafts.

Confer with individual students or groups as needed to support their drafting efforts. Tell students to save their drafts for use in future lessons.

Share

Bring students together. Invite volunteers to share their drafts. Encourage listeners to ask for further explanations as needed.

Strategies to Support ELs

Emerging (Beginning)

 Work with ELs while other students work with partners or independently. Ask students to use "How Rabbit Lost His Tail" on BLMs 14–15 and "How Chipmunk Got Its Stripes" on BLMs 16–18 and draw a picture for each story that shows what happened. Help them write two sentences for the pictures telling how each shows one feature of a pourquoi tale.

Expanding (Intermediate) and Bridging (Advanced)

 Pair ELs with fluent English speakers during the partner activity. Provide the following sentence frames to help students discuss their ideas:

A feature of a pourquoi tale is _____.
One example in this story is _____.

All Levels

 If you have ELs whose first language is Spanish, share these English/Spanish cognates: **character/el character**; **different/diferente**.

Revise and Edit a Response

W.4.2a, W.4.2b, W.4.2c, W.4.2d, W.4.2e, W.4.4, W.4.5, W.4.10, SL.4.1a, SL.4.1b, SL.4.1c, SL.4.1d, SL.4.2, SL.4.3

Objectives

In this mini-lesson, students will:

• Learn how to revise and edit a response to a prompt.

• Apply this strategy to their independent writing to sources.

Preparation

Materials Needed

• "Why Thunder Chases Lightning" (BLMs 8–9)

• "The Story of Lightning and Thunder" (BLMs 10–12)

• "How Rabbit Lost His Tail" (BLMs 14–15)

• "How Chipmunk Got Its Stripes" (BLMs 16–18)

• Students' saved Informative/ Explanatory Planning Guide 1 (BLM 19) from previous lesson

• Students' saved Informative/ Explanatory Planning Guide 2 (BLM 20) from previous lesson

• Conferring Prompts

 **Focus**

Introduce the Mini-Lesson

Tell students that writers look at their drafts to see how they can be revised and edited. When they revise, they should look for ways to make their writing better. They also make sure they have included the right text evidence and enough details to answer the prompt. When they edit their work, writers also check for spelling, grammar, and punctuation errors.

Say: *Today I'll show you how to revise a draft.*

Model Revising a Draft

Display the mini-lesson source texts "Why Thunder Chases Lightning" (BLMs 8–9) and "The Story of Lightning and Thunder" (BLMs 10–12). Also display the sample Informative/Explanatory Planning Guide 1 (BLM 19) and the modeling/practice text. Note that the modeling/practice text has errors inserted into it so that you can model revising it.

"Why Thunder Chases Lightning" and "The Story of Lightning and Thunder" both reflect three features of pourquoi tales. They include a problem and solution that explains something in nature. They both have settings that are critical to the story, and they both have characters who are animals or objects in nature.

The problem and solution in these tales ~~gives~~ explains how lightning and thunder came to be. In "Why Thunder Chases Lightning," a young ram causes trouble in the village. The king's solution is to send the ram and his mother into the sky where they become ~~lightening~~ lightning and thunder. In "The Story of Lightning and Thunder," a ~~Brother~~ brother and ~~Sister~~ sister are abandoned by the other villagers. Happily, they find a new home in the sky.

Both ~~tails~~ tales have important settings. The sheep live in a small village where they cause trouble and the people complain, so the king sends the sheep away. In "The Story of Lightning and Thunder," the children live in a village in the far north. The cold drives the villagers away to find food and the children can't survive on their own. Both settings are important to the story problem.

Finally, both tales include characters who are animals ~~and~~ or objects in nature. The characters in "Why Thunder Chases Lightning" are sheep. The children in "The Story of Lightning and Thunder" turn into objects in nature.

Both of these tales reflect the important features of the pourquoi genre.

Modeling/Practice Text

Model revising a few of the errors in the text.

Read aloud paragraph 1. Say: *My first sentence is not incorrect, but it does not give enough information. Both reflect the features of what? I will insert "of pourquoi tales." Also, if I add the word **both** to the last sentence in the paragraph, I can strengthen my point that the stories share features.*

Grade 4 • ©2017 Benchmark Education Company, LLC

I'll insert **both** *in two places: "They both have settings" and "they both have characters."*

Read aloud sentence 1 in paragraph 2. Say: *The word* **gives** *is awkward here. I'm going to use the word* **explains** *instead. I am writing an explanation of how the two stories reflect the pourquoi genre. The word* **explains** *will tell the reader the purpose of my text.*

Model Editing a Draft

 Continue working with the modeling/practice text to edit for grammar, spelling, and so on. Model correcting one or two errors in the text. Students will finish revising and editing the text in the Rehearse section.

Read aloud sentence 1. Say: *The titles of the stories need to be enclosed in quotation marks. I'll add them around both story titles.*

 Rehearse

Practice Revising a Draft

 Distribute "Why Thunder Chases Lightning" on BLMs 8–9 and "The Story of Lightning and Thunder" on BLMs 10–12. Have students take out their completed Informative/Explanatory Planning Guide 1 on BLM 19. Have students work with a partner to continue revising and editing the text that compares the two explanations of how lightning and thunder came to be.

 If your class includes English learners or other students who need support, use "Strategies to Support ELs."

Share and Discuss

Invite students to share the edits they made. Invite students to listen actively to each other and ask volunteers to speak one at a time to explain their corrections and revisions. Make sure that you address all the errors embedded in the modeling/practice text so that students have correct information.

Independent Writing and Conferring

 Have students take out the independent writing source texts "How Rabbit Lost His Tail" (BLMs 14–15) and "How Chipmunk Got Its Stripes" (BLMs 16–18), their completed Informative/Explanatory Planning Guide 2 (BLM 20), and a copy of their drafts. Explain that they will now edit and revise their drafts. Tell students to check that the text evidence they have written is correct and that their writing fully answers the prompt. They should also edit for spelling, grammar, and punctuation mistakes.

When students have revised and edited their drafts, have them create the final draft of their responses.

 Share

Bring students together. Invite a few volunteers to read aloud their response to the prompt. Ask listeners to provide positive feedback.

Strategies to Support ELs

Emerging (Beginning)

Work one-on-one with ELs to help them revise and edit the sentences they wrote in the drafting lesson to accompany their sketches of Rabbit and Chipmunk.

Expanding (Intermediate) and Bridging (Advanced)

Pair ELs with fluent English speakers during the partner activity.

All Levels

 If you have ELs whose first language is Spanish, share these English/Spanish cognates: **correction/la corrección**; **edit/editar**.

Name _____ Date _____

Why Thunder Chases Lightning

1   Long ago, Thunder and Lightning lived among people in a village on Earth. Thunder was a mother sheep, and her son Lightning was a ram. The sheep and her son often caused trouble in the village, so the king made them move to the end of the village, away from the people.

2   But even though they were at the end of the village, there was still no peace. Lightning had a very bad temper. Whenever he got angry, he set fire to the huts and knocked down trees like he was a bull in a china shop. Sometimes he even damaged the farms and hurt people. Whenever Lightning did these things, Thunder became very angry, and she would call to Lightning in a loud, crackling voice that shook the ground. Her voice made the people tremble like leaves. She scolded Lightning and tried to scare him, but he did not care what she said. So she would chase him through the night and make an awful noise.

3   At last, the people could not stand it any longer, and they went to the king to complain.

Name _____   Date _____

Why Thunder Chases Lightning (page 2)

4   The king ordered Thunder and her son to leave the village and live far away in the bush.

5   This did not do much good. Even far away, Lightning got angry and burned the forests. Then the flames spread to the farms and burned them, too. The people complained again, and this time the king had no choice. He banished Lightning and Thunder from Earth and made them live in the sky. At least there, Lightning would cause less damage. And that is why, to this day, when Lightning is angry, you can see him light up the sky and set fire to Earth, and you can hear his mother, Thunder, chasing and calling after him.

Name _____   Date _____

The Story of Lightning and Thunder

1   One winter, the snow fell hard and long in a village in the north. The people quickly packed up everything and set out for the south where they would be safe and find good hunting grounds. In their haste, the villagers forgot two orphans, a brother and sister, who were out walking in the snow when the villagers left.

2   That night, Brother and Sister returned to an empty village. They searched high and low and although they found no one, Sister did find a flint for lighting fires, which she thought might come in handy.

3   "What shall we do for food?" she asked.

4   "I shall lead us to a wonderful place," said Brother. "First, let me put on my strong sealskin boots which will plow through the snow like a knife through butter."

5   As Brother stomped through the snow, each step caused a loud *boom* that shook the clouds.

Name _____   Date _____

The Story of Lightning and Thunder (page 2)

6   Sister looked up at the night sky. "The stars are twinkling at us, Brother. I think they are inviting us to live with them."

7   "I believe you are right!" said Brother. He kicked his boot heels together and the two children floated up into the sky.

8   "Welcome," said one star. "You may live here if you can show me that you have a magic power."

9   Sister said, "With my flint I can light a fire." A long scrape of the flint produced a fire that crackled and flashed brightly.

10   "Excellent!" exclaimed the delighted star. "You may stay with us. What magic can you do, young man?"

11   "I can make the loudest sound on Earth," answered Brother. He stomped his feet and a boom rippled across the sky. The earth shook and the stars covered their ears.

12   "Magnificent!" said Star. From now on, you shall both be in the sky family, and your names will be Sister Lightning and Brother Thunder."

Name _____ Date _____

The Story of Lightning and Thunder (page 3)

13   The orphans loved their new home and were so happy that they were ecstatic.

14   The next summer, the villagers returned to the north. During a rainstorm, they were overjoyed to see in the sky Brother Thunder and Sister Lightning. They pleaded for the boy and girl to come back, but the orphans would never give up their new home or their magical powers. That is why Lightning and Thunder fill the sky even to this day.

Name _____ Date _____

Story Map

Why Thunder Chases Lightning	The Story of Lightning and Thunder
Beginning:	Beginning:
Middle:	Middle:
End:	End:

Name _____ Date _____

How Rabbit Lost His Tail

1   Rabbit was the most handsome of all the forest animals. He strolled around like a king, showing off his long, wonderful tail to Owl, Deer, and Squirrel. When Squirrel asked if he could have just one strand from Rabbit's tail, Rabbit refused.

2   After hours of showing off his tail, Rabbit was extremely weary. The snow was falling heavily, forming large mounds of white, and it had covered his burrow. All Rabbit could see ahead of him was a small log to rest on, so he climbed onto it and fell asleep. Rabbit snored away for days.

3   When Rabbit finally opened up his eyes, he saw that the sky was blue. He stretched his limbs and looked around. The large mounds of snow had melted away, and he saw that he was not on a log, but on a tree branch high above the ground.

4   Rabbit had to think fast. "Deer," shouted Rabbit, "Please teach me how to leap high into the air and never get hurt when you touch the ground."

5   "Long ago, we could have been good friends and shared so much," Deer said sadly, "but now it is too late for you to learn."

Name _____ Date _____

How Rabbit Lost His Tail (page 2)

6   "Owl," moaned Rabbit, "can you please tell me how you fly?"

7   "I am sorry, but it is too late," said Owl. "I could have taught you how to use your tail like a parachute to land softly, but all you wanted to do was show it off."

8   "Squirrel," pleaded Rabbit, "we are like brothers. We both have wonderful tails and gather food from the forest. Can't you teach me to climb down trees?"

9   Squirrel smiled sadly and shook his head.

10 So, Rabbit had no choice but to close his eyes and let himself fall to the ground. As he fell, his tail caught in a branch and was pulled off, and that is how Rabbit lost his long tail.

11 From that day on, all rabbits have had short, little tails. It is a reminder to them to always be generous with their friends and not to be selfish or boastful.

Name _____ Date _____

How Chipmunk Got Its Stripes

1 One morning Chipmunk came upon Bear, feasting on thousands of ants he had found beneath a log.

2 "Bear," said Chipmunk, "everyone is scared of you and they say that you are the most powerful creature in the world."

3 "Not only am I the biggest and strongest creature around," bragged Bear, "but I am the best at everything, too!"

4 "Everything?" said Chipmunk with a chuckle.

5 In a loud voice, Bear growled, "How dare you laugh at the king of the forest!"

6 "If you are so powerful," said Chipmunk, "then I dare you to stop the sun from shining tomorrow."

7 "*You* dare *me*?" said Bear, the ground shaking with his laughter. "Of course I can stop the sun."

Name _____ Date _____

How Chipmunk Got Its Stripes (page 2)

8   The next morning, it was still dark outside when Bear left his cave and Chipmunk climbed out of his hole. They sat together to see what would happen next. First, the birds began to sing, then daylight appeared and, finally, the sun popped up its head and shone brightly.

9   Chipmunk called out, "I won! The sun is more powerful than Bear!"

10 Bear was furious, and he pounced on Chipmunk, pinning him to the ground with his giant paw. "I may not be as powerful as the sun, but I am more powerful than you! You have seen your last sunrise!"

11 Though Chipmunk was small, he was clever, and no one had been able to capture and eat him yet. "Bear," Chipmunk pleaded, "please let me say a final good-bye to the world."

12 Though Bear was angry, he was not unreasonable. "Say your good-byes," Bear commanded, "but be quick about it."

Name _____ Date _____

How Chipmunk Got Its Stripes (page 3)

13   "Thank you, Bear," Chipmunk gasped, "but could you please lift your paw just a little so I can breathe."

14   Bear lifted his paw a little, but it was just enough for Chipmunk to escape. He darted away as Bear lunged at him. Bear could not grab Chipmunk, but his sharp claws were just long enough to reach Chipmunk's back, leaving three long scratches on his fur. From that day on, all chipmunks have three stripes in their fur to remind them to never, ever make fun of a bear.

Name _____ Date _____

Informative/Explanatory Planning Guide 1

Prompt: Pourquoi tales all share certain features. They have a problem and solution that explains why things in nature are a certain way. The setting is usually important to the story. The characters are usually animals or objects in nature. How do the tales "Why Thunder Chases Lightning" and "The Story of Lightning and Thunder" reflect these features? Write a short text that answers this question. Provide examples from the two tales.

Analyze the Prompt

How does the prompt apply to the sources?	
What does the prompt ask me to do?	

Evidence from the Text

Pourquoi Tale Feature	Why Thunder Chases Lightning	The Story of Lightning and Thunder
Problem		
Solution that explains why things in nature are a certain way		
A setting important to the story		
Characters are usually animals or objects in nature.		

Name _____ Date _____

Informative/Explanatory Planning Guide 2

Prompt: Pourquoi tales all share certain features. They have a problem and solution that explains why things in nature are a certain way. The setting is usually important to the story. The characters are usually animals or objects in nature. How do the tales "How Rabbit Lost His Tail" and "How Chipmunk Got Its Stripes" reflect these features? Write a short text that answers this question. Provide examples from the two tales.

Analyze the Prompt

How does the prompt apply to the sources?	
What does the prompt ask me to do?	

Evidence from the Text

Pourquoi Tale Feature	How Rabbit Lost His Tail	How Chipmunk Got Its Stripes
Problem		
Solution that explains why things in nature are a certain way		
A setting important to the story		
Characters are usually animals or objects in nature.		

Name _____   Date _____

Informative/Explanatory Checklist

Title _____

	Yes	No	Not Sure
1. I researched my topic and organized my information into notes that helped me write my paper.	__	__	__
2. I introduce my topic and use words that grab my readers' attention.	__	__	__
3. I keep my paper organized by grouping information together in a way that makes sense. I use paragraphs and sections.	__	__	__
4. I use headings to organize my sections.	__	__	__
5. The information in my report is accurate.	__	__	__
6. I support my points with facts, definitions, and details.	__	__	__
7. I include graphics to support my information.	__	__	__
8. I include captions that explain each graphic.	__	__	__
9. I use linking words and phrases to connect ideas.	__	__	__
10. My report includes different viewpoints so that I do not sway my readers to think one way.	__	__	__
11. I include a strong conclusion that keeps my readers thinking.	__	__	__
12. I choose words that make my text interesting to read and easy to understand. I include words that connect to the topic.	__	__	__
13. I use at least one primary source.	__	__	__
14. I use a formal voice.	__	__	__

Quality Writing Checklist
I looked for and corrected . . .

	Yes	No	Not Sure
sentence fragments and run-ons.	__	__	__
parts of speech (pronouns, auxiliaries, adjectives, prepositions).	__	__	__
grammar.	__	__	__
indented paragraphs.	__	__	__
punctuation.	__	__	__
capitalization.	__	__	__
spelling.	__	__	__

Informative/Explanatory Teacher Rubric

Score	Planning and Implementation	Evidence of Genre Characteristics	Conventions of Grammar and Usage	Conventions of Mechanics
4	(CCSS W.4.2, W.4.4, W.4.7, W.4.8, W.4.9, L.4.3, L.4.6) The writer's ideas are well organized and well developed. The writer: • thoroughly researches the topic before writing. • includes an introduction, or lead, that grabs readers' attention. • creates and maintains a meaningful organizational structure by introducing the topic and grouping related information. • consistently varies sentence structure to facilitate clear ideas. • uses a wide variety of linking words and phrases to link ideas within categories of information. • uses well-chosen words and phrases and domain-specific vocabulary that add effect and description to the piece. • includes a strong conclusion that keeps readers thinking.	(CCSS W.4.2, W.4.7, W.4.8, W.4.9, L.4.3) The writer demonstrates complete understanding of the features of informative/explanatory writing. The writer: • thoroughly develops the topic by including facts, definitions, details, and examples. • includes unique text and graphic features (headings, charts, illustrations, etc.) that support the information. • includes thoughtfully worded captions that explain each graphic feature. • includes one or more different viewpoints so readers can draw their own conclusions. • includes carefully chosen primary sources. • consistently maintains a formal voice.	(CCSS L.4.1, W.4.5) The writer correctly implements all conventions. The writer: • produces well-developed complete sentences. • efficiently revises and corrects sentence fragments and run-ons. • uses parts of speech in unique ways. • uses grammar conventions in clear and concise ways.	(CCSS W.4.5, L.4.2) The writer correctly implements all conventions. The writer: • always correctly indents paragraphs. • makes no, or few, mechanical mistakes, and they do not hinder overall meaning.
3	The writer's ideas are adequately organized and developed. The writer: • researches the topic before writing. • includes an introduction, or lead. • creates and maintains an organizational structure and groups related information into paragraphs or sections. • varies sentence structure to facilitate clear ideas. • uses linking words and phrases to link ideas within categories of information. • uses words and phrases and domain-specific words that add effect and description to the informational piece. • includes a conclusion.	The writer demonstrates an adequate understanding of the features of informative/explanatory writing. The writer: • develops the topic by including facts, definitions, details, and examples. • includes text and graphic features (headings, charts, illustrations, etc.) that support the information. • includes captions that explain the graphics. • includes one different viewpoint. • includes primary source documents. • maintains a formal voice.	The writer implements most conventions. The writer: • produces complete sentences. • revises and corrects sentence fragments and run-ons most of the time. • uses correct parts of speech most of the time. • uses correct grammar conventions most of the time.	The writer implements most conventions. The writer: • correctly indents paragraphs most of the time. • makes occasional mechanical mistakes, but they do not hinder overall meaning.
2	The writer's ideas are somewhat organized and developed. The writer: • does some research on the project. • includes an introduction, or lead, that is weak. • attempts to create and maintain an organizational structure. Though the writer attempts to group related ideas, they are difficult to follow. • attempts to vary sentence structure. Attempt does not aid understanding. • uses some linking words and phrases to link ideas within categories of information. • uses some words and phrases that add effect and description. Domain-specific words may or may not be included. • includes a weak conclusion.	The writer demonstrates some understanding of the features of informative/explanatory writing. The writer: • somewhat develops the topic by including facts, definitions, details, etc. • includes few text and graphic features to support the information. • includes some captions that explain the graphics. Captions may or may not adequately address the graphic. • attempts to include one different viewpoint. The viewpoint does not necessarily connect to the topic. • includes one primary source document. It may or may not connect to the topic. • inconsistently maintains a formal voice.	The writer implements some conventions. The writer: • produces complete sentences some of the time. • revises and corrects sentence fragments and run-ons some of the time. • uses correct parts of speech some of the time. • uses correct grammar conventions some of the time.	The writer implements some conventions. The writer: • indents paragraphs some of the time. • makes many mechanical mistakes, and they hinder overall meaning.
1	The writer's ideas are disorganized and undeveloped. The writer: • does very little research on the topic. • does not include an introduction, or lead. • does not create or maintain an organizational structure. Ideas may be grouped, but they are difficult to follow. • does not vary sentence structure. • uses few, if any, linking words and phrases to link ideas. • uses few, if any, words and phrases that add effect and description. Writer includes few, if any, domain-specific words. • does not include a conclusion.	The writer demonstrates little, if any, understanding of the features of informative/explanatory writing. The writer: • does not develop the topic. • includes few, if any, text and graphic features to support the information. • includes few, if any, captions. Captions do not necessarily explain the graphics. • does not include different viewpoints. • does not include primary sources. • does not maintain a formal voice.	The writer implements few, if any, conventions. The writer: • rarely produces complete sentences. • rarely revises and corrects fragments and run-ons. • rarely uses correct parts of speech. • rarely uses correct grammar conventions.	The writer implements few, if any, conventions. The writer: • does not attempt to indent paragraphs. • makes many mechanical mistakes that hinder overall meaning.

    Grade 4 • ©2017 Benchmark Education Company, LLC

Grade 4 Informative/Explanatory Writing to Multiple Sources Mini-Lessons at a Glance

MINI-LESSON MENU		PAGE	BLM
Read and Analyze Source Texts	Writing to Informational Sources	140	21, 22, 23, 24, 25, 26, 27, 28
Read and Analyze an Informative/Explanatory Prompt	Writing to Informational Sources	142	30, 31
Read Closely to Find Text Evidence	Writing to Informational Sources	144	21, 22, 23, 24, 26, 27, 28, 29, 30, 31
Draft a Response	Writing to Informational Sources	146	26,27,28,29,30,31
Revise and Edit a Response	Writing to Informational Sources	148	21, 22, 23, 24, 26, 27, 28, 29, 30, 31

MANAGEMENT & ASSESSMENT TOOLS	PAGE
Informative/Explanatory Checklist	161
Informative/Explanatory Teacher Rubric	162

Read and Analyze Source Texts

RI.4.1, RI.4.2, RI.4.3, RI.4.6, W.4.4, SL.4.1a, SL.4.1b, SL.4.1c, SL.4.1d, SL.4.2, SL.4.3

Objectives

In this mini-lesson, students will:

• Listen as a source text is read aloud.

• Find key information from a source text using a main idea chart.

• Apply the mini-lesson independently to a different source text.

Preparation

Materials Needed

• "The Olympic Flame" (BLMs 21–22)

• "Golden Moment" (BLMs 23–24)

• "Katrina" (BLMs 26–27)

• "Higher Ground" (BLMs 28–29)

• Main Idea Chart (BLM 25)

• Conferring Prompts

 **Focus**

Introduce the Mini-Lesson

In this unit, students will focus on writing to multiple informational sources to respond to an informative/explanatory writing prompt. Explain that today's mini-lesson will focus on how to read two informational sources to identify the key details.

 Display and distribute copies of the mini-lesson source texts "The Olympic Flame" (BLMs 21–22) and "Golden Moment" (BLMs 23–24).

Say: *These passages are both about the torch relay that passes the Olympic flame from runner to runner until it reaches the Olympic cauldron where it burns during the Games. One passage is informative/explanatory writing and the other is a firsthand account narrated by a participant in the relay. Before I write about the texts, I must be sure I understand them. Today, I am going to show you how I find the key details in a source passage.*

Read Aloud the Source Texts

Read aloud "The Olympic Flame" and "Golden Moment," stopping at some or all of the places indicated (or at other points you choose) to highlight key ideas. You may wish to model for students how you annotate a text by underlining the key details as you read.

After "The Olympic Flame." Say: *The text recounts the history of burning a flame during the Olympic Games. It describes the Olympic Torch Relay, an event where the flame is carried from runner to runner, and describes how the torch has again become a symbol of the Olympic Games.*

After "Golden Moment." Say: *This passage also is about the Olympic Torch Relay. But it's different from the first passage in some ways. Rather than being a text that just tells information about the topic, this passage tells about one person's experience carrying the torch, from the first person point of view.*

Respond Orally to the Source Texts

Engage students in a text-dependent discussion about the two informational texts, using some or all of the following questions:
• *Describe what you learned about the Olympic Torch Relay.*
• *What details does Abby include in her description of carrying the Torch?*
• *What are some ways these two texts are similar?*
• *What are some ways these two texts are different?*

 **Rehearse**

Analyze the Source Texts

 Distribute the Main Idea Chart (BLM 25). Tell students to work in small groups and complete the chart by listing the most important details from each text. Point out that the main idea for the first text is provided on the chart.

Source Texts	Main Idea	Details
The Olympic Flame	History of the Olympic Torch Relay	Began in Greece thousands of years ago. Tradition continued until the games were banned by a Roman emperor. Games were started again in 1894, but the tradition of lighting a torch didn't begin again until 1928. First Olympic Torch Relay was held in 1936. Flame is passed from runner to runner, until it gets to the setting of current Olympic Games. The torch has again become a symbol of the Olympic Games.
Golden Moment	What it's like to personally carry the torch in the Olympic Torch Relay	Girl waiting in wheelchair to receive the torch; friends and family are with her; her name had been selected from thousands of names. She lights her torch from the torch a young man is carrying. Her friends push her along—she doesn't want to go fast and wants the moment to last. Girl passes the flame to a woman waiting to carry the flame.

Sample Main Idea Chart (BLM 25)

 If your class includes English learners or other students who need support, use "Strategies to Support ELs."

Share Ideas

Invite volunteers to share the details they listed in their Main Idea Charts. Encourage students to ask questions as volunteers share their ideas.

 **Independent Writing and Conferring**

 Distribute copies of the independent writing source texts "Katrina" (BLMs 26–27) and "Higher Ground" (BLMs 28–29). Also give students a blank copy of the Main Idea Chart on BLM 25. Explain that these are the passages that students will write about. Before they write, they need to make sure they understand the ideas in the passages.

Read aloud the passages with students. Then ask students to reread the passages independently to find the most important details and list them on the chart.

 **Share**

Bring students together and ask them to share the details they listed on their Main Idea Charts. Encourage listeners to question speakers if they don't feel they have listed the most important information. Remind students to share their ideas in a positive, helpful way.

Strategies to Support ELs

Emerging (Beginning)

While other students complete the group activity (or during independent writing time), work with ELs to help them understand terms that are key to understanding the text, such as **flame**, **torch**, **ignited**, **Olympic Games**, and **wheelchair**. Have students create an illustrated dictionary for unfamiliar words in these passages. In their dictionaries, have them write the word or phrase and then draw a picture showing the word. Students can also include a translation into their native languages for each term or a sentence that uses the term. Encourage students to use their dictionaries as they complete the activities in this unit.

Expanding (Intermediate) and Bridging (Advanced)

 Pair ELs with English speakers to discuss the key events from both texts. Display simple sentence frames and model how students can use them to talk about the texts. For example:

The first text is about _____.
The second text is about _____.
An important detail is _____.
An important event is _____.

All Levels

 If you have ELs whose first language is Spanish, share this English/Spanish cognate: **different/diferente**.

Read and Analyze an Informative/Explanatory Prompt

W.4.4, SL.4.1a, SL.4.1b, SL.4.1c, SL.4.1d, SL.4.2, SL.4.3

 ## Focus

Objectives

In this mini-lesson, students will:

- Analyze prompts by breaking them into parts.

- Apply this mini-lesson to their independent writing to sources.

Preparation

Materials Needed

- Informative/Explanatory Planning Guide 1 (BLM 30)

- Informative/Explanatory Planning Guide 2 (BLM 31)

- Conferring Prompts

Introduce the Mini-Lesson

Remind students that in the previous mini-lesson they read two text sources. Today, they will focus on reading and analyzing a prompt that asks them to write a response based on information from both of those texts.

Say: *Today we will read and analyze a prompt together. Then you will read and analyze a different prompt during independent writing time.*

Model Reading and Analyzing an Informational Prompt

Display Informative/Explanatory Planning Guide 1 (BLM 30) and read aloud the prompt. Explain to students how you unpack the prompt to find out exactly what it is asking you to do.

Prompt: Compare and contrast "The Olympic Flame" and "Golden Moment." Explain how the two accounts you read are different and how they are similar. Consider each text's topic, genre, point of view, text structure, and purpose. Cite specific details and examples from each text to support your response.

Informative/Explanatory Planning Guide 1 (BLM 30)

Reread sentence 1. Say: *This sentence tells me what I am asked to do—I need to compare and contrast the two texts I read. And it refers to the titles of the two texts.*

Reread sentence 2. Say: *This sentence tells me that I must explain how the two texts are similar and how they are different.*

Reread sentences 3 and 4. Say: *These sentences tell me that I must use details and examples from the passages when I write my compare-and-contrast text.*

 **Rehearse**

Practice Reading and Analyzing an Informational Prompt

 Distribute Informative/Explanatory Planning Guide 1 on BLM 30 to students. Ask them to work in small groups to complete the chart. Tell students to save their partially completed planning guide for future lessons.

Analyze the Prompt	
How does the prompt apply to the sources?	Asks me to compare and contrast the two sources, "The Olympic Flame" and "Golden Moment."
What does the prompt ask me to do?	Explain how the accounts are different and similar; cite specific details and examples from each text.

Sample Informative/Explanatory Planning Guide 1 (BLM 30)

 If your class includes English learners or other students who need support, use "Strategies to Support ELs."

Share and Discuss

Invite groups to read aloud the information they supplied in the chart.

 **Independent Writing and Conferring**

 Distribute copies of Informative/Explanatory Planning Guide 2 (BLM 31). Have students read the prompt they will be writing a response to and break it down to determine what it is asking. Tell them to fill in the Analyze the Prompt section. Tell students to save their partially completed planning guide for future lessons.

 **Share**

Bring students together and ask them to share the information they wrote on their charts.

Strategies to Support ELs

Emerging (Beginning)

Work individually with beginning ELs to develop the concept of alike and different. Use simple items in the classroom as examples, such as a pen and a pencil; an apple and an orange; a cup and a glass. Hold up two items. **Say:** *This is _____. This is _____. They both have _____. This one has _____. But this one has _____.*

Expanding (Intermediate) and Bridging (Advanced)

 Provide sentence frames to help students talk about the prompt with their group:

The first part of the prompt asks me to _____.
The second part of the prompt asks me to _____.
The third part of the prompt asks me to _____.

All Levels

 If you have ELs whose first language is Spanish, share these English/Spanish cognates: **detail/el detalle; example/el ejemplo.**

Read Closely to Find Text Evidence

RI.4.1, RI.4.2, RI.4.3, RI.4.6, W.4.4, SL.4.1a, SL.4.1b, SL.4.1c, SL.4.1d, SL.4.2, SL.4.3

 **Focus**

Objectives

In this mini-lesson, students will:

- Understand what it means to perform a close reading of a text.

- Practice close reading to find evidence to support a response.

- Identify details and examples that can be used to compare and contrast two texts.

- Apply this mini-lesson to their independent writing to sources.

Preparation

Materials Needed

- "The Olympic Flame" (BLMs 21–22)

- "Golden Moment" (BLMs 23–24)

- "Katrina" (BLMs 26–27)

- "Higher Ground" (BLMs 28–29)

- Students' saved Informative/ Explanatory Planning Guide 1 (BLM 30) from previous lesson

- Students' saved Informative/ Explanatory Planning Guide 2 (BLM 31) from previous lesson

- Conferring Prompts

Introduce the Mini-Lesson

Remind students that they have now read two passages and pulled out the key details. They have also read and analyzed a prompt that asks them to explain how the two texts are similar and different. Today you will show students how to closely read a text to find evidence to support a response.

Model Close Reading to Find Text Evidence

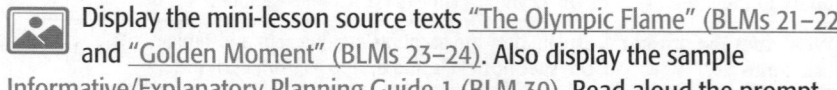 Display the mini-lesson source texts "The Olympic Flame" (BLMs 21–22) and "Golden Moment" (BLMs 23–24). Also display the sample Informative/Explanatory Planning Guide 1 (BLM 30). Read aloud the prompt.

> **Prompt:** Compare and contrast "The Olympic Flame" and "Golden Moment." Explain how the two accounts you read are different and how they are similar. Consider each text's topic, genre, point of view, text structure, and purpose. Cite specific details and examples from each text to support your response.

Informative/Explanatory Planning Guide 1 (BLM 30)

Say: *The prompt is asking me to compare and contrast the two passages I read. That means I will tell how the two passages are similar and how they are different. I will need to go back and reread so I can find specific details and examples that support my idea of how they compare. When we do close reading, we reread and examine a text carefully to look for evidence and to make sure we understand what we are reading.*

Model close reading with the first paragraphs of "The Olympic Flame" and "Golden Moment." Add notes to the planning guide using the sample as a model. Model looking for how the passages are similar and how they are different.

Reread paragraphs 1–2 of "The Olympic Flame." Say: *These paragraphs introduce the topic, the Olympic torch, and then begin to tell about the history and tradition of lighting a torch during the Olympic Games.*

Reread paragraphs 1–2 of "Golden Moment." Say: *These paragraphs are a first-person account about carrying the Olympic flame. The topic is the same as the other passage, the Olympic flame, but the style and information included are very different. This passage includes dialogue. Instead of facts about the history of the Olympic torch, this text includes descriptive details about what it's like to actually carry the torch.*

 **Rehearse**

Practice Close Reading to Find Text Evidence

 Distribute copies of "The Olympic Flame" on BLMs 21–22 and "Golden Moment" on BLMs 23–24 to student pairs. Have them take out their partially complete Informative/Explanatory Planning Guide 1 on BLM 30. Ask them to complete the chart by listing details that compare and contrast the two texts.

Tell students that they should be prepared to explain their choice of details. Tell students to save their completed planning guide for future lessons.

Compare and Contrast

Comparison/ Contrast	The Olympic Flame	Golden Moment
Topic	History of the Olympics and torch runners	One woman's experience as a torch runner
Genre	Informational text	First-hand account
Point of View	Third person, formal	First person
Text Structure	Sequential	Descriptive
Writer's Purpose	Inform readers about the events leading from the ancient to modern Olympic games	Share the sights, sounds, and feelings she experienced as a torch carrier.

Sample Informative/Explanatory Planning Guide 1 (BLM 30)

If your class includes English learners or other students who need support, use "Strategies to Support ELs."**Share and Discuss**

Ask students to discuss their ideas about how to complete the chart.

 **Independent Writing and Conferring**

Distribute copies of the independent writing source texts "Katrina" (BLMs 26–27) and "Higher Ground" (BLMs 28–29). Have students take out their partially completed Informative/Explanatory Planning Guide 2 (BLM 31). Tell students that they are going to reread the text to look for details and examples that show how the two texts are similar and how they are different. They should write this information on the chart. Tell students to save their completed planning guide for future lessons.

During student conferences, observe and support students as they read closely to identify details and examples that compare and contrast the two texts.

 **Share**

Invite volunteers to share the details and examples they found in the texts.

Strategies to Support ELs

Emerging (Beginning)

 Work with ELs while other students work with partners or independently. Reread and discuss the passages about Hurricane Katrina on BLMs 26–27 and BLMs 28–29 with them. Have them retell the passages in any way they can, using words, gestures, pantomime, or sketches.

Expanding (Intermediate) and Bridging (Advanced)

Explain to students that they can use signal words to compare and contrast two things. Provide the following sentence frames that use compare-and-contrast signal words:

Both texts _____.
However, the second text _____.
Unlike the first text, the second text _____.

All Levels

If you have ELs whose first language is Spanish, share this English/Spanish cognate: **experience/la experiencia**.

Draft a Response

W.4.1a, W.4.1b, W.4.1c, W.4.1d, W.4.4, W.4.10, SL.4.1a, SL.4.1b, SL.4.1c, SL.4.1d, SL.4.2, SL.4.3

Objectives

In this mini-lesson, students will:

• Use evidence from a source text to draft a response to a prompt.

• Apply the mini-lesson to their independent writing to sources.

Preparation

Materials Needed

• "Katrina" (BLMs 26–27)

• "Higher Ground" (BLMs 28–29)

• Students' saved Informative/ Explanatory Planning Guide 2 (BLM 31) from previous lesson

• Informative/Explanatory Checklist

• Conferring Prompts

Focus

Introduce the Mini-Lesson

 Display the sample Informative/Explanatory Planning Guide 1 (BLM 30) and tell students that today you will show them how to use the information in the planning guide to draft a well-structured response to the prompt.

Display and read aloud the Informative/Explanatory Checklist. Remind students that well-structured informational texts include these features. Point out that when they write to a source during an assessment or in class, they won't always have the checklist in front of them. Writers need to remember these features for future reference.

Model Writing a Draft

Display the modeling text and read it aloud.

"The Olympic Flame" and "Golden Moment" both help readers understand the significance of the Olympic torch. However, these texts are different, too. They are different genres. They have different points of view. And they were written for different purposes.

"The Olympic Flame" is a third person informational text. It presents sequential facts about the Olympics. For example, readers learn that the first games occurred about 3,000 years ago. To the ancient Greeks the flame represented "the gift of fire from the god Prometheus." This text follows the Olympics from ancient to modern times.

On the other hand, "Golden Moment" is a first person account. It describes one woman's experience as a torch carrier. She writes, "The noise grew louder as the Olympic flame grew nearer. Dozens of flags waved and my heart pounded in my chest." This writer isn't trying to explain. She is describing what she saw, heard, felt, and thought.

Both texts build readers' awareness of the Olympics. One text informs readers with historical facts. The other describes one woman's experience.

Modeling Text

Say: *I noted details and examples that helped me compare and contrast these two texts. I used this information to respond to the prompt. I began by introducing the titles of the passages and stating how the texts are the same and how they are different.*

Remind students that writers use special words, called signal words and phrases, to show comparisons and contrasts in a text. Discuss examples of signal words for comparing (both, too, etc.) and signal words for contrast (however, on the other hand, etc.). Point out how you quote specific evidence from the text that supports your comparisons and contrasts.

Comparisons:
- *Both are about the same topic—the Olympic torch and the Olympic Torch Relay.*
- *Both describe how the Olympic Torch Relay works.*

Contrasts:
- *"The Olympic Flame" describes the history of the Olympic torch tradition from an objective point of view, while "Golden Moment" is a firsthand account about carrying the Olympic torch.*
- *The purpose of "The Olympic Flame" is to inform. The purpose of "Golden Moment" is to share the experiences of one torch carrier.*

Say: *After I included several details and examples that show how the two texts are similar and different, I wrote a paragraph that concludes or wraps up my compare-and-contrast explanation.*

 **Rehearse**

Prepare for Independent Writing

 Distribute the independent writing source texts "Katrina" (BLMs 26–27) and "Higher Ground" (BLMs 28–29). Have students take out their completed Informative/Explanatory Planning Guide 2 (BLM 31). Ask students to refer to their evidence and discuss in a small group what they will draft in response to the prompt asking them to compare and contrast the two texts.

If your class includes English learners or other students who need support, use "Strategies to Support ELs."

Share and Discuss

Invite students to share their ideas for their drafts.

Independent Writing and Conferring

Tell students that they have read and analyzed a source text to make sure they understand it. They have analyzed the prompt so they know what they are supposed to write about. They have found details and examples in the text that they will use in their writing. And they have rehearsed their ideas for their draft with a partner. They are now ready to write their drafts. Distribute the Informative/Explanatory Checklist to students and remind them to refer to it as they write their drafts.

Confer with individual students or groups as needed to support their drafting efforts. Tell students to save their drafts for use in future lessons.

 **Share**

Bring students together. Invite volunteers to share their drafts. Encourage listeners to summarize the key ideas in the speaker's writing.

Strategies to Support ELs

Emerging (Beginning)

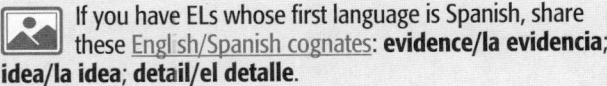 Review the texts "Katrina" on BLMs 26–27 and "Higher Ground" on BLMs 28–29 with students. Talk about what is the same and/or different in the texts. Ask students to draw a picture of something that happens in the nonfiction text and something that happens in the firsthand account. Help them write sentences for their pictures.

Expanding (Intermediate) and Bridging (Advanced)

Pair ELs with fluent English speakers as they rehearse their ideas for their draft.

All Levels

If you have ELs whose first language is Spanish, share these English/Spanish cognates: **evidence/la evidencia**; **idea/la idea**; **detail/el detalle**.

Revise and Edit a Response

W.4.1a, W.4.1b, W.4.1c, W.4.1d, W.4.4, W.4.5, W.4.10, SL.4.1a, SL.4.1b, SL.4.1c, SL.4.1d, SL.4.2, SL.4.3

 **Focus**

Objectives

In this mini-lesson, students will:

• Learn how to revise and edit a response to a prompt.

• Apply this strategy to their independent writing to sources.

Preparation

Materials Needed

• "The Olympic Flame" (BLMs 21–22)

• "Golden Moment" (BLMs 23–24)

• "Katrina" (BLMs 26–27)

• "Higher Ground" (BLMs 28–29)

• Students' saved Informative/ Explanatory Planning Guide 1 (BLM 30) from previous lesson

• Students' saved Informative/ Explanatory Planning Guide 2 (BLM 31) from previous lesson

• Conferring Prompts

Introduce the Mini-Lesson

Tell students that before preparing a final draft, writers work to improve their writing. After drafting, writers revise their work. During this step, writers try to make their writing better by making sure it is clear and well organized. They also make sure they have answered the prompt. Writers also edit their work. During this step, they fix errors in spelling, capitalization, grammar, and punctuation.

Say: *Today I'll show you how to revise a draft.*

Model Revising a Draft

Display the mini-lesson source texts "The Olympic Flame" (BLMs 21–22) and "Golden Moment" (BLMs 23–24). Also display the sample Informative/Explanatory Planning Guide 1 (BLM 30) and the modeling/practice text. Note that the modeling text has errors inserted into it so that you can model revising it.

"The Olympic Flame" and "Golden Moment" both help readers understand the significance of the ~~o~~Olympic torch. However, these texts are different, too. They are different genres. They have different points of view. And they were written for different ~~purposes~~ purposes. ~~I think "Golden Moment is better than "The Olympic Flame."~~

"The Olympic Flame" is a third person informational text. It presents sequential facts about the Olympics. For example, ~~R~~readers learn that the first games occurred about 3,000 years ago. To the ancient ~~g~~Greeks the flame represented "the gift of fire from the god Prometheus." This text follows the Olympics from ancient to modern times.

On the other hand, "Golden Moment" is a first person account. It describes one woman's experience as a torch carrier. She writes, "The noise grew louder as the Olympic flame grew nearer. Dozens of flags waved and my heart pounded in my chest." This writer isn't trying to explain. She is describing what she ~~seen~~ saw, heard, felt, and thought.

Both texts build readers' awareness of the Olympics. One text informs readers with historical facts. The other ~~One~~ describes one woman's experience.

Modeling/Practice Text

Model revising a few of the errors in the text.

Read aloud first paragraph. Say: *The first two sentences are okay. But something is wrong with the last sentence in this paragraph. It states my opinion. But the prompt does not ask for my opinion. I will delete this.*

Read aloud sentence 2 in paragraph 2. Say: *I want to emphasize the evidence from the source, so I'll insert "for example" at the beginning of this sentence.*

Read aloud sentence 1 in paragraph 3. Say: *If I add a comparison signal phrase here, I can make a stronger link to the comparisons I'm making. I'll insert the phrase "on the other hand" at the beginning of the sentence.*

Model Editing a Draft

 Continue working with the modeling/practice text to edit for grammar, spelling, and so on. Model correcting one or two errors in the text. Students will finish revising and editing the text in the Rehearse section.

Read aloud sentence 1. Say: *In the first sentence, the* **o** *in* **Olympic** *needs to be capitalized.*

 ## Rehearse

Practice Revising a Draft

 Distribute the mini-lesson source texts "The Olympic Flame" (BLMs 21–22) and "Golden Moment" (BLMs 23–24). Have students take out their completed Informative/Explanatory Planning Guide 1 on BLM 30. Have students work with a partner to continue revising and editing the modeling/ practice text comparing and contrasting the two passages. Tell students to look for places where they could insert transition words and signal words that tell that two things are being contrasted.

 If your class includes English learners or other students who need support, use "Strategies to Support ELs."

Share and Discuss

Invite students to share the revisions and edits they made. Encourage students to question edits they don't agree with in a positive way and provide alternatives. Make sure that you address all the errors embedded in the modeling/practice text so that students have correct information.

Independent Writing and Conferring

 Have students take out the independent writing source texts "Katrina" (BLMs 26–27) and "Higher Ground" (BLMs 28–29), their completed Informative/Explanatory Planning Guide 2 (BLM 31), and a copy of their draft. Explain that they will now edit and revise their drafts. Tell students to check that the details and examples they have included focus on comparing and contrasting the two texts. Tell them to ask themselves if their writing is clear and well organized and if it makes sense. Tell them to check that they have used words that clearly express what they want to say. Finally, students should also edit for spelling, capitalization, grammar, and punctuation mistakes.

When students have revised and edited their drafts, have them create the final draft of their responses.

 ## Share

Invite a few volunteers to read aloud their response to the prompt. Invite students who are listening to provide feedback and ask clarifying questions.

Strategies to Support ELs

Emerging (Beginning)

Work one on one with ELs while other students revise their writing independently. Read their sentences with them. Ask them if they want to add or change anything in their sentences. Help them make the changes.

Expanding (Intermediate) and Bridging (Advanced)

Pair ELs with fluent English speakers during the partner activity.

All Levels

 If you have ELs whose first language is Spanish, share these English/Spanish cognates: **punctuation/la puntuación; revise/revisar**.

Name _____ Date _____

The Olympic Flame

1 A runner holding an Olympic torch runs into a stadium. The crowd cheers as the runner carries the flame to an enormous Olympic cauldron. Once ignited, it will burn until the final moments of the games. As the flame burns, it represents the passion and dedication of the athletes from around the world who will compete in the games. It is also a fitting tribute to the first Olympic Games held in ancient Greece.

2 The first Olympic Games were held in Greece about 3,000 years ago. At the beginning of the games, the ancient Greeks ignited a flame. They used the sun to ignite the flame on the altar of the goddess Hera. The flame symbolized the gift of fire from the god Prometheus. The flame would burn until the games ended.

3 The Olympic Games continued for 1,200 years until a Roman emperor banned them. Hundreds of years passed. Then in 1894, a Frenchman named Pierre de Coubertin, restored the games. The first modern Olympic Games were held in Athens, Greece, on April 6, 1896. Although the Olympics had returned, the Olympic flame wasn't reignited until the 1928 Summer Olympics in Amsterdam.

Name _____   Date _____

The Olympic Flame (page 2)

4   The first Olympic Torch Relay was held at the 1936 Summer Olympics in Berlin. It was a new, grand way to honor the ancient event. Before the Olympics began, a runner ignited a torch in Greece, the home of the Olympics. Then, it passed from one runner to another until the flame reached the setting for the modern Olympic Games.

5   The Olympic Torch Relay soon became a cherished tradition of the Olympic Games. At first, people might think that runners pass one torch from person to person like a baton in a regular relay race. But that is not the case in the Olympic Torch Relay. In this event, each runner has a torch and passes the flame from one torch to the next until it reaches the final stop—the Olympic Cauldron—where it will burn brightly until the final moments of the Games, just like the flame in ancient Greece.

Name _____ Date _____

Golden Moment

1 I sat in my wheelchair on the road and couldn't believe the day had finally arrived. Cheering crowds lined the street as I waited for my turn to carry the Olympic flame. The long golden torch felt smooth and hard in my hands and I gripped it tightly insuring that the worst of the worst wouldn't happen—dropping the Olympic flame.

2 "It's coming! It's coming, Abby!" shouted someone in my cluster of friends and family who had joined me for this unforgettable moment. The noise grew louder as the Olympic flame grew nearer. Dozens of flags waved and my heart pounded in my chest. I didn't know why I was chosen, only that my friends nominated me and, somehow, my name was selected from thousands of other names.

3 Then suddenly, there it was. A young man dressed in the same white uniform as me jogged up to my wheelchair carrying the flickering flame. I touched my torch to his, and in an instant, *I* was carrying the Olympic flame.

4 My heart nearly burst as I held the torch, and my friends pushed me along through the joyful crowds. A car followed behind our happy group like a grand parade.

Name _____ Date _____

Golden Moment (page 2)

5   "Not too fast!" I warned my laughing friends. I wanted the moment to last forever. I held the precious flame second by second, foot by foot. Each relay runner was only allowed to carry the flame for about half a mile. I would have carried it forever.

6   Up ahead I could see an eager woman waiting for me to pass the flame to her. I rolled the last few feet of my journey. Our torches touched. Her torch ignited and mine was extinguished. Only one person can carry the Olympic flame at a time. Overjoyed, she twirled and danced down the street, as flags waved and cameras flashed.

7   Although her journey had just begun, and mine had ended, I knew we would never forget the golden moment when we carried the Olympic flame.

Name _____   Date _____

Main Idea Chart

Source Texts	Main Idea	Details
The Olympic Flame	History of the Olympic Torch Relay	
Golden Moment		

Name _____ Date _____

Katrina

1   On August 23, 2005, a tropical storm formed in the Caribbean Sea. Soon, the great swirling winds reached hurricane force—75 miles per hour. First, the storm hit the southern tip of Florida, and then it swept across the Gulf of Mexico. The fierce winds grew even stronger. Experts monitored the powerful storm. What would happen next? Would it stay safely out at sea and slowly wind down? Or, would it turn and hit land again?

2   The hurricane turned northwest—towards New Orleans. It would be one of the deadliest and destructive hurricanes in American history. They called it Katrina.

3   Katrina reached the Gulf Coast on the morning of August 29. Winds over 145 miles per hour tore through coastal communities. Water surges as tall as three-story buildings rushed in from the sea and flooded communities unprepared for this hurricane's widespread fury. The coast was hardest hit, yet the destruction stretched inland for hundreds of miles.

Name _____ Date _____

Katrina (page 2)

4   Within hours, the hurricane destroyed nearly everything in its path. Houses, businesses, roads, and bridges were swept away like dominoes. A system of levees in New Orleans that were supposed to protect the community from flooding failed. In the end, more than 1,700 people perished and more than a million people in three states were left without power. Hundreds of thousands lost their homes and fled the cities looking for shelter.

5   After the disaster, many people donated money, time, and materials to start the long process of rebuilding the communities that had been devastated by Katrina. The government set aside billions of dollars, too. But many people complained it was too little, too late. People demanded to know why the levees had failed. They blamed all levels of government for not providing adequate levees before the storm, and greater relief efforts after the storm.

6   Years later, the Gulf Coast is still recovering from Katrina. The storm was so destructive, the name Katrina has been retired. There will be other hurricanes, but there will never be another Hurricane Katrina.

Name _____ Date _____

Higher Ground

1   One August day in 2005, we heard on the news that Hurricane Katrina was coming. I wasn't scared because Uncle Hal and I had been through a few hurricanes already. Our house along the Mississippi Gulf Coast had never flooded before and things had always turned out fine. So when the winds picked up that afternoon, we did what we always did. Uncle Hal got out the generator and we filled a couple of jugs with water, just in case. Then we watched a movie on TV and went to bed.

2   By morning, things had changed.

3   "This looks bad, Nicki," said Uncle Hal, brushing back his thinning hair.

4   We never imagined how bad it would be.

5   I rushed to the window. The sky was thick and dark as if it was a living thing and murky waves of water climbed higher and higher onto our driveway. Spurred on by fear, we scrambled out a window onto the roof and crouched behind a skylight that protected us from the growing wind.

6   "We should be safe up here," said Uncle Hal reassuringly.

Name _____   Date _____

Higher Ground (page 2)

7   I wanted to believe him. I heard glass shattering below us as water poured into the house. It felt like a dream as we watched houses around us collapsing, trees disappearing, and our furniture, cars, and appliances floating away. How could any of this be happening? Gales of gritty wind stung our eyes as we watched the unimaginable unfold.

8   Then, my worst nightmare became real—spiders!

9   Every spider in the yard had the same idea we did—surviving by scurrying to higher ground. At first, I was petrified at the hordes of creepy crawlies that scrambled onto the roof with us, but at the same time, I knew they wanted to survive just as much as we did. So we shared the only patch of dry ground around in the sea of destruction, and we were duly rewarded because none of them bit us.

10   In time, the water receded and we climbed back down. Even though it's hard to explain, we were happy in a weird way. We'd lost everything to Hurricane Katrina and it didn't matter. We were still here.

Name _____   Date _____

Informative/Explanatory Planning Guide 1

Prompt: Compare and contrast "The Olympic Flame" and "Golden Moment." Explain how the two accounts you read are different and how they are similar. Consider each text's topic, genre, point of view, text structure, and purpose. Cite specific details and examples from each text to support your response.

Analyze the Prompt

How does the prompt apply to the sources?	
What does the prompt ask me to do?	

Compare and Contrast

Comparison/ Contrast	The Olympic Flame	Golden Moment
Topic		
Genre		
Point of View		
Text Structure		
Writer's Purpose		

Name _____ Date _____

Informative/Explanatory Planning Guide 2

Prompt: Compare and contrast "Katrina" and "Higher Ground." Explain how the two accounts you read are different and how they are similar. Consider each text's topic, genre, point of view, text structure, and purpose. Cite specific details and examples from each text to support your response.

Analyze the Prompt

How does the prompt apply to the sources?	
What does the prompt ask me to do?	

Compare and Contrast

Comparison/ Contrast	Katrina	Higher Ground
Topic		
Genre		
Point of View		
Text Structure		
Writer's Purpose		

Informative/Explanatory Checklist

Title _____

	Yes	No	Not Sure
1. I researched my topic and organized my information into notes that helped me write my paper.	—	—	—
2. I introduce my topic and use words that grab my readers' attention.	—	—	—
3. I keep my paper organized by grouping information together in a way that makes sense. I use paragraphs and sections.	—	—	—
4. I use headings to organize my sections.	—	—	—
5. The information in my report is accurate.	—	—	—
6. I support my points with facts, definitions, and details.	—	—	—
7. I include graphics to support my information.	—	—	—
8. I include captions that explain each graphic.	—	—	—
9. I use linking words and phrases to connect ideas.	—	—	—
10. My report includes different viewpoints so that I do not sway my readers to think one way.	—	—	—
11. I include a strong conclusion that keeps my readers thinking.	—	—	—
12. I choose words that make my text interesting to read and easy to understand. I include words that connect to the topic.	—	—	—
13. I use at least one primary source.	—	—	—
14. I use a formal voice.	—	—	—

Quality Writing Checklist
I looked for and corrected . . .

sentence fragments and run-ons.	—	—	—
parts of speech (pronouns, auxiliaries, adjectives, prepositions).	—	—	—
grammar.	—	—	—
indented paragraphs.	—	—	—
punctuation.	—	—	—
capitalization.	—	—	—
spelling.	—	—	—

Informative/Explanatory Teacher Rubric

Score	Planning and Implementation	Evidence of Genre Characteristics	Conventions of Grammar and Usage	Conventions of Mechanics
4	(CCSS W.4.2, W.4.4, W.4.7, W.4.8, W.4.9, L.4.3, L.4.6) The writer's ideas are well organized and well developed. The writer: • thoroughly researches the topic before writing. • includes an introduction, or lead, that grabs readers' attention. • creates and maintains a meaningful organizational structure by introducing the topic and grouping related information. • consistently varies sentence structure to facilitate clear ideas. • uses a wide variety of linking words and phrases to link ideas within categories of information. • uses well-chosen words and phrases and domain-specific vocabulary that add effect and description to the piece. • includes a strong conclusion that keeps readers thinking.	(CCSS W.4.2, W.4.7, W.4.8, W.4.9, L.4.3) The writer demonstrates complete understanding of the features of informative/explanatory writing. The writer: • thoroughly develops the topic by including facts, definitions, details, and examples. • includes unique text and graphic features (headings, charts, illustrations, etc.) that support the information. • includes thoughtfully worded captions that explain each graphic feature. • includes one or more different viewpoints so readers can draw their own conclusions. • includes carefully chosen primary sources. • consistently maintains a formal voice.	(CCSS L.4.1, W.4.5) The writer correctly implements all conventions. The writer: • produces well-developed complete sentences. • efficiently revises and corrects sentence fragments and run-ons. • uses parts of speech in unique ways. • uses grammar conventions in clear and concise ways.	(CCSS W.4.5, L.4.2) The writer correctly implements all conventions. The writer: • always correctly indents paragraphs. • makes no, or few, mechanical mistakes, and they do not hinder overall meaning.
3	The writer's ideas are adequately organized and developed. The writer: • researches the topic before writing. • includes an introduction, or lead. • creates and maintains an organizational structure and groups related information into paragraphs or sections. • varies sentence structure to facilitate clear ideas. • uses linking words and phrases to link ideas within categories of information. • uses words and phrases and domain-specific words that add effect and description to the informational piece. • includes a conclusion.	The writer demonstrates an adequate understanding of the features of informative/explanatory writing. The writer: • develops the topic by including facts, definitions, details, and examples. • includes text and graphic features (headings, charts, illustrations, etc.) that support the information. • includes captions that explain the graphics. • includes one different viewpoint. • includes primary source documents. • maintains a formal voice.	The writer implements most conventions. The writer: • produces complete sentences. • revises and corrects sentence fragments and run-ons most of the time. • uses correct parts of speech most of the time. • uses correct grammar conventions most of the time.	The writer implements most conventions. The writer: • correctly indents paragraphs most of the time. • makes occasional mechanical mistakes, but they do not hinder overall meaning.
2	The writer's ideas are somewhat organized and developed. The writer: • does some research on the project. • includes an introduction, or lead, that is weak. • attempts to create and maintain an organizational structure. Though the writer attempts to group related ideas, they are difficult to follow. • attempts to vary sentence structure. Attempt does not aid understanding. • uses some linking words and phrases to link ideas within categories of information. • uses some words and phrases that add effect and description. Domain-specific words may or may not be included. • includes a weak conclusion.	The writer demonstrates some understanding of the features of informative/explanatory writing. The writer: • somewhat develops the topic by including facts, definitions, details, etc. • includes few text and graphic features to support the information. • includes some captions that explain the graphics. Captions may or may not adequately address the graphic. • attempts to include one different viewpoint. The viewpoint does not necessarily connect to the topic. • includes one primary source document. It may or may not connect to the topic. • inconsistently maintains a formal voice.	The writer implements some conventions. The writer: • produces complete sentences some of the time. • revises and corrects sentence fragments and run-ons some of the time. • uses correct parts of speech some of the time. • uses correct grammar conventions some of the time.	The writer implements some conventions. The writer: • indents paragraphs some of the time. • makes many mechanical mistakes, and they hinder overall meaning.
1	The writer's ideas are disorganized and undeveloped. The writer: • does very little research on the topic. • does not include an introduction, or lead. • does not create or maintain an organizational structure. Ideas may be grouped, but they are difficult to follow. • does not vary sentence structure. • uses few, if any, linking words and phrases to link ideas. • uses few, if any, words and phrases that add effect and description. Writer includes few, if any, domain-specific words. • does not include a conclusion.	The writer demonstrates little, if any, understanding of the features of informative/explanatory writing. The writer: • does not develop the topic. • includes few, if any, text and graphic features to support the information. • includes few, if any, captions. Captions do not necessarily explain the graphics. • does not include different viewpoints. • does not include primary sources. • does not maintain a formal voice.	The writer implements few, if any, conventions. The writer: • rarely produces complete sentences. • rarely revises and corrects fragments and run-ons. • rarely uses correct parts of speech. • rarely uses correct grammar conventions.	The writer implements few, if any, conventions. The writer: • does not attempt to indent paragraphs. • makes many mechanical mistakes that hinder overall meaning.

Grade 4 • ©2017 Benchmark Education Company, LLC

Grade 4 Language Mini-Lessons at a Glance

Use Relative Adverbs

L.4.1a

Objectives

In this mini-lesson, students will:

• Identify relative adverbs and their function in sentences.

• Use a relative adverb to replace a preposition + **which** in a sentence.

• Determine which relative adverbs to use in sentences.

Preparation

Materials Needed

• Use Relative Adverbs (BLM 1)

Focus

Explain Relative Adverbs

Say: *An adverb is a describing word. A relative adverb introduces a dependent clause that gives more information about a word or phrase in the sentence. This is called a relative clause because it relates to the word or phrase it describes. A relative adverb can take the place of a preposition plus the word* **which.**

 Display the example Relative Adverbs Chart.

Relative Adverb	Refers To . . .	Replaces a Phrase Such As . . .	Example
where	a place	in which	This is the park <u>where we had our family reunion</u>.
when	a time	on which	I'll never forget the day <u>when I got my first bicycle</u>.
why	a reason	for which	There is the reason <u>why I always have an umbrella in the car</u>.

Example Relative Adverbs Chart

Say: *The relative clause "where we had our family reunion" gives more information about the park. Using* **where** *in place of "in which" makes the sentence sound less formal and more conversational.*

Similarly analyze the remaining two example sentences.

Model Using Relative Adverbs

 Display the modeling text.

I don't understand the reason (<u>why</u>, when) girls can't be on the school football team.

In many states, June is the month (where, <u>when</u>) school ends for the summer.

Modeling Text

Say: *In the first sentence, the relative clause refers to the word* **reason,** *so* **why** *is the correct relative adverb. In the second sentence, the relative clause refers to the word* **month,** *so* **when** *is the correct relative adverb.*

Point out that the clauses "why girls can't be on the school football team" and "when school ends for the summer" give readers valuable information about what the writer doesn't understand and why the month of June is memorable.

Rehearse

Practice Using Relative Adverbs

 Display the practice text.

---

1. The PTA will decide on a _____ when we can plan our school carnival.

2. Mom wanted to know the _____ why I didn't bring home my permission slip.

3. That's the _____ where we had our first book club meeting.

Practice Text

 Ask students to work with a partner to read each sentence and write a word or phrase for the blank that goes with the relative adverb. Remind them to refer to the Relative Adverbs Chart if needed.

 If your class includes English learners or other students who need support, use "Strategies to Support ELs."

Share Practice Sentences

Invite pairs to share their responses. Ask the following questions:

• *What word or phrase did you choose to go with the relative adverb* **when**? *The relative adverb* **why**? *The relative adverb* **where**?

• *How does using relative adverbs help readers and writers?*

Independent Writing and Conferring

Say: *As writers, we can use the relative adverbs* **where, when,** *and* **why** *to give more information about words and phrases in our sentences. Remember to use the correct relative adverb for the situation so your writing will sound right and make sense to your readers.*

 If you would like to give students additional practice recognizing relative adverbs, have them complete Use Relative Adverbs (BLM 1).

Share

 Bring students together. Review and provide corrective feedback based on students' answers to BLM 1. Ask students to share what they learned about relative adverbs.

Strategies to Support ELs

Emerging (Beginning)

 Beginning ELs will need additional support and practice in using relative adverbs. Locate illustrations and photographs that show people, places, and things. Help students form simple sentences about the photographs and then combine them using a relative clause. For example: *This is a store. A girl is buying some shoes. This is the store* where *the girl bought shoes.*

Expanding (Intermediate) and Bridging (Advanced)

Pair ELs with fluent English speakers to complete the practice activity.

Use Relative Pronouns

L.4.1a

 **Focus**

Objectives

In this mini-lesson, students will:

• Identify relative pronouns and their function in sentences.

• Use **who**, **whom**, and **whose** to refer to people and **that** and **which** to refer to things.

• Determine which relative pronouns to use in sentences.

Preparation

Materials Needed

• Use Relative Pronouns (BLM 2)

Explain Relative Pronouns

Say: *We know that a pronoun is a word that refers to a noun. A relative pronoun introduces a dependent clause that gives more information about a word or phrase in the sentence. The clause is called a relative clause because it relates to the word or phrase it describes.*

 Display the example Relative Pronouns Chart.

Relative Pronoun	Refers To . . .	Example
who	people	I like to visit my friend who lives down the road.
whom	people	This is the speaker for whom we were waiting.
whose	people	Every student whose permission slip is signed may go on the field trip.
that	things	The wheat rolls that we bought will be perfect for sandwiches.
which	things	The cat, which is my neighbor's pet, sat on the fence.

Example Relative Pronouns Chart

Say: *The relative clause "who lives down the road" gives more information about the friend. The relative clause "for whom we were waiting" gives more information about the speaker.*

Similarly analyze the remaining three example sentences.

Model Using Relative Pronouns

 Display the modeling text.

> The woman (<u>who</u>, which) came to the door was delivering a package.
>
> I frosted the cake (whom, <u>that</u>) I baked for Mom's birthday.

Modeling Text

Say: *In the first sentence, the relative clause refers to the word* **woman**, *so* **who** *is the correct relative pronoun. In the second sentence, the relative clause refers to the word* **cake,** *so* **that** *is the correct relative pronoun.*

Point out that the clauses "who came to the door" and "that I baked for Mom's birthday" give readers valuable information about the person and the cake.

Rehearse

Practice Using Relative Pronouns

 Display the practice text.

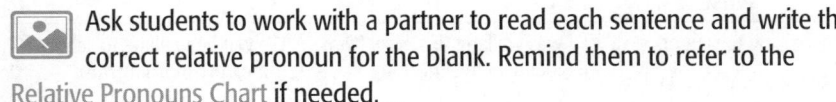

1. This is the window _that_ my neighbor accidentally broke when he hit a baseball.
2. The person _who_ most closely estimates the number of beans in the jar wins a prize.
3. The garage sale, _which_ closed at 6:00, was a huge success.
4. My brother, _whose_ book you borrowed, would like for you to return it on Thursday.

Practice Text

 Ask students to work with a partner to read each sentence and write the correct relative pronoun for the blank. Remind them to refer to the Relative Pronouns Chart if needed.

 If your class includes English learners or other students who need support, use "Strategies to Support ELs."

Share Practice Sentences

Invite pairs to share their responses. Ask the following questions:
- *What word or phrase is being described in each sentence? What did you need to consider when choosing its matching relative pronoun?*
- *How does using relative pronouns help readers and writers?*

Independent Writing and Conferring

Say: *As writers, we can use the relative pronouns* **who, whom, whose, that,** *and* **which** *to give more information about words and phrases in our sentences. Remember to use the correct relative pronoun for the situation so your writing will sound right and make sense to your readers.*

 If you would like to give students additional practice recognizing relative pronouns, have them complete Use Relative Pronouns (BLM 2).

 **Share**

 Bring students together. Review and provide corrective feedback based on students' answers to BLM 2. Ask students to share what they learned about relative pronouns.

Strategies to Support ELs

Emerging (Beginning)

 Beginning ELs will need additional support and practice in using relative pronouns. Locate illustrations and photographs that show people, places, and things. Help students form simple sentences about the photographs and then combine them using a relative clause. For example: *This is a kite. The boy flew the kite. This is the kite that the boy flew.*

Expanding (Intermediate) and Bridging (Advanced)

Pair ELs with fluent English speakers to complete the practice activity.

Use Progressive Verb Tenses

L.4.1b

Objectives

In this mini-lesson, students will:

• Understand verb tense.

• Identify the progressive verb tenses in sentences.

• Correctly use progressive verb tenses in their writing.

Preparation

Materials Needed

• Use Progressive Verb Tenses (BLM 3)

 **Focus**

Explain Progressive Verb Tense

Say: *Verbs are a category of words. Most verbs show action, while other verbs are "to be" verbs. The tense of a verb shows when the action is happening.*

Remind students that present tense verbs tell about actions that are happening right now or actions that are continued or repeated. Past tense verbs show that an action or situation already happened. Future tense verbs tell about something that hasn't happened yet, a plan or prediction. Explain that today you will discuss present, past, and future progressive verb tense.

 Display the example Progressive Verb Tense Chart.

Present Progressive Tense	Past Progressive Tense	Future Progressive Tense
I am walking to school. My brother is walking with me. We are walking together.	I was walking to school from 8:00–8:15 this morning. My brother and I were walking together.	We will be walking to school tomorrow morning, too.

Example Progressive Verb Tense Chart

Say: *The present progressive tense sentences tell about an ongoing action, it is happening as you say or write it. We form the present progressive verb tense by using the "to be" verb* **am, is,** *or* **are** *with the* **-ing** *form of an action verb.*

Similarly analyze the remaining verb tenses, pointing out that past progressive tense tells about something that took place over a period of time and is formed by using the "to be" verb **was** or **were** with an **-ing** verb. Future progressive tense tells about an action that will take place at a later time and is formed by using the "to be" verbs **will be** with an **-ing** verb.

Model Using Progressive Verb Tense

 Display the modeling text.

> My friend and I <u>will be going</u> to the recreation center every day after school. We <u>are renting</u> a locker so we can keep our sports gear there. Dad made me a necklace key chain, because he once lost his locker key when he <u>was jogging</u>.

Modeling Text

Say: *This passage has present, past, and future progressive tense verbs.*

Together, analyze each underlined verb to determine its verb tense. Point out that past progressive tense sometimes indicates an action that occurred at the same time as another action.

Remind students that using different verb tenses helps writers express when something happened, is happening, or will happen in a fiction or nonfiction text.

 **Rehearse**

Practice Using Progressive Verb Tense

 Display the practice text.

Present Progressive Tense	Past Progressive Tense	Future Progressive Tense
am, is, are walking are renting	was, were walking was jogging	will be walking will be going

Practice Text

Say: *Here are the present, past, and future progressive tense verbs we have discussed so far. Let's think of other progressive tense verbs that we can add to the chart. Then we will use some of the verbs in sentences.*

Work with students to add more progressive tense verbs in each column. Then invite students to work with a partner to choose one verb from each column to use in a written sentence.

 If your class includes English learners or other students who need support, use "Strategies to Support ELs."

Share Practice Sentences

Invite pairs to share their responses. Ask the following questions:
- *Which sentence tells about an ongoing action happening right now? Which sentence tells about something that already happened? Which sentence tells about something planned for the future?*
- *Why is it important to use the correct verb tense in our speaking and writing?*

Independent Writing and Conferring

Say: *Today we reviewed present, past, and future progressive tense verbs. Remember to pay close attention to verb tense as you write so your readers will understand when an action or situation happens.*

 If you would like to give students additional practice using progressive verb tense, have them complete Use Progressive Verb Tenses (BLM 3).

Share

Bring students together. Review and provide corrective feedback based on students' answers to BLM 3. Ask students to share what they learned about progressive verb tense.

Strategies to Support ELs

Emerging (Beginning)

Help beginning ELs see the difference between present, past, and future progressive tense verbs. Focus on common action verbs they are likely to use in oral language. Create a three-column chart with the heads "Now (am, is, are)"; "In the Past (was, were)"; and "In the Future (will be)." Write the present, past, and future progressive tense forms of the verbs in the columns. Read the words with students and use them in simple sentences as you pantomime their meanings to build understanding.

Expanding (Intermediate) and Bridging (Advanced)

Pair ELs with fluent English speakers to complete the practice activity.

Use Modal Auxiliaries

L.4.1c

Objectives

In this mini-lesson, students will:

• Understand modal auxiliaries.

• Identify modal auxiliaries and their function in sentences.

• Determine which modal auxiliaries to use in sentences.

Preparation

Materials Needed

• Use Modal Auxiliaries (BLM 4)

 **Focus**

Explain Modal Auxiliaries

Say: *The word* **modal** *is a grammar term that expresses a "mood" such as possibility or necessity. The word* **auxiliary** *refers to something that helps or supports. A* **modal auxiliary** *is a verb that helps a main verb express a particular meaning or idea.*

 Display the example Modal Auxiliary Chart.

Modal Auxiliary	Refers To Concepts Such As . . .	Example
can	ability, offer	I <u>can bring</u> the supplies for our science project tomorrow. We <u>can start</u> on it after school if that works for you.
could	request, ability, possibility	<u>Could</u> you <u>help</u> me figure out these directions, please? I <u>could do</u> the first part, but the second part is confusing. It <u>could take</u> a long time to finish.
would	offer, obstacle, opinion or preference	<u>Would</u> you <u>like</u> Dan to turn in your project to Mr. Brown? I <u>would do</u> it, but I have to leave, too. I know you <u>would like</u> Mr. Brown to get it before the due date.
may	permission, probability	<u>May</u> I <u>share</u> some good news? My friend Kammi <u>may win</u> the election for class president!
might	possibility	If it snows, we <u>might postpone</u> the field trip until Friday.
must	necessity, deduction	Mom said we <u>must finish</u> breakfast before we go. She <u>must be worried</u> that we'll get hungry before lunch.
should	advisability, expectation	You <u>should wear</u> sunscreen to the park. We <u>should be able</u> to find a shady spot while we eat lunch.
will	invitation or request, plan of action, prediction	<u>Will</u> you <u>join</u> us at the basketball game? If so, we <u>will pick</u> you up at 6:00. I think our team <u>will win</u> the tournament this year, don't you?

Example Modal Auxiliary Chart

Say: *The modal auxiliary* **can** *adds the concept of ability to the verb* **bring** *and the concept of possibility to the verb* **start.** *The modal auxiliary* **could** *turns the verb* **help** *into a request and expresses ability when paired with the verb* **do.**

Similarly analyze the remaining example sentences, pointing out that the modal auxiliaries may have additional meanings in certain situations.

Model Using Modal Auxiliaries

 Display the modeling text.

I see a package on the porch! It <u>could be</u> for me! It <u>might be</u> the book Mom ordered yesterday. It <u>may be</u> for Jed, because his birthday is this week. Yes, it <u>should be</u> Jed's package, since Grandma always sends gifts through the mail. That <u>must be</u> it . . . I'm sure the package <u>will be</u> for Jed. Now I <u>can see</u> the address. It's for Jed!

Modeling Text

Say: *In the example text, the writer uses seven different modal auxiliaries, each with a different degree of certainty. This demonstrates the power that these small words have over the verbs they support and how important it is to choose just the right modal auxiliary to express what we want our readers to understand as they read our fiction and nonfiction texts.*

 ## Rehearse

Practice Using Modal Auxiliaries

 Display the practice text.

---

1. I'm a great swimmer! In fact, I _could_ swim when I was five years old!

2. Kareem _can_ play the guitar better than anyone I know.

3. Mr. Fisher said we _should_ knock on his back door when we finish weeding and he will pay us.

4. _Can_ I check out more than two books this week, please?

5. We _must_ return our permission slips in order to go on the field trip.

6. I _would_ enjoy going to a movie on Saturday if you can go, too.

Practice Text

 Ask students to work with a partner to read each sentence and write an appropriate modal auxiliary for the blank. Remind them to refer to the Modal Auxiliary Chart if needed.

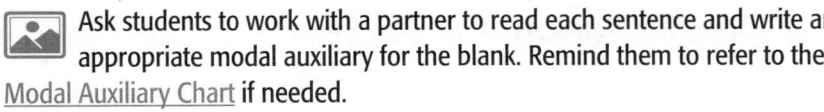 If your class includes English learners or other students who need support, use "Strategies to Support ELs."

Share Practice Sentences

Invite pairs to share their responses. Ask the following questions:
• *What did you need to consider when choosing an appropriate modal auxiliary?*
• *How does using and understanding the meanings of modal auxiliaries help readers and writers?*

Independent Writing and Conferring

Say: *As writers, we can use modal auxiliaries such as* **can, could, would, may, might, must, should,** *and* **will** *to add meaning to verbs in our sentences. Remember to use the correct modal auxiliary for the situation so your writing will sound right and make sense to your readers.*

 If you would like to give students additional practice recognizing modal auxiliaries, have them complete Use Modal Auxiliaries (BLM 4).

Share

Bring students together. Review and provide corrective feedback based on students' answers to BLM 4. Ask students to share what they learned about modal auxiliaries.

Strategies to Support ELs

Emerging (Beginning)

Beginning ELs will need additional support and practice in using modal auxiliaries. Locate illustrations and photographs that show people, places, and things. Help students form simple sentences about the photographs using different modal auxiliaries. For example: *The boy can run fast. He may be running a race. I wish I could race with him, too.*

Expanding (Intermediate) and Bridging (Advanced)

Pair ELs with fluent English speakers to complete the practice activity.

Order Adjectives Within Sentences

L.4.1d

 **Focus**

Objectives

In this mini-lesson, students will:

• Understand that adjectives modify nouns.

• Order adjectives within sentences according to conventional patterns.

• Choose appropriate adjectives in oral and written language.

Preparation

Materials Needed

• Order of Adjectives Chart (BLM 5)

• Order Adjectives Within Sentences (BLM 6)

Explain Adjectives

Say: *Adjectives describe nouns. In English, adjectives usually come before the nouns they modify. Sometimes writers use more than one adjective at a time. When this happens, we usually follow a certain order for these adjectives.*

Explain that English speakers often follow this conventional pattern because it sounds right, while a different order often sounds wrong.

 Display the example text.

My grandmother doesn't like heavy purses, so she carries a <u>red small bag</u>.

My grandmother doesn't like heavy purses, so she carries a <u>small red bag</u>.

Example Text

Say: *When I read the first sentence aloud, the words "red small bag" don't sound right. The adjectives sound better in the second sentence—"small red bag." I can learn some rules about the order of adjectives to help me when I write my own sentences.*

Model Ordering Adjectives Within Sentences

 Display the Order of Adjectives Chart (BLM 5), and distribute a copy to students.

Opinion	nice, lovely, expensive, delicious
Size	big, little, long, short
Feels/ Looks	hot, dry, soft, shiny
Age	old, young, ancient, antique
Shape	square, skinny, round, chunky
Color	blue, white, clear, colorful
Nationality	American, Canadian, Mexican, Italian
Material	wooden, silver, silk, plastic
Purpose	gardening (gloves), baseball (players), book (report), city (hall)

Order of Adjectives Chart (BLM 5)

Say: *This chart shows a typical order for adjectives within a sentence. We would never use this many adjectives in a row. However, a good rule is to use no more than four to describe a particular noun. Often, fewer are better, since a long list can become dull for our readers.*

Model using the Order of Adjectives Chart to compose some oral sentences, such as *My aunt gave me a lovely old silver locket* or *The pillow was made of a soft blue silk fabric.* Then explain that it is acceptable to vary the adjectives' locations if you have a reason. For example, to emphasize that a cat is skinny and a car is big, you might say *Mr. Smith took the skinny little kitten to the vet in his big, expensive car.* Mention also that this chart doesn't include every possible type of adjective.

 ## Rehearse

Practice Ordering Adjectives Within Sentences

 Display the practice text.

1. I found some ~~wooden old round~~ old round wooden boxes in the attic.
2. The clown wore a ~~polka-dotted pointy gigantic~~ gigantic pointy polka-dotted hat.
3. My sister went to a concert for the ~~Italian popular opera new~~ popular new Italian opera singer.

Practice Text

Ask students to work with a partner to read each sentence and rearrange the adjectives in conventional order. Remind them to use the Order of Adjectives Chart for assistance.

 If your class includes English learners or other students who need support, use "Strategies to Support ELs."

Share Practice Sentences

Invite pairs to share their responses. Ask the following questions:
- *How did you rearrange each set of adjectives? Why?*
- *Do the sentences sound better with the adjectives in the new order? Why or why not?*

 # Independent Writing and Conferring

Say: *As writers, we sometimes use more than one adjective to describe a single noun. This can make our texts more interesting or informative for our readers. Reading our work aloud can help us find places where we might need to rearrange adjectives to make a sentence sound better. Remember not to overdo multiple adjectives. Occasionally using two, three, or perhaps four at a time is usually sufficient.*

If you would like to give students additional practice ordering adjectives within sentences, have them complete Order Adjectives Within Sentences (BLM 6).

 ## Share

Bring students together. Review and provide corrective feedback based on students' answers to BLM 6. Ask students to share what they learned about ordering adjectives within sentences.

Strategies to Support ELs

Emerging (Beginning)

Beginning ELs will need additional support and practice to understand adjective order. Display items from your desk and model simple sentences about them with two adjectives, such as *I have a long green pencil.* Write the adjectives and noun on self-stick notes and place them on the objects. Then invite students to display and describe items from their own desks or backpacks. Help them form simple statements about the items using two conventionally ordered adjectives.

Expanding (Intermediate) and Bridging (Advanced)

Pair ELs with fluent English speakers to complete the practice activity.

All Levels

 If you have ELs whose first language is Spanish, share this English/Spanish cognate: **adjective/el adjetivo**.

Use Prepositional Phrases

L.4.1e

Objectives

In this mini-lesson, students will:

• Understand the purpose of prepositions.

• Identify prepositional phrases in sentences.

• Form and use prepositional phrases in writing.

Preparation

Materials Needed

• Use Prepositional Phrases (BLM 7)

 **Focus**

Explain Prepositional Phrases

Say: *Prepositions are words we use to show relationships between words in a sentence. Prepositions introduce phrases that answer questions like where, when, what, and how.*

Remind students of the frequently occurring prepositions they have previously studied, such as **to**, **from**, **in**, **out**, **on**, **off**, **for**, **of**, **by**, **with**, **during**, **beyond**, and **toward**. Explain, however, that these are only a few of the prepositions in the English language.

 Display the example Prepositional Phrases Chart.

Questions	Example
Where?	We stayed <u>in</u> a cottage <u>beside</u> the beach.
When?	<u>During</u> the bus ride, I discovered that the museum wouldn't be open <u>until</u> the next day.
What?	<u>For</u> the cover, choose any piece <u>of</u> paper <u>except</u> plain white.
How?	<u>To</u> everyone's amazement, the shy young man sang his solo <u>with</u> gusto.

Example Prepositional Phrases Chart

Say: *Think how the sentences would sound and how their meanings would change without the prepositional phrases: We stayed. I discovered that the museum wouldn't be open. Choose any piece. The shy young man sang his solo. Using prepositional phrases makes our writing clearer by giving readers necessary information about the people, places, objects, and events in our texts.*

Model Using Prepositional Phrases

 Display the modeling text.

- Get eight bottles <u>of</u> the same size <u>with</u> narrow necks.
- Put the bottles <u>in</u> a row.
- Fill each bottle <u>with</u> water <u>from</u> a little <u>to</u> a lot as you go <u>down</u> the row.
- Put the bottom edge <u>of</u> your lower lip <u>against</u> the lip <u>of</u> one bottle and blow <u>across</u> the top.
- Do the same <u>for</u> all eight bottles.
- If you can't get a sound, tap each bottle <u>with</u> a spoon.
- What is the pattern <u>of</u> the sounds?

Modeling Text

Say: *This passage gives directions for an experiment with sound. Imagine if the writer tried to explain this procedure without using prepositional phrases.*

Together, analyze each prepositional phrase, the question it answers, and the information it adds to the text.

 **Rehearse**

Practice Using Prepositional Phrases

 Display the practice text.

---

1. **Where** is your school?
2. **When** does your school start each morning?
3. **What** is in your school library?
4. **How** can students be successful at your school?

Practice Text

Ask students to work with a partner to read each question and write an answer in a complete sentence that includes a prepositional phrase.

 If your class includes English learners or other students who need support, use "Strategies to Support ELs."

Share Practice Sentences

Invite pairs to share their responses. Ask the following questions:
- *How did you answer each question? What prepositional phrase did you use in each answer?*
- *Why is it important for writers to understand and use prepositional phrases?*

Independent Writing and Conferring

Say: *Prepositional phrases add valuable information to our writing, whether we are writing narratives, opinion/argument pieces, or informational texts. As you write, revise, and edit, look for places where you can use prepositional phrases effectively to give your readers where, when, what, and how details that will help them better understand and enjoy your texts.*

 If you would like to give students additional practice identifying and using prepositional phrases, have them complete Use Prepositional Phrases (BLM 7).

Share

 Bring students together. Review and provide corrective feedback based on students' answers to BLM 7. Ask students to share what they learned about prepositional phrases.

Strategies to Support ELs

Emerging (Beginning)

To support beginning ELs in understanding prepositional phrases, ask them to bring familiar fiction and nonfiction books to share with the group. Together, locate sentences that include prepositional phrases. Write each phrase, boxing the preposition, and discuss what question the phrase answers and what information it adds to the text. When appropriate, act out the phrase. Repeat with examples from each student's book.

Expanding (Intermediate) and Bridging (Advanced)

Provide simple sentences to help ELs use prepositions. For example:

The dog barked.
The dog barked at me.
The dog barked in the back yard.
The dog barked during the night.

Use Complete Sentences

L.4.1f

Objectives

In this mini-lesson, students will:

• Identify simple, compound, and complex sentences.

• Identify sentence fragments and run-on sentences.

• Correct incomplete sentences by adding appropriate punctuation and/or conjunctions.

Preparation

Materials Needed

• Use Complete Sentences (BLM 8)

Focus

Explain Complete Sentences

Say: *We have learned about three kinds of sentences: simple, compound, and complex. Each type of sentence has a different construction, but they all contain a subject, verb, and complete thought. Sometimes when we revise and edit, we find incomplete sentences that we need to correct.*

 Display the example Complete Sentences Chart.

Complete Sentences		Incomplete Sentences	
Simple Sentence: an independent clause	The gardener planted a rose bush.	**Sentence Fragment:** does not contain an independent clause (missing a subject or verb)	Planted a rose bush.
Compound Sentence: two independent clauses joined by a comma and coordinate conjunction	The gardener planted a rose bush, and he waters it daily.	**Run-On Sentence:** more than one complete sentence joined with no mid-sentence punctuation (such as an em dash or semicolon) or conjunctions	The gardener planted a rose bush he waters it daily.
Complex Sentence: an independent clause joined to a dependent clause that begins with a subordinate conjunction	The gardener planted a rose bush that he waters daily.		

Example Complete Sentences Chart

Say: *As writers, we use complete sentences except for some instances where we're writing character dialogue or have a particular reason to write a sentence fragment for emphasis. As always, vary your writing by including different types of complete sentences, and reread your text to check for sentence fragments and run-ons.*

Demonstrate different ways to correct the run-on sentence, such as making it into two separate sentences, turning it into a compound or complex sentence, or using mid-sentence punctuation.

Model Using Complete Sentences

 Display the modeling texts. Read aloud the first modeling text.

Sometimes you send a birthday card to a friend or give a family member a holiday gift. When you take the time to make your own greeting cards and gifts. You really show that you care. That's because a card or gift that you make yourself has a personal touch that only you can put into it it's one of a kind!	Sometimes you send a birthday card to a friend or give a family member a holiday gift. When you take the time to make your own greeting cards and gifts, you really show that you care. That's because a card or gift that you make yourself has a personal touch that only you can put into it. It's one of a kind!

Modeling Text 1   Modeling Text 2

Say: *This passage has some complete sentences, but some of them are incomplete. The incomplete sentences make the text hard to read and make it hard to figure out exactly what the writer means. Let's see how the writer corrects the sentence fragment and run-on during revision and editing.*

Read aloud the second modeling text.

Say: *The writer joined the sentence fragment with the next sentence to form a complex sentence and divided the run-on sentence into two complete sentences. Now the passage is easy to read and understand.*

 ## Rehearse

Practice Using Complete Sentences

 Display the practice text.

> A map is not very helpful if you can't find the information you need. To make information easier to find. Maps are often divided into squares. The squares are drawn with faint lines they don't interfere with the contents of the map. Called grid squares.

Practice Text

Ask students to work with a partner to rewrite the paragraph and correct any sentence fragments or run-ons.

 If your class includes English learners or other students who need support, use "Strategies to Support ELs."

Share Practice Sentences

Invite pairs to share their responses. Ask the following questions:
- *How did you correct the sentence fragments? How did you correct the run-on sentence?*
- *Do your corrections make the text easier to read and understand? How?*

 # Independent Writing and Conferring

Say: *When you write, you will almost always use a mixture of simple, compound, and complex sentences with no sentence fragments or run-ons. This ensures that each of your sentences will have a complete thought, making it easy for readers to comprehend your ideas. Remember to check for sentence fragments and run-ons when you revise and edit.*

Remind students that they can combine sentences, divide sentences, and use punctuation and conjunctions to make sure their sentences are complete.

If you would like to give students additional practice using complete sentences, have them complete Use Complete Sentences (BLM 8).

 ## Share

Review and provide corrective feedback based on students' answers to BLM 8. Ask students to share what they learned about complete sentences.

Strategies to Support ELs

Emerging (Beginning)
Beginning ELs will need additional support and practice to produce complete sentences. Together, brainstorm a list of familiar nouns and verbs. Model how to choose a noun and verb and use them in simple, compound, and complex sentences, such as *The cat played with the plant; The cat played with the plant, and he knocked it off the table; While playing with the plant, the cat knocked it off the table.* Then use the complete sentences to demonstrate incomplete sentences, such as *Played with the plant* (fragment) and *The cat played with the plant he knocked it off the table* (run-on).

Expanding (Intermediate) and Bridging (Advanced)
Pair ELs with fluent English speakers to complete the practice activity.

Use Frequently Confused Words

L.4.1g

Objectives

In this mini-lesson, students will:

• Understand why homophones are frequently confused.

• Identify homophones in sentences.

• Correctly use homophones in writing, consulting a dictionary as needed.

Preparation

Materials Needed

• Use Frequently Confused Words (BLM 9)

 **Focus**

Explain Homophones

Say: *Homophones are words that are pronounced the same but have different spellings and meanings. For example, on television, we can see an ad for a product—**a-d.** But in math, we add numbers—**a-d-d.** Because both words sound the same, they are easy to confuse in writing.*

Explain that writers must be sure to choose the homophone that fits the intended meaning.

 Display the example Homophone Chart.

Homophones	Meanings	Example Sentences
to, too, two	direction	We'll be on our way to the zoo by 8:00 a.m.
	also	Let's stop for lunch, and we'll go for a walk, too.
	number after one	This T-shirt is on sale for only two dollars!
there, their, they're	place	The shop is on State Street, but I don't know how to get there.
	belonging to them	Grandpa and Grandma will ride their motorcycles to the picnic.
	they are	The children are in bed, but I'm not sure if they're asleep.
by, bye, buy	beside	You can leave your wet umbrella by the front door.
	short for "goodbye"	"Mom!" called Ginny. "The school bus is here! Bye!"
	purchase	I got some money for my birthday, so I'm going to buy a book.

Example Homophone Chart

Say: *This chart lists three sets of common homophones. You can see that using the wrong word in a sentence would leave readers confused about the intended meaning. Any time you're unsure which spelling of a word to use, you can use a dictionary to make sure the spelling matches the correct definition.*

Model Using Homophones

 Display the modeling text.

"I love camping on this isle," said Marta. "I rode here on the road over the bridge."

"I'm glad to hear there's a bridge," said Zoe. "We rowed here in a boat. It was so crowded that I had to sit in the aisle! I'll come by car next time."

Modeling Text

Say: *The writer used three sets of homophones. The first one is **isle, aisle,** and **I'll. I-s-l-e** is a small island, **a-i-s-l-e** is a passageway between seating areas, and **I-apostrophe-l-l** is the contraction for "I will."*

Similarly analyze the homophones **rode/road/rowed** and **here/hear**. Discuss the importance of using the correct spellings to match the writer's intended meanings.

 ## Rehearse

Practice Using Homophones

 Display the practice text.

> 1. I could tell by my brother's (pail, <u>pale</u>) face that he wasn't feeling well.
> 2. Drinks in glass containers are (band, <u>banned</u>) from the swimming pool.
> 3. Remember to (<u>cite</u>, sight) your source when you take research notes.
> 4. The (<u>scent</u>, cent) in the flower garden attracted many bees and butterflies.
> 5. Let's invite the (principle, <u>principal</u>) to watch our poetry performances.

Practice Text

Ask students to work with a partner to read each sentence and choose the correct homophone. Remind them to use a dictionary to help them if needed.

 If your class includes English learners or other students who need support, use "Strategies to Support ELs."

Share Practice Sentences

Invite pairs to share their responses. Ask the following questions:
- *What word did you choose for each sentence? Why did you choose that word?*
- *Why are homophones frequently confused? How can writers avoid this confusion?*

Independent Writing and Conferring

Say: *The English language has many homophones, words that are pronounced the same but have different spellings and meanings. As writers, we need to take time to consult a dictionary if we're unsure of the spelling that matches the meaning of a sentence. Doing this helps ensure that our readers can enjoy our texts without becoming confused.*

 If you would like to give students additional practice using homophones, have them complete Use Frequently Confused Words (BLM 9).

Share

 Bring students together. Review and provide corrective feedback based on students' answers to BLM 9. Ask students to share what they learned about homophones.

Strategies to Support ELs

Emerging (Beginning)

Beginning ELs will need additional support and practice to understand homophones. Prepare a matching game by writing homophones on separate index cards. Once students have matched all the pairs, help them use each word in an oral sentence, acting it out if possible. Following are some homophone pairs you might use: **ant/aunt, meat/meet, flower/flour, son/sun, high/hi, won/one, for/four, so/sew,** and **blew/blue**.

Expanding (Intermediate) and Bridging (Advanced)

Pair ELs with fluent English speakers to complete the practice activity.

Use Correct Capitalization

L.4.2a

Objectives

In this mini-lesson, students will:

• Distinguish between common and proper nouns.

• Review categories of proper nouns.

• Properly capitalize proper nouns in sentences.

Preparation

Materials Needed

• Use Correct Capitalization (BLM 10)

 **Focus**

Explain Proper Nouns

Say: *Almost every sentence includes a noun. A common noun names a person, place, or thing. A proper noun names a specific person, place, or thing and begins with a capital letter. Following are some categories of proper nouns.*

 Display the example Capitalization Chart.

Category	Words We Capitalize	Examples
dates	day, month	Monday, January 17, 1987
names and titles	all names and titles	Tanya Fisher, Mrs. Lockhart, Mayor Ellis, Dr. Wilson, Uncle Joe, General Pace
holidays	all words in name of holiday	Thanksgiving, Memorial Day, Veterans Day
product names	usually all words, depending on official trademarked name	Tasty Treats, Jammin' Jumprope, Hiker's Choice Backpack
place and geographic names	all words	Watson City Park, Grand Canyon, Maple Avenue, Atlantic Ocean, Kansas City, Missouri, Canada, Asia
buildings, stores, organizations, and institutions	all words except some conjunctions and prepositions	Empire State Building, Lincoln Elementary School, Eisenhower Museum, Sports World, Boys & Girls Clubs of America
languages and nationalities	all words	French, English, Italian, Spanish, Latin
book and movie titles	first word, last word, nouns, pronouns, verbs, adjectives, adverbs, first word in a subtitle	*A is for America, James and the Giant Peach, Thomas Edison: A Brilliant Designer* (italics when typed; underlined when written by hand)

Example Capitalization Chart

Say: *Look at the holidays category. If I say, "I love holidays," I have used a common noun. But if I say, "I visit my grandmother every Thanksgiving," I have used a proper noun. Common nouns begin with lowercase letters. Proper nouns begin with capital letters no matter where they appear in a sentence.*

Repeat the process with examples from other rows.

Model Capitalizing Proper Nouns

 Display the modeling texts. Read aloud the first modeling text.

My family plants a new tree every <u>arbor day</u>. After digging the hole, we fill it with <u>fast-grow fertilizer</u>. Then we go to the nursery in <u>rush city</u> to buy a baby tree.	My family plants a new tree every <u>Arbor Day</u>. After digging the hole, we fill it with <u>Fast-Grow Fertilizer</u>. Then we go to the nursery in <u>Rush City</u> to buy a baby tree.
Modeling Text 1	**Modeling Text 2**

Say: *These sentences have some errors. The first sentence has a holiday, Arbor Day. The second sentence has a product name, Fast-Grow Fertilizer. The third sentence has a geographic name, Rush City.* **Arbor Day, Fast-Grow Fertilizer,** *and* **Rush City** *are proper nouns, so these words must be capitalized.*

Read aloud the second modeling text.

Say: *The writer corrected the proper nouns by beginning them with capital letters. This makes the text easy to read. Now it is clear that we are reading about a holiday, product name, and geographic location.*

Rehearse

Practice Capitalizing Proper Nouns

 Display the practice text.

1. On sSaturday, I took my cat fFluffy to dDr. rRoscoe's office on vViola sStreet.
2. A sSpanish teacher came to my gGirl sScout meeting at the cCarson rRecreation cCenter to teach us about her native country.
3. I read cCharlie and the cChocolate fFactory to my little brother, and then we watched the movie with dad and mom on nNew yYear's eEve.

Practice Text

Ask students to work with a partner to read each sentence and correctly write the words that are proper nouns.

 If your class includes English learners or other students who need support, use "Strategies to Support ELs."

Share Practice Sentences

Invite pairs to share their responses. Ask the following questions:
- *Which words are proper nouns? How do you know?*
- *How did you correct each proper noun? How will this help readers better understand the sentences?*

Independent Writing and Conferring

Say: *Proper nouns name specific people, places, and things. It is important for writers to remember to capitalize proper nouns. Capitalizing these words helps us make our meaning clear and helps readers better understand what we are referring to as we write.*

 If you would like to give students additional practice recognizing and writing proper nouns, have them complete Use Correct Capitalization (BLM 10).

Share

Bring students together. Review and provide corrective feedback based on students' answers to BLM 10. Ask students to share what they learned about capitalizing proper nouns.

Strategies to Support ELs

Emerging (Beginning)

To support beginning ELs, collect a variety of ads. Model how to use self-stick notes to label proper nouns such as dates and names of people, products, geographic places, and stores. Point out the capital letters in each proper noun. Then provide old newspapers and magazines and invite students to search for additional examples.

Expanding (Intermediate) and Bridging (Advanced)

Provide realia for a proper noun search, such as a calendar for dates and holidays, products for product names, and maps or globes for geographic names. Remind students that these are different categories of proper nouns and that proper nouns begin with capital letters.

Use Commas and Quotation Marks

L.4.2b

Objectives

In this mini-lesson, students will:

- Identify direct speech and quotations in texts.
- Identify the speaker in direct speech and quotations.
- Use commas and quotation marks to mark direct speech and quotations from a text.

Preparation

Materials Needed

- Computers or print resources
- Use Commas and Quotation Marks (BLM 11)

 **Focus**

Explain Direct Speech and Quotations

Say: *Direct speech is the words a character says in a story. A quotation is the words a real or fictional person says as quoted, or repeated, by another speaker or writer. In writing, quotation marks show the exact words the character or person speaks.*

Explain that writers tell the names of speakers outside the quotation marks and the punctuation the writer uses depends on where the speaker's name appears.

 Display the example Direct Speech and Quotations Chart.

Features	direct speech or quotation?	speaker	quotation marks	comma	period
Finding me in front of the TV, Mom said, "It's time to clean your room."	direct speech	identified before the direct speech	around exact words Mom said	after the word **said**	at the end of the direct speech inside the quotation marks
"It's time to clean your room," said Mom when she found me in front of the TV.	direct speech	identified after the direct speech	around exact words Mom said	after direct speech inside the quotation marks	after the words "said Mom" and the accompanying description
Former British Prime Minister Benjamin Disraeli once said, "Cleanliness and order are not matters of instinct . . . you must cultivate a taste for them."	quotation	identified before the quotation	around quoted words	after the word **said**	at the end of the quotation inside the quotation marks
Former British Prime Minister Benjamin Disraeli believed that people "must cultivate a taste" for order.	quotation	identified before the quotation	around an excerpt from speaker's quotation	no comma necessary because the quoted phrase is embedded in the sentence	at the end of the sentence

Example Direct Speech and Quotations Chart

Say: *Here we find two ways to write direct speech and two ways to write a quotation. Notice that quotation marks always surround the speaker's exact words, but the placement of the comma depends on the sentence's construction. Good writers learn to use commas and quotation marks correctly so that readers can easily determine who is speaking and what that person says.*

Model Using Commas and Quotation Marks

 Display the modeling text.

> I recently found a book full of interesting facts about sea animals. On page 6, the author says, "A full-grown whale shark is as big as a school bus." I also like the section about seahorses, which are "the slowest known fish" and "definitely aren't long-distance swimmers." I showed the book to my teacher and said, "I'd like to borrow this book for my next science report."

Modeling Text

Say: *The writer put quotation marks around one full quotation and two excerpts from a book. The writer also put quotation marks around his or her own words to the teacher. Both the quotation and the direct speech require commas. Using punctuation correctly makes the writer's thoughts easier to understand.*

 ## Rehearse

Practice Using Commas and Quotation Marks

 Display the practice text. Ask students to work with a partner to research, discuss, and write the practice assignment.

> Using online or print resources, locate a quotation that you like. Write the quotation or an excerpt from it two different ways. Be sure to include the original speaker's name in each sentence.

Practice Text

 If your class includes English learners or other students who need support, use "Strategies to Support ELs."

Share Practice Sentences

Invite pairs to share their responses. Ask the following questions:
- *Why are quotations important in a text? Why is it important for writers to know how to punctuate quotations correctly?*

 # Independent Writing and Conferring

Say: *Stories are more realistic and engaging when writers include characters' direct speech. Nonfiction texts are more interesting and authentic when they include quotations from people with experience, interest, or expertise in the topic. Remember to use commas and quotation marks when you write direct speech and quotations so readers will know who is speaking and the exact words each person says.*

 If you would like to give students additional practice using commas and quotation marks, have them complete Use Commas and Quotation Marks (BLM 11).

Share

 Bring students together. Review and provide corrective feedback based on students' answers to BLM 11. Ask students to share what they learned about writing direct speech and quotations.

Strategies to Support ELs

Emerging (Beginning)

Beginning ELs will need additional support and practice to understand punctuation for direct speech and quotations. Write a simple direct speech statement or quotation on index cards, one word per card. Write the words **said** and **said that**, a name, and any other needed words on other cards. Draw a comma, period, and left and right quotation marks on half cards. Work together to assemble the cards in different ways and read the resulting sentences.

Expanding (Intermediate) and Bridging (Advanced)

Pair ELs with fluent English speakers to complete the practice activity.

Use Commas in Compound Sentences

L.4.2c

 **Focus**

Objectives

In this mini-lesson, students will:

- Identify coordinating conjunctions.
- Understand how a compound sentence is formed and punctuated.
- Combine two sentences into a compound sentence with a coordinating conjunction.

Preparation

Materials Needed

- Use Commas in Compound Sentences (BLM 12)

Explain Compound Sentences

Say: *We have learned about coordinating conjunctions such as **and, but,** and **or.** Sometimes we use these conjunctions to combine words or phrases. Today we will use coordinating conjunctions to combine two sentences into compound sentences.*

 Display the example Coordinating Conjunction Chart.

Coordinating Conjunction	Purpose	Compound Sentence
and	connect similar ideas	I went to the library for a book, <u>and</u> I also checked out a movie.
or	show an alternative	Should I read my book first, <u>or</u> should I go ahead and watch the movie?
but	show a contrast	I could invite my brother to watch the movie with me, <u>but</u> he'd probably rather play basketball.
yet	show a contrast	My brother and I hardly ever spend time together, <u>yet</u> he always treats me kindly.
so	show a cause and effect	I'd like to do something with my brother, <u>so</u> I'll see if he wants to come watch the movie.
nor	show a negative	My brother can't watch the movie today, <u>nor</u> will he be able to watch it tomorrow.
for	introduce a reason	I'm as happy as can be, <u>for</u> my brother said he'd watch the movie with me on Saturday!

Example Coordinating Conjunction Chart

Say: *In each example sentence, the writer has combined two short sentences with the appropriate coordinating conjunction.*

Point out that when we form a compound sentence, we use a comma before the conjunction. Explain that the comma tells the reader to pause very briefly before continuing and shows where one complete thought ends and the next begins.

Model Compound Sentences

 Display the modeling texts. Read aloud the first modeling text.

Matter can be a solid. It can be a liquid or gas. Your desk is a solid. The milk you drink with your lunch is a liquid. Sometimes matter changes! Juice is a liquid. Juice pops are a solid. Water can be all three states of matter. It is special!	Matter can be a solid, <u>or</u> it can be a liquid or gas. Your desk is a solid, <u>and</u> the milk you drink with your lunch is a liquid. Sometimes matter changes! Juice is a liquid, <u>but</u> juice pops are a solid. Water can be all three states of matter, <u>so</u> it is special!
Modeling Text 1	**Modeling Text 2**

Say: *Using all short, simple sentences makes the writing choppy. Listen to the difference when the writer combines some of these sentences.*

Read aloud the second modeling text. Then discuss the use of conjunctions, underlining each coordinating conjunction in the modeling text.

Say: *The writer combined the first two sentences with a comma and the coordinating conjunction **or** to show a contrast. The writer also combined sentences using the conjunction **and** to connect examples, the conjunction **but** to show a contrast, and the conjunction **so** to show a cause and effect.*

Point out that the coordinating conjunctions help the sentences flow smoothly and that varying our sentence structures makes our writing more interesting.

 **Rehearse**

Practice Compound Sentences

 Display the practice text.

1. I drew some pictures, _and_ I hung them on the refrigerator.
2. My class might read to the first-graders today, _or_ we might go tomorrow.
3. My sister likes to play soccer, _but_ my brother likes to play baseball.
4. We were out of bread, _so_ we went to the store.

Practice Text

Ask students to work with a partner and read each sentence. Ask them to write a coordinating conjunction for each sentence.

 If your class includes English learners or other students who need support, use "Strategies to Support ELs."

Share Practice Sentences

Invite pairs to share their responses. Ask the following questions:
- *What two sentences are combined in each compound sentence?*
- *What coordinating conjunction did you choose for each sentence?*

Independent Writing and Conferring

Say: *You can use coordinating conjunctions to combine sentences into compound sentences when you write. Using a combination of sentence types gives your writing variety, makes it more interesting, and better holds your readers' attention.*

 If you would like to give students additional practice producing compound sentences, have them complete Use Commas in Compound Sentences (BLM 12).

Share

Bring students together. Review and provide corrective feedback based on students' answers to BLM 12. Ask students to share what they learned about compound sentences.

Strategies to Support ELs

Emerging (Beginning)

Beginning ELs will need additional support and practice to understand compound sentences. Write the coordinating conjunctions on individual index cards and hold them up one at a time as you say and pantomime simple compound sentences. Help students form and pantomime simple compound sentences about themselves using various coordinating conjunctions as well.

Expanding (Intermediate) and Bridging (Advanced)

Pair ELs with fluent English speakers to complete the practice activity.

Use Spelling Reference Materials

L.4.2d

 **Focus**

Objectives

In this mini-lesson, students will:

• Explore a variety of spelling reference materials.

• Look up words in a dictionary.

• Use a word's definition to help check and correct spellings.

Preparation

Materials Needed

• Dictionaries

• Use Spelling Reference Materials (BLM 13)

Explain Spelling Reference Materials

Say: *Sometimes when we write, we're not sure how to spell a word. When that happens, we can use different types of reference materials to help us.*

 Display the example Spelling References Chart.

Look back! Is the word in the text you are reading? If the book has a glossary, can you find the word there? Is the word in a question you are answering?

Look at classroom word banks. Is the word in a theme or topic poster in your classroom?

Look at classroom spelling rules charts. Does the word fit a spelling rule you have learned? Might it have a known letter pattern, prefix, or suffix?

Look at other print items in the classroom. For example, you can use a calendar to check the spelling of days of the week and months of the year or use the classroom schedule to see how to spell the names of classes and activities.

Use the spell-checker on your computer. Remember, though, that the spell-checker might not pick up a correctly spelled word that is misused, such as **here** in place of **hear**.

Use a print or digital dictionary. Write down different ways your word might be spelled. Then see if you can find the words in the dictionary. Read the definitions to make sure you choose the right word.

Example Spelling References Chart

Say: *Each of these reference materials is valuable to writers. Today we will focus on using a dictionary to check and correct our spelling.*

Model Using a Dictionary

 Display the modeling text.

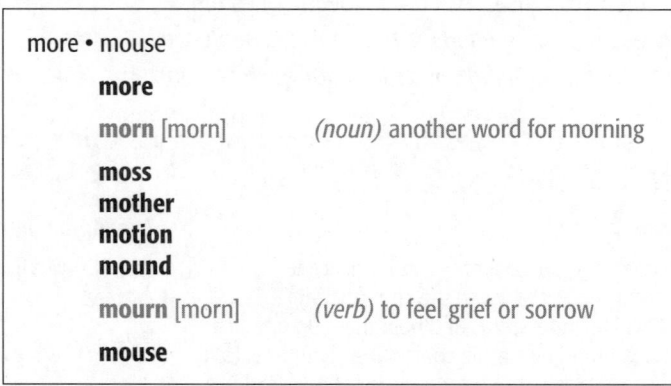

Modeling Text

Say: *All of these words are on one page of a print dictionary. The first word,* **more**, *and the last word,* **mouse**, *are also listed at the top of the page as guide words. These guide words help us figure out if the word we are looking for is on that page. Today we are focusing on the words* **morn** *and* **mourn**.

Explain that if you weren't sure how to spell the word **mourn**, you could look it up in a dictionary. Does it begin with **m-o-r** or **m-o-u-r**? You can read the definitions of both words to determine that the word **mourn** has the correct meaning and spelling. Then display an online dictionary and demonstrate how to type your spelling tries into the search bar and check what pops up.

 **Rehearse**

Practice Using a Dictionary

 Display the practice text.

> My word is _____.
>
> My word is on page _____.
>
> The guide words on this page are _____ and _____.
>
> One meaning of my word is _____.
>
> Here is a sentence using this meaning of my word: _____

Practice Text

Pair students and give each pair a dictionary. Ask each pair to choose a word that would be interesting and fill in the information about the word.

 If your class includes English learners or other students who need support, use "Strategies to Support ELs."

Share Selected Words

Invite pairs to share their responses. Ask the following questions:
- *Why did you choose this word?*
- *Why do you think this word might be confusing for some people to spell?*
- *How can writers use a dictionary to check and correct their spelling?*

Independent Writing and Conferring

Say: *We have discussed different types of spelling reference materials, such as texts, word banks, spelling rules charts, other classroom print items, computer spell-checkers, and print or digital dictionaries. When using a spell-checker or dictionary, it is important to make sure the word's definition matches the word we are using, too. Remember that good spelling is a courtesy to our readers and helps them better enjoy and understand our texts.*

 If you would like to give students additional practice using spelling reference materials, have them complete Use Spelling Reference Materials (BLM 13).

 **Share**

Bring students together. Review and provide corrective feedback based on students' answers to BLM 13. Ask students to share what they learned about using a dictionary.

Strategies to Support ELs

Emerging (Beginning)

Support beginning ELs by working together to look up simple words in a dictionary. If needed, preteach alphabetical order skills. For each word, read the definition together and use it in an oral sentence. Once students are more confident, help them look up and compare familiar but easily confused words such as **wait/weight**, **vary/very**, **role/roll**, and **threw/through**.

Expanding (Intermediate) and Bridging (Advanced)

Pair ELs with fluent English speakers to complete the practice activity.

All Levels

Invite students to bring any dictionaries they have in their homes to share with the class.

Use Precise Words and Phrases

L.4.3a, L.4.6

 **Focus**

Objectives

In this mini-lesson, students will:

• Understand the meaning of the term **precise**.

• Use precise nouns, verbs, adjectives, and adverbs.

• Choose the most accurate word to help readers visualize what is being described in a text.

Preparation

Materials Needed

• Thesauruses

• Use Precise Words and Phrases (BLM 14)

Explain Precise Words and Phrases

Say: *We use many nouns, verbs, adjectives, and adverbs in our speaking, reading, and writing. Many of the words we use have related meanings but create very different pictures in our minds.*

Explain that writers must choose the most precise, exact, accurate, specific, particular, and clear-cut words and phrases to express what they mean. Display a thesaurus, and read and discuss the other synonyms for the noun **speak**.

 Display the example Precise Words Chart.

Nouns	Verbs	Adjectives	Adverbs
color	quiver	rich	proudly
hue	tremble	wealthy	confidently
tint	shake	affluent	smugly
shade	shudder	prosperous	conceitedly
stain	shiver	well-to-do	pompously

Example Precise Words Chart

Say: *Each of these nouns, verbs, adjectives, and adverbs has a similar meaning and a more specific meaning of its own. In your writing, you would choose the word or phrase that most precisely represents the situation you are describing. This helps readers visualize the scene and better understand the text.*

Model Using Precise Words and Phrases

 Display the sample Using Precise Words and Phrases Chart.

Part of Speech	General Word or Phrase	Passage	More Specific Word or Phrase	Passage Using More Precise Words and Phrases
noun	a woman	I watched the little girl and <u>a helpful woman playing happily</u> at the park.	her babysitter	I watched the little girl and <u>her attentive babysitter swinging merrily</u> at the park.
verb	playing		swinging	
adjective	helpful		attentive	
adverb	happily		merrily	

Sample Using Precise Words and Phrases Chart

Say: *What do you visualize in the first passage? What do you visualize in the second one? Using the most precise, accurate words and phrases possible adds meaningful details to our writing and helps it have the greatest effect on our readers.*

Rehearse

Practice Using Precise Words and Phrases

 Display the practice text.

---

1. The visitor's (hat, <u>fedora</u>) flew off as he scurried to catch the bus.
2. "I adore how the stars (<u>sparkle</u>, glow) in the night sky," said my poetic sister.
3. The little boy stomped vigorously through the (wet, <u>slushy</u>) puddle.
4. My cousin's (funny, <u>sarcastic</u>) brand of humor sometimes hurts people's feelings.

Practice Text

Ask students to work with a partner and read each sentence. Ask them to write the word or phrase they feel is more precise in the sentence.

 If your class includes English learners or other students who need support, use "Strategies to Support ELs."

Share Practice Sentences

Invite pairs to share their responses. Ask the following questions:
- *Which noun, verb, adjective, and adverb did you choose? Why did you choose each one?*
- *As a writer, why is using the most precise word or phrase important?*

Independent Writing and Conferring

Say: *Many nouns, verbs, adjectives, and adverbs are related to other words with similar definitions. Some of the words are more powerful and interesting than others, or their specific meaning fits a situation more accurately. Choosing words and phrases with the most precise meanings helps readers visualize what we describe.*

Remind students that they can use a thesaurus to help them find precise words and phrases to use in their writing.

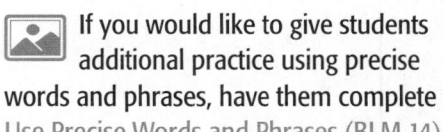 If you would like to give students additional practice using precise words and phrases, have them complete Use Precise Words and Phrases (BLM 14).

 Share

Bring students together. Review and provide corrective feedback based on students' answers to BLM 14. Ask students to share what they learned about using precise words and phrases.

Strategies to Support ELs

Emerging (Beginning)

 Beginning ELs will need additional support and practice to understand the concept of precise words and phrases. Display some photographs that depict familiar items or situations. For each one, orally state a "plain" sentence and one in which you use different, more precise words or phrases, such as *The man is helping/The police officer is assisting*. Invite each student to choose a photograph, and help him or her create a set of oral sentences.

Expanding (Intermediate) and Bridging (Advanced)

Pair ELs with fluent English speakers to complete the practice activity.

Use Punctuation for Effect

L.4.3b

Objectives

In this mini-lesson, students will:

• Review end punctuation and commas.

• Identify the names and purposes of lesser-used types of punctuation.

• Use colons, semicolons, em dashes, ellipses, and parentheses for effect.

Preparation

Materials Needed

• Use Punctuation for Effect (BLM 15)

 **Focus**

Explain Using Punctuation for Effect

Say: *Today you will learn about five types of end punctuation: colons, semicolons, em dashes, ellipses, and parentheses. Writers must choose just the right punctuation to express what they mean. This is called "writing for effect."*

 Display the example Punctuation Chart.

Type of Punctuation	Purpose	Example
colon	to introduce examples, details, or related information	We grow many types of vegetables in our garden: tomatoes, beans, peas, and zucchini.
semicolon	to show a close relationship between independent clauses not joined by a comma and conjunction	Benjamin Franklin wrote many proverbs; he included many of them in *Poor Richard's Almanac.*
em dash	to break into the main thought of a sentence with new information, examples, or details, either in the middle or at the end	We will research all 50 states–their symbols, geography, industry, and unique features–to learn more about the United States.
	to show that one character interrupts another in dialogue	Joel smiled. "I have all the invitations ready to send out for Ray's–"
ellipses	to show where we have omitted words or sentences, such as when shortening a long quote	"With malice toward none, with charity for all . . . let us strive on to finish the work we are in, to bind up the nation's wounds." (Abraham Lincoln)
	to show a pause in dialogue	"Hi, Dad! I . . . um . . . er . . . had to stay after school," stammered Lon.
	to show an unfinished thought	"I just wish I knew what she wanted . . ." murmured Alice.
parentheses	to add a comment or piece of information; to add pronunciations and alternative measurements	Tickets are available at the door. (The box office opens at 5:00.)
		People saw cocoons woven by the Bombyx mori (bahm-BIKS MOR-ee) moth.
		Capua, Italy, is a town 130 miles (209 kilometers) south of Rome.

Example Punctuation Chart

Say: *You have probably seen all of these punctuation marks in your reading, but now you can begin using them to add variety to your writing as well.*

Point out the following: If the information after a colon is an independent clause, it begins with a capital letter. However, the independent clause after a semicolon begins with a lowercase letter (unless it is a proper noun). When parentheses contain a complete sentence, use end punctuation inside the parentheses.

Model Using Punctuation for Effect

 Display the sample Using Punctuation for Effect Chart. Ask students which way of presenting information is best and why.

	Your eyes, ears, nose, tongue, and skin are the parts of your body that allow you to sense the world around you. That's why sight, hearing, smell, taste, and touch are called the five senses.
colon	Five parts of your body allow you to sense the world around you: your eyes for sight, ears for hearing, nose for smell, tongue for taste, and skin for touch.
semicolon	Your eyes, ears, nose, tongue, and skin are the parts of your body that allow you to sense the world around you; that's why sight, hearing, smell, taste, and touch are called the five senses.
em dash	Your five senses—sight, hearing, smell, taste, and touch—are possible because your eyes, ears, nose, tongue, and skin help you sense the world around you.
ellipses	"Your eyes, ears, nose, tongue, and skin . . . allow you to sense the world about you . . . sight, hearing, smell, taste, and touch . . ."
parentheses	Your eyes, ears, nose, tongue, and skin are the parts of your body that allow you to sense the world around you (sight, hearing, smell, taste, and touch).

Sample Using Punctuation for Effect Chart

 ## Rehearse

Practice Using Punctuation for Effect

 Display the practice text. Ask students to work with a partner to rewrite the information at least two different ways using the punctuation marks described on the Punctuation Chart.

> A bird's-eye view is a view from above. It is from the perspective of a bird. Most maps are bird's-eye views of things.

Practice Text

 If your class includes English learners or other students who need support, use "Strategies to Support ELs."

Share Practice Sentences

Invite pairs to share their responses.

 ## Independent Writing and Conferring

Say: *Colons, semicolons, em dashes, ellipses, and parentheses are punctuation marks we can use to vary our sentence structures and to make our texts more informative and interesting to read. As you write, revise, and edit, look for places where you can use these punctuation marks for effect.*

If you would like to give students additional practice with colons, semicolons, em dashes, ellipses, and parentheses, have them complete Use Punctuation for Effect (BLM 15).

 ## Share

Bring students together. Review and provide corrective feedback based on students' answers to BLM 15. Ask students to share what they learned about using punctuation for effect.

Strategies to Support ELs

Emerging (Beginning)

Beginning ELs will need additional support and practice to use punctuation for effect. Using self-stick notes, invite students to search through familiar fiction and nonfiction books for examples of colons, semicolons, em dashes, ellipses, and parentheses. Discuss each sentence, pointing out the role of the punctuation mark.

Expanding (Intermediate) and Bridging (Advanced)

Pair ELs with fluent English speakers to complete the practice activity.

Use Formal and Informal English

L.4.3c

 **Focus**

Objectives

In this mini-lesson, students will:

• Identify the purposes of formal and informal English.

• Compare formal and informal uses of English.

• Compose examples of formal and informal English.

Preparation

Materials Needed

• Formal and Informal English Chart (BLM 16)

• Use Formal and Informal English (BLM 17)

Explain Formal and Informal English

Say: *We talk and write differently in various situations. For example, a student who is giving a presentation usually has well-thought-out ideas and uses more complete sentences than a student who is in a small-group discussion.*

 Display the Formal and Informal English Chart (BLM 16), and distribute a copy to students.

When giving a presentation . . .	In a small-group discussion . . .
• You are likely the only person speaking, so all the attention is on you.	• Several people carry the conversation.
• Your tone is more serious.	• The tone is more casual.
• Your sentences are complete, and your grammar is correct.	• Participants may use some incomplete sentences, so grammar rules are sometimes "bent."
• You use fewer contractions and little or no slang or idioms.	• Participants use frequent contractions and may use some slang or idioms.
• You likely use a larger, more specific vocabulary.	• Participants may use a smaller vocabulary.
• You rely less on body language and facial expressions; instead, your meaning is in the words themselves.	• Participants rely on body language and facial expressions to reinforce meaning.
• You plan and compose your thoughts before stating them, but you're not always aware if your listeners accurately hear or understand what you say.	• Ideas are often exchanged rapidly with little planning, but participants can easily repeat or reword their thoughts if others don't hear or understand.

Formal and Informal English Chart (BLM 16)

Say: *Speakers and writers must consider the situations they are in to determine whether formal or informal language is appropriate.*

Model Using Formal and Informal Language

 Display the modeling texts. Read aloud the first modeling text.

> "Can we discuss the main character?" asked Miranda. "I liked Audrey! I felt like I knew her . . ."
>
> ". . . but not because the author described her, right?" asked Tasha. "Actions and dialogue . . . that's what brought her to life."
>
> "Yeah," said Michael. "I guess that's what Ms. Busby means by 'show, don't tell' in our own writing."
>
> "Exactly!" said Miranda.
>
> "I was surprised a lot," said Tasha. "How about you guys?"
>
> "Me, too," said Michael. "I kept making predictions, but they didn't all turn out the way I thought they would."
>
> "Well, I like surprises in a book," said Miranda. "I wonder if we have any more books by that author in the library? I want to see if they're just as good."

Modeling Text 1

"My reading group read and discussed *The Girl on the Hill* by Grace Crane," said Miranda. "This book has a strong main character named Audrey. The author portrays Audrey through her actions and dialogue rather than through specific description, which we thought was a creative way to help readers visualize what she is like. We were also pleasantly surprised when some of our predictions about the story came true and some did not. We appreciate an author who has enough surprises to keep our attention. We look forward to reading more books by this author to see if she uses some of these same techniques."

Modeling Text 2

Say: *Miranda, Tasha, and Michael use informal language to discuss a book in their reading group. Let's see how Miranda's language changes when she reports her group's discussion in front of the whole class.*

Read aloud the second modeling text. Point out that here Miranda uses more formal language, including complete sentences, correct grammar, and a wider vocabulary.

 **Rehearse**

Practice Using Formal and Informal English

 Display the practice text. Ask students to work with a partner and complete each activity.

(1) Briefly discuss a topic you are studying in math, science, or social studies. Write down one example of informal language you used in your conversation.

(2) Now imagine you are giving a presentation to the class about this same topic. Write down one example of formal language you might use in your presentation.

Practice Text

 If your class includes English learners or other students who need support, use "Strategies to Support ELs."

Share Practice Sentences

Invite pairs to share their responses. Ask the following questions:
- *What is your example of informal language? In what ways is it informal?*
- *What is your example of formal language? In what ways is it formal?*
- *How does formal and informal language apply to writing?*

Independent Writing and Conferring

Say: *We have learned that different situations call for different language styles. Sometimes we can use informal English, such as to depict conversations in stories. Other times, we need to use more formal English in our writing. Both types of language are appropriate when used at the right time. Remember to consider your audience and setting when deciding whether to use formal or informal English as you speak or write.*

 If you would like to give students additional practice using formal and informal English, have them complete Use Formal and Informal English (BLM 17).

 **Share**

 Bring students together. Review and provide corrective feedback based on students' answers to BLM 17. Ask students to share what they learned about formal and informal language.

Strategies to Support ELs

Emerging (Beginning)

 Beginning ELs will need additional support and practice to compare formal and informal English. Locate clear examples of each style in fiction and nonfiction books students have already read. Read the examples out loud and use BLM 16 to help students analyze whether each one is formal or informal and why.

Expanding (Intermediate) and Bridging (Advanced)

Pair ELs with fluent English speakers to complete the practice activity.

Use Context Clues

L.4.4a

Objectives

In this mini-lesson, students will:

• Identify different types of context clues used in reading.

• Understand why writers include context clues.

• Write sentences that contain context clues.

Preparation

Materials Needed

• Use Context Clues (BLM 18)

 **Focus**

Explain Context Clues

Say: *When we read, we use context clues to help us figure out the meaning of new words. As writers, we can include context clues for our readers, too. We can use information from a dictionary or thesaurus.*

 Display the example Types of Context Clues Chart.

Word: ringmaster	
Type of Context Clue	**Example**
definition	All eyes were on the ringmaster as he <u>announced each event in the circus</u>.
description	To be a ringmaster, you must <u>love the circus and enjoy hosting, announcing, and making presentations with flair</u>.
example	The ringmaster, <u>wearing a bright red coat and tall hat</u>, introduced the performers and their acts.
synonym	A ringmaster, or <u>master of ceremonies</u>, helps direct the crowd's attention to what is happening in the circus ring.
antonym	The ringmaster's assistant didn't need a microphone but <u>quietly helped behind the scenes</u>.

Example Types of Context Clues Chart

Say: *A context clue can be a definition, description, example, synonym, or antonym.*

Discuss each example, pointing out how the bold-faced words and phrases give more information about the meaning of the word **ringmaster**. They also help readers visualize who a ringmaster is and better understand where he works, how he acts, and what he does.

Model Using Context Clues

 Display the modeling text.

I used a wheelbarrow—<u>a cart with three wheels and two handles</u>—to carry the bricks to the garden.

My family does many fun seasonal activities, such as <u>camping in the summer</u> and <u>picking apples in autumn</u>.

You may think adding extra practices will motivate the team, but instead it may <u>discourage</u> them.

Modeling Text

Say: *Each of these sentences has a word that might be new to a reader, so the writer included one or more context clues that tell more about the word.*

Help students determine that the first sentence contains a definition or description of the word **wheelbarrow**, the second sentence contains examples that help describe the word **seasonal**, and the third sentence uses antonyms, or opposites, to help explain the word **motivate**.

 **Rehearse**

Practice Using Context Clues

 Display the practice text.

merchandise
quantity
distribute

Practice Text

 Ask students to work with a partner, choose one of the words, and write a sentence using that word along with at least one context clue that gives more information about the word's meaning. Tell them to use the Context Clues Chart to help them remember different types of context clues they can use.

 If your class includes English learners or other students who need support, use "Strategies to Support ELs."

Share Practice Sentences

Invite pairs to share their responses. Ask the following questions:
- *What does your word mean?*
- *What context clue(s) did you include in your sentence?*
- *How will your context clue(s) help readers better understand your word?*

Independent Writing and Conferring

Say: *You already use context clues as a reader. The definitions, descriptions, examples, synonyms, and antonyms that writers add to their sentences help you picture and understand what new words mean. Now it's time to start helping your readers by adding context clues for tricky words. This extra information will make the tricky words easier to figure out and make your writing more effective than ever.*

 If you would like to give students additional practice adding context clues to their writing, have them complete Use Context Clues (BLM 18).

 **Share**

 Bring students together. Review and provide corrective feedback based on students' answers to BLM 18. Ask students to share what they learned about context clues.

Strategies to Support ELs

Emerging (Beginning)

Beginning ELs will need additional support and practice to understand context clues. Display a simple adjective, such as **cold**. Together create a list of context clues for the word—a definition and/or description, some examples, and a synonym and antonym. Then invite students to dictate sentences using the clues as you record them on the board, such as **The cold air made it too chilly to sit outside.** Repeat the process with additional adjectives students need to learn.

Expanding (Intermediate) and Bridging (Advanced)

Pair ELs with fluent English speakers to complete the practice activity.

Use Greek and Latin Roots and Affixes

L.4.4b

Objectives

In this mini-lesson, students will:

- Identify related words based on their Greek or Latin root.
- Use common Greek and Latin roots and affixes as clues to the meaning of a word.
- Given a root, add affixes to create new words.

Preparation

Materials Needed

- Use Greek and Latin Roots and Affixes (BLM 19)

 **Focus**

Explain Greek and Latin Roots and Affixes

Say: *Many words in the English language are based on Greek and Latin roots. Many of our common prefixes and suffixes come from the Greek and Latin languages as well. Learning these word units helps us figure out the meanings of new words as readers and select and spell appropriate words as writers.*

 Display the example Greek and Latin Roots Chart.

Root	Meaning	Examples
aud (Latin)	hear	<u>aud</u>ible, <u>aud</u>ience, <u>aud</u>iovisual, <u>aud</u>itorium
graph (Greek)	write	auto<u>graph</u>, bio<u>graph</u>y, phono<u>graph</u>, photo<u>graph</u>
lab (Latin)	work	col<u>lab</u>orate, e<u>lab</u>orate, <u>lab</u>or, <u>lab</u>oratory
photo (Greek)	light	<u>photo</u>genic, <u>photo</u>graph, <u>photo</u>synthesis, tele<u>photo</u>
scop (Greek)	see	micro<u>scop</u>e, peri<u>scop</u>e, stetho<u>scop</u>e, tele<u>scop</u>e

Example Greek and Latin Roots Chart

Say: *These are just a few of the many examples of Greek and Latin influence on the English language. Notice that sometimes roots are combined, such as in the word photograph.*

Discuss each root, adding other related words you and your students think of to the chart.

Model Using Greek and Latin Roots and Affixes

 Display the modeling text.

> uni ("one") + cycle = unicycle
>
> bi ("two") + cycle = bicycle
>
> tri ("three") + cycle = tricycle
>
> mot ("move") + or ("state of") + cycle = motorcycle
>
> re ("again") + cycle = recycle

Modeling Text

Say: *The Greek root cycl means "circle" or "ring." We can use what we know about the root cycl to help us determine the meaning of words that have this root. For example, the affix uni- means "one." So a unicycle is a vehicle with one wheel.*

Review the remaining affixes with students, modeling how to use what you know about the root and the affix to figure out the meaning of a word. Note that other related words are **cyclone**, a storm of rotating winds, and simply the word **cycle**.

Rehearse

Practice Using Greek and Latin Roots and Affixes

 Display the practice text.

---

1. **act** ("do"): "Please try to (enact, <u>react</u>, transact) with surprise when Aunt Millie gives you the same birthday gift you get every year," said Mom.

2. **script** ("write"): Joe wrote a colorful (<u>description</u>, prescription, subscription) of his activities during summer vacation.

3. **aqua** ("water"): Our swim club meets at the (aquarium, aquamarine, <u>aquatic</u>) center for practice and competitions.

4. **port** ("carry"): Dad hired a moving van to (import, <u>transport</u>, report) our belongings to our new apartment.

5. **volv** ("turn"): I hope my sister doesn't (revolve, evolve, <u>involve</u>) me in her latest craft project, or I'll have to help clean it up, too.

Practice Text

Ask students to work with a partner to read each sentence and write the word that makes sense, using a dictionary as needed.

 If your class includes English learners or other students who need support, use "Strategies to Support ELs."

Share Practice Sentences

Invite pairs to share their responses. Ask the following questions:

- *What do the word choices in each sentence have in common? How did you choose the correct word?*
- *How does knowing Greek and Latin roots and affixes help us as readers? As writers?*

Independent Writing and Conferring

Say: *We use words with Greek and Latin roots and affixes daily in our speaking, reading, and writing. The more we learn about them, the wider our vocabularies will be. A good way to become proficient in these word parts is to pay special attention to them when you read and set aside a page in your writing notebook to begin collecting examples to use in your own texts.*

 If you would like to give students additional practice using Greek and Latin root and affixes, have them complete Use Greek and Latin Roots and Affixes (BLM 19).

Share

Bring students together. Review and provide corrective feedback based on students' answers to BLM 19. Ask students to share what they learned about Greek and Latin roots and affixes.

Strategies to Support ELs

Emerging (Beginning)

Beginning ELs will need additional support and practice to understand Greek and Latin roots and affixes. Use alphabet manipulatives or letter cards to spell some simple roots, adding letters at the front and back to demonstrate how to form new words from the root, such as **loc** ("place")—**local**, **locate**, **location**, **locomotion**, **dislocate**. Use each form of the word in a simple sentence and act out its meaning, when possible.

Expanding (Intermediate) and Bridging (Advanced)

Pair ELs with fluent English speakers to complete the practice activity.

Use Dictionaries, Glossaries, and Thesauruses

L.4.4c

Objectives

In this mini-lesson, students will:

- Compare and contrast dictionaries, glossaries, and thesauruses.
- Consult these reference materials to find words' pronunciations.
- Consult these reference materials to determine or clarify the precise meaning of key words and phrases.

Preparation

Materials Needed

- Dictionaries, nonfiction books with glossaries, thesauruses
- Use Dictionaries, Glossaries, and Thesauruses (BLM 20)

 Focus

Explain Dictionaries, Glossaries, and Thesauruses

Say: *Sometimes when we write, we need to check a word's meaning before we use it. Other times, we need to see if we can find a more accurate, specific word to use or check a word's pronunciation so we'll know how to read it aloud. When these situations occur, we can use a print or digital dictionary, glossary, or thesaurus to help us.*

 Display the example Reference Materials Chart.

Questions	Dictionary	Glossary	Thesaurus
Where do you find it?	digital versions available online; print versions available in classrooms, libraries, offices, and many homes	at the end of many print and digital nonfiction books	digital versions available online; print versions available in classrooms, libraries, offices, and many homes
What words does it include?	some, many, or most words from a particular language	selected words used in the book; these words are often bold-faced in the text	words that have synonyms and antonyms
How are the words organized?	in alphabetical order	in alphabetical order	in alphabetical order
What information does it provide about the word?	pronunciation, syllabication, definitions for all parts of speech, and etymology (history of the word)	pronunciation, syllabication, and definition used in the book	brief definitions, synonyms, and antonyms for the words' different parts of speech

Example Reference Materials Chart

Say: *Dictionaries, glossaries, and thesauruses are all valuable to writers. Let's use a dictionary entry to find the pronunciation of a word and to determine or clarify its meaning.*

Model Using a Dictionary

 Display the modeling text.

> **com•press** [kuhm-PREHS]
>
> *(verb)* to squeeze together or flatten
>
> (from the Old French word *compresser*, meaning "put under pressure")

Modeling Text

Say: *Imagine you are writing a report about an experiment but you're not sure if **compress** is the correct verb to describe one of the steps. You can use a* *dictionary to find the meaning of **compress** and make sure you know how to pronounce the word correctly when you read your report aloud.*

Display an online dictionary and demonstrate how to type the word **compress** into the search box, and then read the results together. If available, share a print or online science book in which the word **compress** is bold-faced and display the word's entry in the glossary.

 ## Rehearse

Practice Using Reference Materials

 Display the practice text.

> I would like to write a _____ about _____.
>
> I would like to use the word _____ in my text.
>
> I found the word on page _____ of a (glossary, thesaurus, dictionary).
>
> The meaning of the word I will use is _____.
>
> Here is a sentence using this meaning of my word: _____

Practice Text

Have students work with a partner, and provide them with thesauruses, dictionaries, and books with glossaries. Ask each pair to choose an interesting word and fill in the information about the word.

 If your class includes English learners or other students who need support, use "Strategies to Support ELs."

Share Selected Words

Invite pairs to share their responses. Ask the following questions:
- *Why did you choose this word?*
- *Does the word have more than one meaning? Which meaning did you choose? Why?*
- *How can writers use dictionaries, glossaries, and thesauruses to make their writing better?*

 ## Independent Writing and Conferring

Say: *Dictionaries, glossaries, and thesauruses are three different tools that you can use to determine or clarify the meaning and pronunciation of words you want to use in your texts. If you're writing about a specific topic, you can often find a word you need in the glossary of a nonfiction book about that topic. Otherwise, you can look up the word in a print or digital dictionary or thesaurus. Making sure that our words mean what we think they mean is a courtesy to our readers and helps them better enjoy and understand our texts.*

If you would like to give students additional practice using reference materials, have them complete Use Dictionaries, Glossaries, and Thesauruses (BLM 20).

 ## Share

Bring students together. Review and provide corrective feedback based on students' answers to BLM 20. Ask students to share what they learned about using dictionaries, glossaries, and thesauruses.

Strategies to Support ELs

Emerging (Beginning)

Support beginning ELs by working together to look up words in a glossary of a very familiar book they have already read, a thesaurus, and a dictionary. For each word, read the pronunciation and definition together and use it in an oral sentence.

Expanding (Intermediate) and Bridging (Advanced)

Pair ELs with fluent English speakers to complete the practice activity.

All Levels

Invite students to bring any dictionaries they have in their homes to share with the class.

Use Similes and Metaphors

L.4.5a

Objectives

In this mini-lesson, students will:

- Understand the purpose of and differences in similes and metaphors.

- Explain the meaning of simple similes and metaphors.

- Identify similes and metaphors in sentences and use them in writing.

Preparation

Materials Needed

- Use Similes and Metaphors (BLM 21)

 **Focus**

Explain Similes and Metaphors

Say: *Authors often use special techniques called figurative language to make their writing more colorful and interesting. When we read these expressions, we sometimes have to use our imaginations to help us picture what the author means. Two types of figurative language are similes and metaphors.*

Explain that a simile compares two things using the word **like** or **as**, while a metaphor compares them by saying that one actually is the other.

 Display the example Similes and Metaphors Chart.

	What does it do?	What are the key words?	What is an example?	What does it mean?
simile	compares two things with some characteristics in common	**like** or **as**	The princess looked as pretty as a picture.	The princess was exceptionally pretty.
metaphor	compares two unlike things	**is**, **are**, **was**, or **were**	The Internet is a treasure chest of information.	The Internet is full of valuable items, such as facts, maps, videos, and photographs.

Example Similes and Metaphors Chart

Say: *The simile uses the word **as** to compare a pretty princess to a pretty picture. The metaphor uses the word **is** to speak about the Internet as if it is an actual treasure chest. Both types of figurative language paint pictures in our minds that help us understand what the author is trying to describe.*

Model Using Similes and Metaphors

 Display the modeling texts. Read aloud the first modeling text.

Laura's hair was shiny.	Laura's red hair shone like a penny.
The playground has a lot of activity.	The playground was a beehive of activity.

Modeling Text 1   Modeling Text 2

Say: *These sentences sound a little dull and boring. Let's see what happens when the writer uses a simile and metaphor to give them more pizzazz.*

Read aloud the second modeling text.

Say: *The writer used the word **like** to create a simile in the first sentence, comparing Laura's red hair to a shiny penny. The writer then used a metaphor in the second sentence by calling a playground another busy place—a beehive.*

The simile and metaphor help us better visualize and understand this character and setting. We would never turn every sentence into a simile or metaphor.

 **Rehearse**

Practice Using Similes and Metaphors

 Display the practice text.

Similes

1. The circus swept through the town like a tornado.

2. Once I burrowed under my blankets, I was as warm as toast.

Metaphors

1. The fog was a gray wall between the house and the street.

2. Worries are weeds in the garden of your mind.

Practice Text

Ask students to work with a partner to read each sentence and write what the simile or metaphor compares and what it means.

 If your class includes English learners or other students who need support, use "Strategies to Support ELs."

Share Practice Sentences

Invite pairs to share their responses. Ask the following questions:

- *What key words do you see in the similes? What do they compare? What do they mean?*
- *What key words do you see in the metaphors? What do they compare? What do they mean?*
- *Why is it important for writers to learn about similes and metaphors? How do similes and metaphors benefit readers?*

 # Independent Writing and Conferring

Say: *You can use similes and metaphors in your writing to make it more descriptive and inviting. Both of these types of figurative language can help readers visualize, make connections, and make inferences about the characters, plot, and setting of a story. A good way to become proficient in using similes and metaphors is to pay special attention to those you hear and read. You can also set aside a page in your writing notebook to begin collecting examples to use in your own texts.*

 If you would like to give students additional practice using similes and metaphors, have them complete Use Similes and Metaphors (BLM 21).

 **Share**

 Bring students together. Review and provide corrective feedback based on students' answers to BLM 21. Ask students to share what they learned about similes and metaphors.

Strategies to Support ELs

Emerging (Beginning)

Beginning ELs will need additional support and practice to understand similes and metaphors. Write the key words **like** and **as** (similes) and **is, are, was,** and **were** (metaphors) on index cards. Hold up the correct card as you state a simple simile or metaphor, such as *The night seemed as dark as ink* or *The baby's smile was sunshine on a rainy day.* Help students form simple similes and metaphors as well, suggesting familiar objects and ideas they might use in their comparisons.

Expanding (Intermediate) and Bridging (Advanced)

Pair ELs with fluent English speakers to complete the practice activity.

Use Idioms, Adages, and Proverbs

L.4.5b

Objectives

In this mini-lesson, students will:

- Understand the purposes of idioms, adages, and proverbs.
- Explain the meaning of common idioms, adages, and proverbs.
- Identify idioms, adages, and proverbs in sentences and use them in writing.

Preparation

Materials Needed

- Use Idioms, Adages, and Proverbs (BLM 22)

 **Focus**

Explain Idioms, Adages, and Proverbs

Say: *Authors often use special techniques called figurative language to make their writing more colorful and interesting. When we read these expressions, we sometimes have to use our imaginations to help us picture what the author means. Today we will discuss idioms, adages, and proverbs.*

Explain that these types of figurative language are all sayings in which we need to look beyond their literal meanings.

 Display the example Idioms, Adages, and Proverbs Chart.

	What is it?	What is an example?	What does it mean?
idiom	a saying that addresses someone or describes a person, object, or situation	Shake a leg! My famous chocolate chip cookies will knock your socks off!	Hurry up! You will be amazed!
adage or proverb	a saying that shares an observation, advice, or wisdom gained from personal experience	Don't judge a book by its cover.	Don't form opinions based on how someone looks; get to know them.

Example Idioms, Adages, and Proverbs Chart

Say: *This idiom has nothing to do with socks, and this adage or proverb has nothing to do with books. Instead, the listener or reader has to understand or figure out the true meaning of the words.*

Point out that the words **adage** and **proverb** are often used interchangeably. Then explain that different cultures have different idioms, adages, and proverbs and that learning the meaning of these sayings is an important part of learning that culture's beliefs, customs, and language.

Model Using Idioms, Adages, and Proverbs

 Display the modeling texts. Read aloud the first modeling text.

"My brother still hasn't apologized for losing my book," said Courtney. "That makes me so mad! I'm going to march right in there and tell him how I feel." "I don't think you should mention it again," said Marisa. "I happen to know that he's saving his allowance to buy you a new copy."	"My brother still hasn't apologized for losing my book," said Courtney. "That really gets my goat! I'm going to march right in there and tell him how I feel." "I think you should let sleeping dogs lie," said Marisa. "I happen to know that he's saving his allowance to buy you a new copy."
Modeling Text 1	**Modeling Text 2**

Grade 4 • ©2017 Benchmark Education Company, LLC

Say: *This conversation presents an interesting scene. However, the writer has underlined two places where an idiom, adage, or proverb would fit. Let's see what happens when the writer uses some old sayings.*

Read aloud the second modeling text. Point out that Courtney used the idiom "That really gets my goat" to describe her feelings. Marisa used the proverb "let sleeping dogs lie" to give advice to Courtney. The idiom and proverb express the same ideas in a more creative way.

 ## Rehearse

Practice Using Idioms, Adages, and Proverbs

 Display the practice text. Ask students to work with a partner to read each sentence and write what the underlined idiom, adage, or proverb might mean.

> 1. "You said you'd contribute to mom's birthday gift," said Taylor. "Put your money where your mouth is!"
>
> 2. "Don't worry about memorizing your solo yet," said Tim's trumpet teacher. "We'll cross that bridge when we come to it."
>
> 3. "I'm going to try to read another chapter of my book while the baby naps," said Mom. "I've got to make hay while the sun shines!"

Practice Text

 If your class includes English learners or other students who need support, use "Strategies to Support ELs."

Share Practice Sentences

Invite pairs to share their responses. Ask the following questions:
- *What do you think each idiom, adage, or proverb means?*
- *Why is it important for writers to learn about idioms, adages, and proverbs?*
- *What do these types of figurative language add to our texts?*

 # Independent Writing and Conferring

Say: *You can use idioms, adages, and proverbs in your writing to make it more descriptive and to convey—or have your characters convey—observations, advice, and wisdom. Careful use of these types of figurative language can make your writing more interesting and inviting, too. A good way to become proficient in idioms, adages, and proverbs is to pay special attention to those you hear and read. You can also set aside a page in your writing notebook to begin collecting examples to use in your own texts.*

If you would like to give students additional practice using idioms, adages, and proverbs, have them complete Use Idioms, Adages, and Proverbs (BLM 22).

 ## Share

Review and provide corrective feedback based on students' answers to BLM 22. Ask students to share what they learned about idioms, adages, and proverbs.

Strategies to Support ELs

Emerging (Beginning)

To help beginning ELs better understand idioms, adages, and proverbs, provide several examples that have clear literal and nonliteral meanings. One by one, sketch or act out the literal meaning. Then sketch or act out the actual meaning. Invite students to join you in thinking of situations where you might use each one. Following are some examples: *Don't cry over spilt milk. An apple a day keeps the doctor away. If the shoe fits, wear it. The grass is always greener on the other side. Quit horsing around! I have butterflies in my stomach. It's raining cats and dogs!*

Expanding (Intermediate) and Bridging (Advanced)

Pair ELs with fluent English speakers to complete the practice activity.

Use Synonyms and Antonyms

L.4.5c

Objectives

In this mini-lesson, students will:

- Recognize synonyms and antonyms in texts.
- Demonstrate understanding of words by relating them to their synonyms and antonyms.
- Write sentences that contain synonyms and antonyms as context clues.

Preparation

Materials Needed

- Dictionaries and thesauruses
- Use Synonyms and Antonyms (BLM 23)

 **Focus**

Explain Synonyms and Antonyms

Say: *When we read, we use synonyms and antonyms to help us figure out the meaning of new words. As writers, we can include synonyms and antonyms as context clues for our readers, too. We can use information from a dictionary or thesaurus as well.*

 Display the example Synonyms and Antonyms Chart.

Word: unique	
synonyms: words with similar but not identical meanings	The antique store downtown specializes in unique, one-of-a-kind furniture and knickknacks, while the store on State Street carries more common, run-of-the-mill items.
antonyms: words with opposite meanings	

Example Synonyms and Antonyms Chart

Say: *By using synonyms and antonyms in these sentences, the writer supports the meaning of the word* **unique** *while clearly describing how the two antique stores have different goals and purposes.*

Model Using Synonyms and Antonyms

 Display the modeling text.

I'd probably destroy anything I tried to create on the sewing machine, but my friend Krista can fashion beautiful cushions out of things like old sweaters and shirts.

Some people think my brother is industrious and hard-working, but he was just plain lazy when it was time to clean the garage.

Modeling Text

Say: *Each of these sentences has both a synonym and antonym to support the meaning of the boxed word.*

Help students determine that **create** is a synonym for **fashion** and **destroy** is an **antonym**, and **hard-working** is a synonym for **industrious** and **lazy** is an **antonym**. Remind them that using synonyms and antonyms is a good way to provide context clues for words readers might find unfamiliar.

 **Rehearse**

Practice Using Synonyms and Antonyms

 Display the practice text.

> sympathetic
> glistening
> proclamation
> tranquil
> inconsiderate

Practice Text

Ask students to work with a partner, choose one of the words, and write a sentence using that word along with at least one synonym or antonym that gives more information about the word's meaning. Remind them that they can use a dictionary or thesaurus to help them.

 If your class includes English learners or other students who need support, use "Strategies to Support ELs."

Share Practice Sentences

Invite pairs to share their responses. Ask the following questions:
- *What does your word mean?*
- *What synonym(s) and/or antonym(s) did you include in your sentence?*
- *How will these context clue(s) help readers better understand your word?*

 # Independent Writing and Conferring

Say: *You already use synonyms and antonyms as a reader. The similar and opposite meanings that writers add to their sentences help you picture and understand what new words mean. Now it's time to start helping your readers by adding synonyms and antonyms as context clues for tricky words. This extra information will make the tricky words easier to figure out and make your writing more effective than ever.*

If you would like to give students additional practice using synonyms and antonyms to their writing, have them complete Use Synonyms and Antonyms (BLM 23).

 **Share**

Bring students together. Review and provide corrective feedback based on students' answers to BLM 23. Ask students to share what they learned about synonyms and antonyms.

Strategies to Support ELs

Emerging (Beginning)

Support beginning ELs in using synonyms and antonyms by looking up words in a thesaurus, listing the synonyms and antonyms, and using them in oral sentences. Then invite students to dictate sentences using one word as a context clue to another as you record them on the board, such as *The elderly man seemed young again as he played with his grandson.* Repeat the process with additional words.

Expanding (Intermediate) and Bridging (Advanced)

Pair ELs with fluent English speakers to complete the practice activity.

Use Domain-Specific Words

L.4.6

 **Focus**

Objectives

In this mini-lesson, students will:

- Understand the concept of domain-specific words.
- Identify and generate domain-specific words.
- Use domain-specific words in their writing.

Preparation

Materials Needed

- Use Domain-Specific Words (BLM 24)

Explain Domain-Specific Words

Say: *When authors write about a particular topic, they use many words that relate to that topic. These are called domain-specific words. For example, if you read a text about animal preservation, you are likely to see the words* **wildlife, conservation,** *and* **endangered.** *Using domain-specific words helps us write more accurately and with greater detail.*

 Display the example text.

> In colonial America, not all children went to school. Those who did started in what was called a dame school. Because books were very expensive, young children often learned their letters from a hornbook, a piece of wood with the alphabet on one side and a story on the other. Towns with more than fifty families were required to build common schools.

Example Text

Say: *This writer used the domain-specific words* **colonial, dame school, hornbook,** *and* **common schools** *in this passage. Without these words, the text would be much less interesting and informative. Often writers acquire the domain-specific words they need for their texts while doing research on their topics. In nonfiction books, these words are often defined in the text and/or included in the glossary.*

Model Using Domain-Specific Words

 Display the sample Domain-Specific Words Chart.

Topic: Solar System	
solar system	the sun and all the bodies that orbit it
planets	large bodies in space that orbit the sun
moons	bodies that orbit a planet
comets	balls of ice, rock, and dust that orbit the sun
asteroids	chunks of rock that orbit the sun
meteoroids	asteroids that come near Earth
meteors	meteoroids that burn as they move through Earth's atmosphere
meteorites	meteors that fall to the Earth
stars	gigantic, burning balls of gas that produce heat and light
sun	the star at the center of our solar system

Sample Domain-Specific Words Chart

Say: *This chart shows how one writer took notes on domain-specific words to use while writing about the solar system. You can create a chart like this when you are doing research for your next writing assignment.*

Rehearse

Practice Using Domain-Specific Words

 Display the practice text.

ocean life
rattlesnakes
Egypt
rainforests
magnets
lightning

Practice Text

Have students work with a partner. Ask each pair to choose one of the topics on the list (or one of their own choosing), do some basic research, and make a chart with at least three domain-specific words and their definitions.

 If your class includes English learners or other students who need support, use "Strategies to Support ELs."

Share Charts

Invite pairs to share their responses. Ask the following questions:
- *What topic did you choose? What domain-specific words did you choose?*
- *How is each word connected to the topic? How would using these words make an informational text about your topic more interesting and informative?*

Independent Writing and Conferring

Say: *Today we discussed, identified, and located domain-specific words for various topics. Effective writers take notes about domain-specific words they want to include in their texts. Using these words gives our informational texts the detail they need to keep our readers' attention and help them learn more about the topics we choose.*

 If you would like to give students additional practice using domain-specific words, have them complete Use Domain-Specific Words (BLM 24).

Share

Bring students together. Review and provide corrective feedback based on students' answers to BLM 24. Ask students to share what they learned about domain-specific words.

Strategies to Support ELs

Emerging (Beginning)

Help beginning ELs better understand the concept of domain-specific words by studying the glossaries of familiar nonfiction texts. Locate the words in the text and read the sentences they are used in. If the words are bold-faced at first use, point that out as well. Discuss how each word is connected to the topic and what readers learn from the author's use of the word. Finally, name a topic you have studied this year and ask students to help you generate a list of domain-specific words they learned.

Expanding (Intermediate) and Bridging (Advanced)

Pair ELs with fluent English speakers to complete the practice activity.

Name _____   Date _____

Use Relative Adverbs

Directions: Read each sentence. On the line, write the relative adverb that correctly replaces the underlined phrase.

1. _____ The West is the region <u>in which</u> Nevada is located.

2. _____ Montana, another state in the West, has land <u>on which</u> archeologists have dug up dinosaur bones.

3. _____ One reason <u>for which</u> the West was difficult to settle is the presence of the Sierra Nevada mountain range.

4. _____ The 1930s were a time <u>in which</u> many dams were built across rivers in the West.

5. _____ The Sonoran Desert is the area <u>at which</u> you can experience the highest temperatures in North America.

6. _____ August 21, 1959, was the day <u>on which</u> Hawaii joined the West as the fiftieth state in the United States.

7. _____ Hollywood is one reason <u>for which</u> people are drawn to Los Angeles in the West.

Name _____   Date _____

Use Relative Pronouns

Directions: Read each sentence. Find the relative pronoun and draw a line under the relative clause it introduces. Then draw a circle around the word or phrase the relative clause describes.

1. A group of people whom we call the Aztec once ruled a powerful empire in Mexico.

2. Their capital was a large city that stood where Mexico City is today.

3. An eagle, which stood on a cactus eating a snake, showed them where to build their city.

4. The farmers, who were able to grow more food than they needed, used the extra food to trade with other people.

5. In 1376, the Aztec chose a king whose ancestors were very important people.

6. Armies led by a man named Cortés conquered the lands that belonged to the Aztec in 1521.

7. Archeologists who have excavated the area have found around 6,000 objects from the time of the Aztec.

Name _____   Date _____

Use Progressive Verb Tenses

A. Directions: Read each sentence. Then write if the sentence is written in present progressive, past progressive, or future progressive tense.

1. _____ I <u>am waiting</u> impatiently for the mail carrier.

2. _____ Paul <u>was making</u> some delicious pies and cakes for the bake sale.

3. _____ People <u>will be paying</u> my aunt to knit sweaters for them.

4. _____ My grandparents <u>were enjoying</u> a vacation to the mountains last week.

5. _____ The boys, though they are best friends, <u>are fighting</u> like cats and dogs.

B. Directions: Complete the chart.

Present Progressive Tense	Past Progressive Tense	Future Progressive Tense
am throwing		
	was recovering	
is listening		

Name _____   Date _____

Use Modal Auxiliaries

Directions: Read the passage. Draw a circle around the modal auxiliary that best fits the meaning of each sentence.

Have you ever been in an earthquake? If not, perhaps you (may can) imagine how startling it is when the ground begins to shake. Even during a small earthquake, you (will would) feel a little shaking. Pictures hanging on the walls (might should) move back and forth. Dishes (must may) rattle. Tall, lightweight objects like lamps (would could) fall over.

A stronger earthquake (would should) be even more frightening—and dangerous. In these situations, police officers, firefighters, medics, specially trained dogs, and military personnel (must might) spring into action. We (may should) also express our admiration for groups like the Red Cross who provide rescue workers, tents, blankets, food, water, and medicine to earthquake victims around the world.

Name _____ Date _____

Order of Adjectives Chart

Opinion	nice, lovely, expensive, delicious
Size	big, little, long, short
Feels/Looks	hot, dry, soft, shiny
Age	old, young, ancient, antique
Shape	square, skinny, round, chunky
Color	blue, white, clear, colorful
Nationality	American, Canadian, Mexican, Italian
Material	wooden, silver, silk, plastic
Purpose	gardening (gloves), baseball (players), book (report), city (hall)

Name _____   Date _____

Order Adjectives Within Sentences

Directions: Complete each sentence by adding at least two appropriate adjectives and the noun they describe on the blank. Refer to the Order of Adjectives Chart to make sure your adjectives are in conventional order.

1. My grandmother discovered a _____ in a secondhand store.

2. We were impressed when our food arrived on _____ _____.

3. My sister and I made some _____ to take to the party.

4. "This _____ needs to go in the rag bag," said Mom.

5. Our family adopted a _____ from the animal shelter.

6. My cousin was curious when a _____ arrived in the mail.

Name _____ Date _____

Use Prepositional Phrases

A. Directions: Read the passage. Circle the prepositions and underline the prepositional phrases that they introduce.

The first cattle in North America came from Spain. The Spanish brought longhorn cattle to Mexico when they settled there in the 1500s. The cattle were not fenced, and many strayed from their owners in a search for grass and water. Over hundreds of years, some longhorns roamed north to Texas. The abundant grasslands on the Texas plains could feed many head of cattle. In time, there were millions of longhorn cattle in Texas.

B. Directions: Using prepositions from the passage above, write two sentences that each include at least one prepositional phrase. Draw a circle around each preposition you use.

1. _____

_____

2. _____

_____

Name _____   Date _____

Use Complete Sentences

Directions: These sentences or pairs of sentences contain fragments or run-ons. Rewrite them on the lines as complete sentences.

1. You can help your body fight disease. By making it as strong as possible.

   _____

2. You need to eat a balanced diet and get enough sleep and exercise you must follow good health habits.

   _____

   _____

3. You grow your body's needs will change.

   _____

4. Just as it is important to do the right things for your body. It is important not to do the wrong things.

   _____

   _____

5. You've only got one body you need to treat it right.

   _____

Name _____ Date _____

Use Frequently Confused Words

Directions: Read each set of homophones. Write a sentence that includes both words, circling the homophones. Use a dictionary to clarify the words' meanings if needed.

1. see, sea

_____

2. board, bored

_____

3. pair, pear

_____

4. paws, pause

_____

5. clothes, close

_____

6. hour, our

_____

Name _____   Date _____

Use Correct Capitalization

A. Directions: Draw a circle around the proper nouns in each sentence.

1. Our family used to live on cactus court by the walmoth river in baldwin, tennessee.

2. Author ludwig bemelmens wrote a famous book called *madeline* about a parisian schoolgirl.

3. In the united states, labor day is the first monday in september.

4. We used *let's investigate marvelously meaningful maps* as a resource for our research project in mr. gardner's class at kennedy intermediate school.

5. My sister kira bought some rad red razzamatazz to serve at the valentine's day party.

B. Directions: Write a sentence that includes words from at least three categories of proper nouns.

_____

_____

_____

Name _____   Date _____

Use Commas and Quotation Marks

Directions: Read each sentence. Rewrite the sentence as direct speech or a quotation using commas and quotation marks.

DIRECT SPEECH

1. Marta whispered to her brother Brad that he should take off his cap.

_____

2. Mom remarked that she'd never experienced such a cold winter.

_____

QUOTATIONS

3. Wayne Gretzky said that you miss 100 percent of the shots you never take.

_____

4. Benjamin Franklin declared that well done is better than well said.

_____

Name _____   Date _____

Use Commas in Compound Sentences

Directions: Combine each pair of sentences into a compound sentence. Use the coordinating conjunction that best fits the meaning of the sentence. Remember to use a comma before the conjunction.

| for | and | nor | but | or | yet | so |

1. Millions of types of organisms live on Earth. Scientists developed a way to classify them by traits.

_____

2. The original classification had only two groups inside each kingdom. Now there are six.

_____

3. Anthropologists are experts on fossils, ancient bones, and artifacts. They still have much to learn about human life long ago.

_____

4. A skeleton discovered in Africa in 1974 gave us valuable information. It is the most complete skeleton ever found of an early human.

_____

_____

Name _____ Date _____

Use Spelling Reference Materials

Directions: Think of a word that fits each description, and write it on the line. Look up the word in a print or digital dictionary or other available reference. Check the word to make sure you've spelled it correctly. If needed, correct your spelling.

1. An animal that uses quills to protect itself _____

2. Something two things have in common; the opposite of **difference** _____

3. A school where people go to study after high school; sometimes called a college _____

4. A skilled worker who knows how to install and repair wiring in a house or other building _____

5. To go faster, especially in a vehicle _____

6. A trait that describes a person who always wonders about things and wants answers to his or her questions _____

Name _____   Date _____

Use Precise Words and Phrases

A. Directions: Read each word or phrase. Beside it, write a related word or phrase that is more interesting or precise. If needed, use a thesaurus to help you.

pet	
look at	
large	
nicely	
test	
laugh	
red	
sadly	

B. Directions: Choose three words from the right column above. Use each word in a sentence.

1. _____

2. _____

3. _____

Name _____   Date _____

Use Punctuation for Effect

Directions: Read each sentence. Name the punctuation mark used to connect, introduce, or add information. Then write what the punctuation mark does in that sentence.

Sentence	Name of Punctuation Mark	What the Punctuation Mark Does
The word **photography** comes from the Greek language; it means "to write or draw with light."		
Photography shows us how nature looks in far parts of the world—such as exotic animals, plants, and environments.		
Nature photographers pay attention to the same things artists do: colors, lines, curves, and layout.		
Many people enjoy photographing nature. (For some people, it's a career.)		
"In this book you will learn about . . . scenery that can be found in nature . . . the living things that inhabit nature . . . and . . . the power of nature."		

Name _____   Date _____

Formal and Informal English Chart

When giving a presentation . . .	In a small-group discussion . . .
You are likely the only person speaking, so all the attention is on you.	Several people carry the conversation.
Your tone is more serious.	The tone is more casual.
Your sentences are complete, and your grammar is correct.	Participants may use some incomplete sentences, so grammar rules are sometimes "bent."
You use fewer contractions and little or no slang or idioms.	Participants use frequent contractions and may use some slang or idioms.
You likely use a larger, more specific vocabulary.	Participants may use a smaller vocabulary.
You rely less on body language and facial expressions; instead, your meaning is in the words themselves.	Participants rely on body language and facial expressions to reinforce meaning.
You plan and compose your thoughts before stating them, but you're not always aware if your listeners accurately hear or understand what you say.	Ideas are often exchanged rapidly with little planning, but participants can easily repeat or reword their thoughts if others don't hear or understand.

Name _____   Date _____

Use Formal and Informal English

Directions: The letter below is very informal. However, the situation calls for more formal language. On the lines below, rewrite the letter to better represent the style and tone that a proposal from a student should reflect.

Dear Mrs. Carlin,

I heard you fell and broke your ankle . . . yikes! My class needs to do our weekly service project, so we thought we'd ask if we could come help you. Off the top of my head, I'd say you could use someone to walk the dog, sweep the floor, and weed the garden. Right? Anyway, please call 316-7758 if you're up to it. Talk soon!

Your neighbor,
Maria

_____

_____

_____

_____

_____

_____

Name _____   Date _____

Use Context Clues

Directions: Read the sentences. Add words or phrases that provide context clues about the underlined words. Use a dictionary or thesaurus if needed.

1. An animal's <u>instinct</u> is _____.
(definition or description)

2. Some animals must live in or around <u>seawater</u>, while other animals

require a _____ habitat.
(antonym)

3. Some animals protect themselves with different forms of

<u>camouflage</u>, such as _____
(examples)

_____.

4. A predator is an animal that <u>survives</u>, or _____,
(synonym)

by hunting and eating other animals.

Name _____ Date _____

Use Greek and Latin Roots and Affixes

Directions: Read each Greek or Latin root. List at least three words that contain the root, using a dictionary if needed. Then choose one of your words to use in a sentence.

Root	Word List	Sentence
bio ("life")		
gram ("letter, written")		
vac ("empty")		

Name _____   Date _____

Use Dictionaries, Glossaries, and Thesauruses

Directions: Read each pair of easily confused words. Write the correct word on the line to complete each sentence. Use reference materials as needed.

1. **preposition   proposition**

    We made a _____ to our teacher about how to spend indoor recess.

2. **moral   morale**

    The _____ of the fable is to be happy with what you have, because you will miss it when it's gone.

3. **latter   later**

    I could have checked out a sports book or a science book,

    but I decided on the _____.

4. **incredible   incredulous**

    I was _____ when I heard that Kristen and I won first place at the science fair.

5. **envelop   envelope**

    Because the temperature is expected to fall below freezing,

    we're going to _____ the plants in plastic overnight.

Name _____ Date _____

Use Similes and Metaphors

A. Directions: Read each sentence. Write an **S** if it includes a simile. Write an **M** if it includes a metaphor.

1. _____ My big brother's stomach is a bottomless pit.

2. _____ The dew on the flowers sparkled like diamonds.

3. _____ Quit sitting there like a bump on a log and help me rake the leaves!

B. Directions: Complete each sentence using a known or original simile.

1. Put on these mittens; your hands are as _____.

2. My cousin got the lead in the musical because she sings like

_____.

3. The seats in these bleachers are as _____.

C. Directions: Complete each sentence using a known or original metaphor.

1. The raindrops were _____.

2. I like having Jules in my project group because he's

_____.

3. Mom is getting a new computer since hers is _____.

Name _____ Date _____

Use Idioms, Adages, and Proverbs

Directions: Choose three of the idioms, adages, or proverbs. For each one, write a sentence or pair of sentences that uses the figurative language in a way that expresses its true meaning.

If it isn't broken, don't fix it.

Don't cry over spilled milk.

I'm going to turn over a new leaf.

He tried to pull the wool over my eyes.

It's time to throw in the towel.

Two wrongs don't make a right.

A good beginning makes a good ending.

I'm going to hit the books.

That makes me see red!

If the shoe fits, wear it.

1. _____

_____

2. _____

_____

3. _____

_____

Name _____ Date _____

Use Synonyms and Antonyms

Directions: Complete the chart. Use a dictionary or thesaurus for help as needed.

Word	Synonym	Antonym	Example Sentences
inconsiderate			
valiant			
baffled			
famished			
skeptical			
trudged			
nuisance			
agitated			

Name _____   Date _____

Use Domain-Specific Words

Directions: Read each passage. Draw a circle around the domain-specific words.

Your brain is the control center of the body. The brain sends and receives messages from all the other parts of your body through pathways that contain nerve cells. The brain consists of three main parts. One part is the brain stem, which connects the brain to the spinal cord. The other two parts are the cerebrum and the cerebellum.

Different kinds of maps present information about different topics. However, some features appear in most maps. The most common map features are scale (the relationship between a distance on a map and the actual distance); symbols and keys (pictures that represent information on a map); coordinates (a system that locates things on a map in a grid); and relief (the height of land as shown on a map).

Sound waves in air act like waves in water. The highest part of a wave is the crest. The lowest part is the trough. The distance from crest to crest or trough to trough is the wavelength. A wave with a short wavelength passes a fixed point frequently, so we say it has a high frequency. A wave with a long wavelength has a low frequency.

Answer Keys for Language BLMs 1–4

LANGUAGE BLM 1

Name _____ Date _____

Use Relative Adverbs

Directions: Read each sentence. On the line, write the relative adverb that correctly replaces the underlined phrase.

1. _**where**_ The West is the region in which Nevada is located.

2. _**where**_ Montana, another state in the West, has land on which archeologists have dug up dinosaur bones.

3. _**why**_ One reason for which the West was difficult to settle is the presence of the Sierra Nevada mountain range.

4. _**when**_ The 1930s were a time in which many dams were built across rivers in the West.

5. _**where**_ The Sonoran Desert is the area at which you can experience the highest temperatures in North America.

6. _**when**_ August 21, 1959, was the day on which Hawaii joined the West as the fiftieth state in the United States.

7. _**why**_ Hollywood is one reason for which people are drawn to Los Angeles in the West.

LANGUAGE BLM 2

Name _____ Date _____

Use Relative Pronouns

Directions: Read each sentence. Find the relative pronoun and draw a line under the relative clause it introduces. Then draw a circle around the word or phrase the relative clause describes.

1. A (group of people) whom we call the Aztec once ruled a powerful empire in Mexico.

2. Their capital was a large (city) that stood where Mexico City is today.

3. An (eagle,) which stood on a cactus eating a snake, showed them where to build their city.

4. The (farmers,) who were able to grow more food than they needed, used the extra food to trade with other people.

5. In 1376, the Aztec chose a (king) whose ancestors were very important people.

6. Armies led by a man named Cortés conquered the (lands) that belonged to the Aztec in 1521.

7. (Archeologists) who have excavated the area have found around 6,000 objects from the time of the Aztec.

LANGUAGE BLM 3

Name _____ Date _____

Use Progressive Verb Tenses

A. Directions: Read each sentence. Then write if the sentence is written in present progressive, past progressive, or future progressive tense.

1. _present progressive_ I am waiting impatiently for the mail carrier.

2. _past progressive_ Paul was making some delicious pies and cakes for the bake sale.

3. _future progressive_ People will be paying my aunt to knit sweaters for them.

4. _past progressive_ My grandparents were enjoying a vacation to the mountains last week.

5. _present progressive_ The boys, though they are best friends, are fighting like cats and dogs.

B. Directions: Complete the chart.

Present Progressive Tense	Past Progressive Tense	Future Progressive Tense
am throwing	was throwing, were throwing	will be throwing
am recovering, is recovering, are recovering	was recovering	will be recovering
is listening	was listening, were listening	will be listening

LANGUAGE BLM 4

Name _____ Date _____

Use Modal Auxiliaries

Directions: Read the passage. Draw a circle around the modal auxiliary that best fits the meaning of each sentence.

Have you ever been in an earthquake? If not, perhaps you (may can) imagine how startling it is when the ground begins to shake. Even during a small earthquake, you (will would) feel a little shaking. Pictures hanging on the walls (might should) move back and forth. Dishes (must may) rattle. Tall, lightweight objects like lamps (would could) fall over.

A stronger earthquake (would should) be even more frightening—and dangerous. In these situations, police officers, firefighters, medics, specially trained dogs, and military personnel (must might) spring into action. We (may should) also express our admiration for groups like the Red Cross who provide rescue workers, tents, blankets, food, water, and medicine to earthquake victims around the world.

Answer Keys for Language BLMs 6–9

Name _____ Date _____

Order Adjectives Within Sentences

Directions: Complete each sentence by adding at least two appropriate adjectives and the noun they describe on the blank. Refer to the Order of Adjectives Chart to make sure your adjectives are in conventional order.
[SAMPLE RESPONSES]

1. My grandmother discovered a _beautiful shiny red rocking chair_ in a secondhand store.

2. We were impressed when our food arrived on _fancy china serving plates_ _____.

3. My sister and I made some _scrumptious soft sugar cookies_ to take to the party.

4. "This _holey old striped T-shirt_ needs to go in the rag bag," said Mom.

5. Our family adopted a _sweet furry English sheepdog_ from the animal shelter.

6. My cousin was curious when a _large flat cardboard envelope_ arrived in the mail.

Name _____ Date _____

Use Prepositional Phrases

A. Directions: Read the passage. Circle the prepositions and underline the prepositional phrases that they introduce.

The first cattle (in) North America came (from) Spain. The Spanish brought longhorn cattle (to) Mexico when they settled there (in) the 1500s. The cattle were not fenced, and many strayed (from) their owners (in) a search (for) grass and water. Over hundreds (of) years, some longhorns roamed north (to) Texas. The abundant grasslands (on) the Texas plains could feed many head (of) cattle. (In) time, there were millions (of) longhorn cattle (in) Texas.

B. Directions: Using prepositions from the passage above, write two sentences that each include at least one prepositional phrase. Draw a circle around each preposition you use.
[SAMPLE RESPONSES]

1. I removed the sticker (from) the vase and filled it (full) of flowers.

2. We moved (to) this city when I was (in) kindergarten.

Name _____ Date _____

Use Complete Sentences

Directions: These sentences or pairs of sentences contain fragments or run-ons. Rewrite them on the lines as complete sentences.
[SAMPLE RESPONSES]

1. You can help your body fight disease. By making it as strong as possible.

   You can help your body fight disease by making it as strong as possible.

2. You need to eat a balanced diet and get enough sleep and exercise you must follow good health habits.

   You need to eat a balanced diet, get enough sleep and exercise, and follow good health habits.

3. You grow your body's needs will change.

   As you grow, your body's needs will change.

4. Just as it is important to do the right things for your body. It is important not to do the wrong things.

   It is just as important not to do the wrong things to your body as it is to do the right things.

5. You've only got one body you need to treat it right.

   You've only got one body, so you need to treat it right.

Name _____ Date _____

Use Frequently Confused Words

Directions: Read each set of homophones. Write a sentence that includes both words, circling the homophones. Use a dictionary to clarify the words' meanings if needed.
[SAMPLE RESPONSES]

1. see, sea

   I can't wait to (see) my cousin Lenny and hear about the (sea) animals he observed on his vacation to the ocean.

2. board, bored

   I love to draw, so I'm never (bored) when I have a dry-erase (board) and markers in my hands.

3. pair, pear

   We had three bananas, a (pair) of apples, and one (pear) left in the fruit bowl.

4. paws, pause

   Please (pause) a moment to wipe the dog's muddy (paws) before you walk on the carpet.

5. clothes, close

   I'm going to (close) the closet door after I put the rest of my (clothes) away.

6. hour, our

   I'm so excited (our) awards assembly begins in less than an (hour).

Answer Keys for Language BLMs 10–13

LANGUAGE BLM 10

Name _____ Date _____

Use Correct Capitalization

A. Directions: Draw a circle around the proper nouns in each sentence.

1. Our family used to live on (cactus court) by the (walmoth river) in (baldwin, tennessee.)

2. Author (ludwig bemelmens) wrote a famous book called (madeline) about a (parisian) schoolgirl.

3. In the (united states,) (labor day) is the first (monday) in (september.)

4. We used (let's investigate marvelously meaningful maps) as a resource for our research project in (mr. gardner's) class at (kennedy intermediate school.)

5. My sister (kira) bought some (rad red razzamatazz) to serve at the (valentine's day) party.

B. Directions: Write a sentence that includes words from at least three categories of proper nouns.
[SAMPLE RESPONSE]
My baby brother Andrew was born on March 14 at St. Andrew's Hospital near Grandma Lou's house.

LANGUAGE BLM 11

Name _____ Date _____

Use Commas and Quotation Marks

Directions: Read each sentence. Rewrite the sentence as direct speech or a quotation using commas and quotation marks.
[SAMPLE RESPONSES]

DIRECT SPEECH

1. Marta whispered to her brother Brad that he should take off his cap.

   Marta whispered, "Brad, you should take off your cap."

2. Mom remarked that she'd never experienced such a cold winter.

   "I've never experienced such a cold winter," Mom remarked.

QUOTATIONS

3. Wayne Gretzky said that you miss 100 percent of the shots you never take.

   Wayne Gretzky said, "You miss 100 percent of the shots you never take."

4. Benjamin Franklin declared that well done is better than well said.

   "Well done is better than well said," declared Benjamin Franklin.

LANGUAGE BLM 12

Name _____ Date _____

Use Commas in Compound Sentences

Directions: Combine each pair of sentences into a compound sentence. Use the coordinating conjunction that best fits the meaning of the sentence. Remember to use a comma before the conjunction.

for	and	nor	but	or	yet	so

[SAMPLE RESPONSES]

1. Millions of types of organisms live on Earth. Scientists developed a way to classify them by traits.

   Millions of types of organisms live on Earth, so scientists developed a way to classify them by traits.

2. The original classification had only two groups inside each kingdom. Now there are six.

   The original classification had only two groups within each kingdom, but now there are six.

3. Anthropologists are experts on fossils, ancient bones, and artifacts. They still have much to learn about human life long ago.

   Anthropologists are experts in the study of human beings, yet they still have much to learn about life long ago.

4. A skeleton discovered in Africa in 1974 gave us valuable information. It is the most complete skeleton ever found of an early human.

   A skeleton discovered in Africa in 1974 gave us valuable information, for it is the most complete skeleton ever found of an early human.

LANGUAGE BLM 13

Name _____ Date _____

Use Spelling Reference Materials

Directions: Think of a word that fits each description, and write it on the line. Look up the word in a print or digital dictionary or other available reference. Check the word to make sure you've spelled it correctly. If needed, correct your spelling.

1. An animal that uses quills to protect itself _____ porcupine

2. Something two things have in common; the opposite of **difference** _____ similarity

3. A school where people go to study after high school; sometimes called a college _____ university

4. A skilled worker who knows how to install and repair wiring in a house or other building _____ electrician

5. To go faster, especially in a vehicle _____ accelerate

6. A trait that describes a person who always wonders about things and wants answers to his or her questions _____ curiosity

---

Answer Keys for Language BLMs 14–18

Name _____ Date _____

Use Precise Words and Phrases

A. Directions: Read each word or phrase. Beside it, write a related word or phrase that is more interesting or precise. If needed, use a thesaurus to help you.

[SAMPLE RESPONSES]

pet	parakeet
look at	observe
large	sizeable
nicely	agreeably
test	assessment
laugh	guffaw
red	scarlet
sadly	miserably

B. Directions: Choose three words from the right column above. Use each word in a sentence.

[SAMPLE RESPONSES]

1. In science class, we learn to observe processes and take notes.

2. "Yes, you may borrow my colored pencils for your project," Connor said agreeably.

3. The scarlet cardinals swarmed to the birdfeeder and brightened our snowy backyard.

Name _____ Date _____

Use Punctuation for Effect

Directions: Read each sentence. Name the punctuation mark used to connect, introduce, or add information. Then write what the punctuation mark does in that sentence.

Sentence	Name of Punctuation Mark	What the Punctuation Mark Does
The word **photography** comes from the Greek language; it means "to write or draw with light."	semicolon	separates two closely related independent clauses
Photography shows us how nature looks in far parts of the world—such as exotic animals, plants, and environments.	em dash	breaks into the end of the sentence with examples of nature in far parts of the world
Nature photographers pay attention to the same things artists do: colors, lines, curves, and layout.	colon	introduces details about what nature photographers pay attention to
Many people enjoy photographing nature. (For some people, it's a career.)	parentheses	adds a piece of information about nature photographers
"In this book you will learn about . . . scenery that can be found in nature . . . the living things that inhabit nature . . . and . . . the power of nature."	ellipses	shorten a quote

Name _____ Date _____

Use Formal and Informal English

Directions: The letter below is very informal. However, the situation calls for more formal language. On the lines below, rewrite the letter to better represent the style and tone that a proposal from a student should reflect.

Dear Mrs. Carlin,

I heard you fell and broke your ankle . . . yikes! My class needs to do our weekly service project, so we thought we'd ask if we could come help you. Off the top of my head, I'd say you could use someone to walk the dog, sweep the floor, and weed the garden. Right? Anyway, please call 316-7758 if you're up to it. Talk soon!

Your neighbor,
Maria

[SAMPLE RESPONSE]

Dear Mrs. Carlin,

The students in my class are very sorry to hear that you fell and broke your ankle. That must be very painful and inconvenient. If you are willing, we would like to come help you for our service project this week. For example, we could walk your dog, sweep your floor, and weed your garden. If you agree that we could be of assistance, please call 316-7758. We look forward to hearing from you soon!

Your neighbor,

Maria

Name _____ Date _____

Use Context Clues

Directions: Read the sentences. Add words or phrases that provide context clues about the underlined words. Use a dictionary or thesaurus if needed.

[SAMPLE RESPONSES]

1. An animal's instinct is a behavior that is not learned
(definition or description)

2. Some animals must live in or around seawater, while other animals require a freshwater habitat.
(antonym)

3. Some animals protect themselves with different forms of camouflage, such as body parts that look like plants or rocks; skin, feather,
(examples)
or fur color; and stripes, dots, or patterns that help them blend with their environment

4. A predator is an animal that survives, or lives
(synonym)
by hunting and eating other animals.

Answer Keys for Language BLMs 19–22

Name _____ Date _____

Use Greek and Latin Roots and Affixes

Directions: Read each Greek or Latin root. List at least three words that contain the root, using a dictionary if needed. Then choose one of your words to use in a sentence.

[SAMPLE RESPONSES]

Root	Word List	Sentence
bio ("life")	biology biography biochemistry biopsy biosphere biome	We study biology to learn about living things.
gram ("letter, written")	telegram diagram anagram monogram hologram grammar	My uncle has his monogram, or initials, on his luggage.
vac ("empty")	vacant vacation vacuum vacate evacuate medevac	The medevac rescued the injured soldiers and flew them to the nearest military hospital.

Name _____ Date _____

Use Dictionaries, Glossaries, and Thesauruses

Directions: Read each pair of easily confused words. Write the correct word on the line to complete each sentence. Use reference materials as needed.

1. **preposition   proposition**

   We made a _____proposition_____ to our teacher about how to spend indoor recess.

2. **moral   morale**

   The _____moral_____ of the fable is to be happy with what you have, because you will miss it when it's gone.

3. **latter   later**

   I could have checked out a sports book or a science book, but I decided on the _____latter_____.

4. **incredible   incredulous**

   I was _____incredulous_____ when I heard that Kristen and I won first place at the science fair.

5. **envelop   envelope**

   Because the temperature is expected to fall below freezing, we're going to _____envelop_____ the plants in plastic overnight.

Name _____ Date _____

Use Similes and Metaphors

A. Directions: Read each sentence. Write an **S** if it includes a simile. Write an **M** if it includes a metaphor.

1. __M__ My big brother's stomach is a bottomless pit.

2. __S__ The dew on the flowers sparkled like diamonds.

3. __S__ Quit sitting there like a bump on a log and help me rake the leaves!

B. Directions: Complete each sentence using a known or original simile.
[SAMPLE RESPONSES]
1. Put on these mittens; your hands are as _cold as ice_.

2. My cousin got the lead in the musical because she sings like _a nightingale_.

3. The seats in these bleachers are as _hard as rocks_.

C. Directions: Complete each sentence using a known or original metaphor.
[SAMPLE RESPONSES]
1. The raindrops were _ping-pong balls bouncing off our windshield_.

2. I like having Jules in my project group because he's _a fountain of creative ideas_.

3. Mom is getting a new computer since hers is _a dinosaur_.

Name _____ Date _____

Use Idioms, Adages, and Proverbs

Directions: Choose three of the idioms, adages, or proverbs. For each one, write a sentence or pair of sentences that uses the figurative language in a way that expresses its true meaning.

> If it isn't broken, don't fix it.
> Don't cry over spilled milk.
> I'm going to turn over a new leaf.
> He tried to pull the wool over my eyes.
> It's time to throw in the towel.
> Two wrongs don't make a right.
> A good beginning makes a good ending.
> I'm going to hit the books.
> That makes me see red!
> If the shoe fits, wear it.

[SAMPLE RESPONSES]

1. I've been lazy about practicing the piano, but starting today I'm going to turn over a new leaf.

2. Keisha should have asked before using your computer, but please don't pay her back by deleting her project. Two wrongs don't make a right!

3. I'm glad I got to sleep in, but now I need to do my homework. I'm going to hit the books.

Answer Keys for Language BLMs 23–24

Name _____ Date _____

Use Synonyms and Antonyms

Directions: Complete the chart. Use a dictionary or thesaurus for help as needed.

[SAMPLE RESPONSES]

Word	Synonym	Antonym	Example Sentences
inconsiderate	rude	polite	The inconsiderate student suddenly turned polite when the principal entered the room.
valiant	brave	frightened	The valiant firefighter reassured the frightened residents that she could lead them to safety.
baffled	confused	certain	I was confused by the first math problem, and I'm even more baffled by this one.
famished	hungry	stuffed	Are you as hungry as I am? I'm famished!
skeptical	uncertain	confident	Although some people are skeptical about the T-shirt design, I'm confident that it will be a popular item in our shop.
trudged	plodded	strode	The tired hikers trudged and plodded down the last hill.
nuisance	pest	delight	My little sister can be a nuisance sometimes, but she's always a delight to my grandparents.
agitated	upset	calm	Our calm dog only gets agitated when he sees a cat.

Name _____ Date _____

Use Domain-Specific Words

Directions: Read each passage. Draw a circle around the domain-specific words.

Your (brain) is the control center of the body. The brain sends and receives messages from all the other parts of your body through pathways that contain (nerve cells). The brain consists of three main parts. One part is the (brain stem), which connects the brain to the (spinal cord). The other two parts are the (cerebrum) and the (cerebellum).

Different kinds of (maps) present information about different topics. However, some features appear in most maps. The most common map features are (scale) (the relationship between a (distance) on a map and the actual distance); (symbols) and (keys) (pictures that represent information on a map); (coordinates) (a system that locates things on a map in a (grid); and (relief) (the height of land as shown on a map).

(Sound waves) in air act like waves in water. The highest part of a wave is the (crest). The lowest part is the (trough). The distance from crest to crest or trough to trough is the (wavelength). A wave with a short wavelength passes a fixed point frequently, so we say it has a high (frequency). A wave with a long wavelength has a low frequency.

Responsive Conferring Prompts to Support and Scaffold Writers

Responsive **Conferring Prompts** to Support and Scaffold Writers

Skilled writers apply their understanding of genre, text structure, author's craft, and grammar and conventions as they formulate ideas and develop them through the stages of process writing.

Use the gradual-release prompts and tools provided in this flip chart to scaffold student writers toward independent writing across a range of genres and text types.

Text Types	Definition	Examples of Genres
Informational **I**	Informational texts provide facts and details about a topic. They reflect one or more nonfiction text structures: sequence of events, compare/contrast, problem/solution, cause/effect, descriptive. Informational texts may include a range of text and graphic features to support the facts and details.	• Informational Reports • Procedural Texts • Biographies • Research Reports
Narrative **N**	Narrative texts tell a fictional story or an account of a factual sequence of events. Narrative texts usually include characters or real people, a setting, a problem, and a resolution. The events may be told from the first- or third-person point of view.	• Historical Fiction • Journals • Memoirs • Personal Narratives • Realistic Fiction • Science Fiction
Persuasive **P**	Persuasive texts are designed to influence the audience. The writer states a position and provides supporting facts as well as emotional appeals to convince the audience to support his or her point of view.	• Book Reviews • Persuasive Essays • Persuasive Letters

Dear Teacher,

In school and beyond, your students will be required to read, understand, and write a wide range of genres. These genres fall into three major text types. This flip chart is designed to help you support students' writing development across these genres and text types by conducting meaningful writer's workshop conferences and differentiating your interactions to match students' needs as they progress through the gradual release stages toward writing proficiency.

Process Writing Steps

Brainstorm Ideas

Good writers use their knowledge, memories, experiences, and feelings to generate ideas for a text.

▶ Goal Oriented

I I will look at these [books, photos, websites] to get my ideas flowing.

N I need to think about interesting problems a character could have.
N I will use photographs to remind me of events in my life.

P I will list issues I feel strongly about.
P I will think about books I want to evaluate for others.

▶ Directive and Corrective Feedback

I Think of topics you know about.
I Name subjects you think readers will want to learn about. Write those down.

N What are some real-life problems a character could have?
N Imagine if you lived in ____. What problems might you have?
N Close your eyes and look at your past like a movie. What do you see?

P Tell me an issue you feel strongly about. What is your position?
P What is something you would like to change at school or at home?

▶ Self-Monitoring and Reflection

I What could you do to help yourself think about informational topics?
I Did you try remembering topics [you have studied/you know about]?

N How did you use your own experiences to help you find ideas?
N How could visualizing help you brainstorm?

P What strategies helped you think of ideas for your [review, letter, essay]?

▶ Validating and Confirming

I I noticed the way you looked at [books, magazines, websites] to get ideas.
I I would be interested in reading about those topics! Nice brainstorming!

N You closed your eyes and visualized. That was a great strategy to use!
N You brainstormed some very interesting problems a character could have.

P I watched you talk with your peers to help you formulate ideas. That seemed to help you a lot.
P It's not easy to think of issues. You really worked hard at it.

Brainstorm Ideas

Brainstorming List

1.
2.
3.
4.
5.
6.

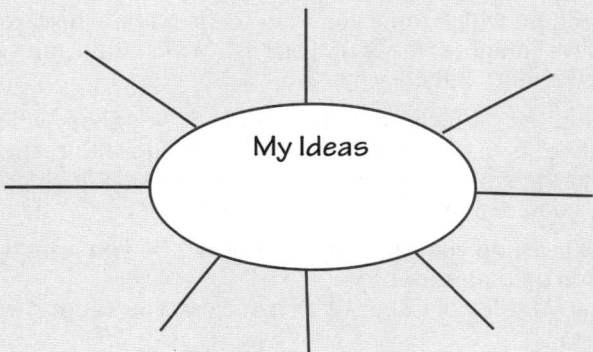

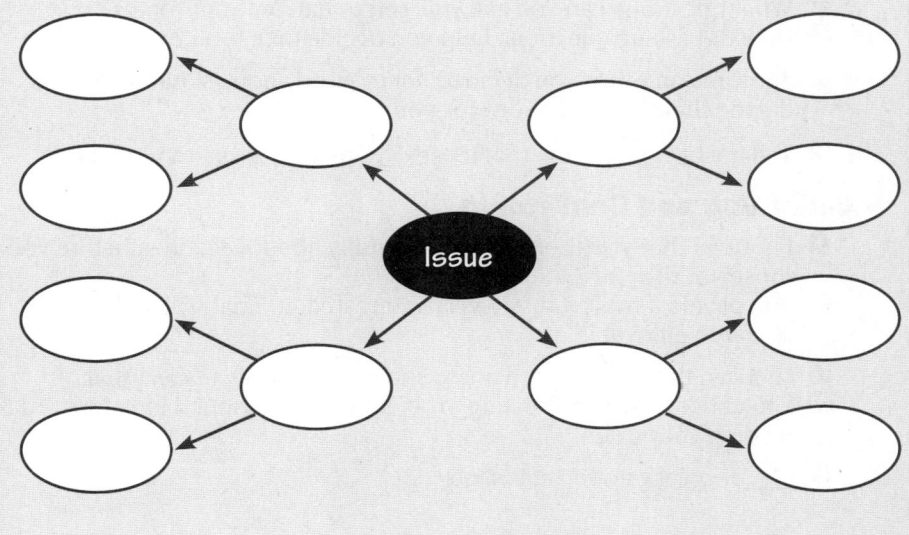

Narrow the Focus

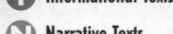
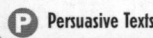

I Informational Texts
N Narrative Texts
P Persuasive Texts

Good writers ask questions to help them evaluate and choose the best idea for them to write about.

▶ Goal Oriented

I I will think about which topic I am most interested in researching.

N I'm going to think about which event I am most interested in sharing.

P I will think about which issue I can support with two or three good arguments.

▶ Directive and Corrective Feedback

I Think about which topic you want to spend time researching.
I You have [number] ideas on your list. Which topic are you most excited about? Tell me why.

N Ask yourself, "Which event in your life do you think will make the best narrative? Is that a subject you want to share with readers?"
N Look at the story problems you brainstormed. Which problem can you find a good resolution for?

P Which issue do you care about the most? Do you want to share your position on that issue?
P Look at your list of issues. Which one can you support with solid facts and details?

▶ Self-Monitoring and Reflection

I What questions can you ask yourself to narrow your topics?
I How did asking questions help you decide on a topic?

N Show me an event you decided *not* to write about. What made you decide that wasn't the idea for you?

P Tell me how you came to choose _____ as your issue to write about.

▶ Validating and Confirming

I I noticed that you thought very carefully about each idea before you chose your topic.
I You picked a topic you are very interested in. That will make doing research enjoyable.

N I noticed that you decided not to share _____. I really respect that.
N You chose a very interesting problem to write about. I look forward to reading your draft.

P _____ is a very important issue!

Ideas	Question 1	Question 2	Question 3

Ideas	Yes	No	Maybe

Process Writing Steps

Research

**Good writers conduct research to support their
ideas and opinions.**

▶ Goal Oriented

I I will look at many sources, including nonfiction books, magazine articles, and reliable websites to find out about ____.

I I am going to take notes and document my sources as I conduct research.

N My story is set in ____. I will find out about how people lived in that time and place by ____.

N I will find out about [subject] by reading and interviewing [his/her] family.

P I need to look for facts that support my position.

P I need to interview sources that people will respect.

▶ Directive and Corrective Feedback

I You want to research ____. Where can you find information about that?

I Who could you interview about ____? Tell me three things you could ask.

N What questions can guide your research about that time and place?

N Your story has a character who ____. What should you know about that topic before you start writing?

P You want me to believe that ____. What [facts, data, statistics] would convince me?

P Who could you interview about this issue? What kind of quote would help you make your case?

▶ Self-Monitoring and Reflection

I Tell me your plan for gathering information. What sources will you use?

I Look at your research questions. Will these questions help you get the information you need for an interesting report? Why, or why not?

N Tell me what you need to know about ____ to make your story believable.

P How will you gather facts that support your point of view?

▶ Validating and Confirming

I Your research questions are well constructed!

I You found reliable [university, museum, government] Internet sources.

N Reading about daily life in [historical time period] was a great way to help you imagine what your characters' daily lives would be like.

N Researching [scientific topic] helped you make your sci-fi plot plausible.

P You developed some very strong arguments for your [letter, essay]. I look forward to reading your draft!

Outline

I. First topic sentence: _____

  A. First supporting detail

  B. Second supporting detail

  C. Add more entries as needed.

2. Second topic sentence: _____

  A.

  B.

  C.

3. Third topic sentence: _____

  A.

  B.

  C.

Subject	Source 1	Source 2	Source 3
Question:			
Question:			
Question:			

Organize Ideas

Good writers use many strategies and tools to organize their ideas before they draft.

(I) Informational Texts
(N) Narrative Texts
(P) Persuasive Texts

▶ Goal Oriented

(I) I am going to categorize my information to help me structure the paragraphs in my report.

(I) I will think about the order of my steps so my procedure makes sense.

(N) I'll use a sequence of events chart to jot down the events I'll write about.

(P) I need to think of two or three good arguments to support my position.

(P) My judgment about this book is ____. I'll jot down the evidence I'll use to support that judgment.

▶ Directive and Corrective Feedback

(I) Put your facts into categories. The categories can be the sections of your report.

(I) Visualize the steps in your procedure. Write them down in order.

(N) Think of events that will lead from the problem to the resolution.

(N) You decided to write about ____. Now think about the sequence of events you will include.

(P) Think about the facts and details you will use to make your case.

(P) Jot down your judgment of the book. Plan the specific evidence you'll use to support your judgment.

▶ Self-Monitoring and Reflection

(I) What could you do to help yourself organize your research findings?

(I) Take a look at your main ideas and details. Do you feel you are ready to draft? Why, or why not?

(N) What graphic organizer could help you organize your story events?

(N) Tell me how you went about organizing your narrative.

(P) Now that you have a [persuasive letter, essay] topic, how will you organize your ideas?

(P) How did organizing your [persuasive letter, essay, review] help you get ready to write?

▶ Validating and Confirming

(I) You organized your report into [number] well-defined sections.

(I) You generated very interesting facts to support your main ideas!

(N) You developed a detailed sequence. This will be very helpful as you draft.

(N) The events you organized lead to a [surprising, fun, etc.] resolution.

(P) You planned some strong arguments for your [letter, essay].

Organize Ideas

Problem:

Position:

Audience:

Arguments/ Reasons	Facts/ Evidence

Solution:

Topic:

Specific Focus:

Research Question:

Research Findings	Details
1.	a.
	b.
	c.
2.	a.
	b.
	c.
3.	a.
	b.
	c.

Solution:

Subject:

Important Life Events:

Date	Events

Personality/Characteristics:

Trail	Examples

Conclusions:

Event	What I saw...	What I heard...	What I smelled...	What I felt...	What I tasted...

Conclusion:

I Informational Texts
N Narrative Texts
P Persuasive Texts

Beginning to Draft

Good writers use their research, their organizing charts, and their creativity to get ideas on paper.

▶ Goal Oriented

I I'm going to use the research I organized to help me start to draft.
I I'm not going to worry about my spelling or punctuation right now. I'll just get my ideas on paper.

N I will use my [type of organizing chart] to help me get started.
N I will think of an interesting beginning that will get my readers hooked.

P I will state my position right at the beginning of my [letter, essay].
P When I write a review, I need to identify the book title right away.

▶ Directive and Corrective Feedback

I How could you introduce your topic in a way that gets readers interested?
I Look at your organizing chart. What is the first fact you want to share?

N Imagine you're the character. What is happening at the beginning of the story? Remember to develop the problem.
N Visualize the setting. What do you want readers to see in their minds?

P Tell me what your position is on _____. How can you say that in the beginning of your [essay, letter] so that readers pay attention?
P Remember the features of a [review, letter, essay] that your draft needs to include.

▶ Self-Monitoring and Reflection

I Did you look at your organizing chart? How did it help you?
I Did you use any strategies, like visualizing or asking yourself questions, to help you? Tell me about that.

N Show me where you used sequence signal words in your narrative.
N Show me how you gave information about your characters and setting.

P What was the hardest part of beginning your [review, letter, essay]?
P Show me where you've stated your position. Now show me what facts you are using to support your position. Where will you go from here?

▶ Validating and Confirming

I Your lead got me interested right away. Keep going!
I You made good progress today getting your facts down.

N I can visualize where your [narrative, story] takes place. You've included some nice details about the setting.

N You've developed an interesting problem in your [narrative, story]. I'm curious to find out what happens next.

P You stated your position right up front. That really got me to pay attention.
P You used some good supporting facts. You really got me thinking about the issue.

Draft Genre Texts Features of Informational Genres

Biography	Informational Report
☐ Starts with a strong hook ☐ Tells the subject's date and place of birth ☐ Tells about the subject's family, childhood, and important events ☐ Describes the subject's personality and characteristics ☐ Quotes the subject and/or people who knew the subject ☐ Describes the subject's impact on the world	☐ Has a strong beginning that hooks the reader ☐ Information is accurate and the facts have been checked ☐ Uses primary sources when appropriate ☐ Includes graphics that support the text ☐ Has a logical organization of major concepts ☐ Includes multiple perspectives so that a reader can draw his or her own conclusions ☐ Has a strong ending that keeps readers thinking
Procedural Texts	**Research Report**
☐ The title clearly identifies the topic ☐ The introduction tells why the reader will want to make or do the activity or project ☐ Supplies or equipment are listed in the order they are used ☐ Directions are given as numbered steps or in short paragraphs with signal words ☐ Most sentences are short and direct and begin with verbs.	☐ Has a strong beginning that hooks the reader ☐ Information is accurate and the facts have been checked ☐ Uses primary sources when appropriate ☐ Includes graphics that support the text ☐ Has a logical organization of major concepts ☐ Includes multiple perspectives so that a reader can draw his or her own conclusions ☐ Has a strong ending that keeps readers thinking

During Drafting

Good writers use their research, their organizing charts, and their creativity to get ideas on paper.

▶ Goal Oriented

I I'm going to think about what I want my readers to know about ____.
I I need to be very clear about my steps so my readers can follow them.

N I'm going to watch the scene in my mind and then write what I see.
N I need to concentrate on how my character will resolve [his/her] problem.

P I will make sure I support the position I stated in the beginning of my [letter, essay].
P I just thought of a new argument to support my position. It's not on my organizing chart, but I will use it anyway.

▶ Directive and Corrective Feedback

I If you're stuck, go back to your organizing chart. Look at the main ideas you wanted to include.

N What happens next in your narrative? What do you want to say?
N Tell me what you felt when ____. Now add that to your draft.

P Go back and reread what you wrote so far. That will help you figure out what do say next.
P What information can you add to make me want to agree with you about ____ ?

▶ Self-Monitoring and Reflection

I Have you included all of the facts you want to share about ____?
I Have you thought about how you will end your report?

N Show me how you're making the sequence of events easy to follow?
N In the beginning, you set up the problem. How are you planning to develop that problem and move toward the resolution?

P You're arguing that ____. What would somebody who doesn't agree with you say? How can you use that to help your argument?
P A review includes [title, author, summary, opinions, supporting details]. Remember to check that you are addressing [this feature] as you draft.

▶ Validating and Confirming

I Your writing is answering a lot of my questions about ____ as I read!
I I can see every step of this process. I know I could follow these directions.
I I learned something new from reading this!

N This part made me want to [laugh, cry, get angry, etc.].
N These details draw a picture in my mind of ____.
N I think this character is ____ because of the way you said ____.

P Your arguments are making me stop and think about this issue.
P It was very effective when you gave the other side's argument and explained why it was wrong.

Draft Genre Texts Features of Narrative Genres

Historical Fiction	Memoir
☐ Takes place in an authentic historical setting ☐ The events did occur or could have occurred in the setting ☐ At least one character deals with a conflict ☐ The story is told from a first- or third-person point of view ☐ Dialogue is made up but may be based on letters, a diary, or a report	☐ Is written in the first person ☐ Focuses on a short period of time or several related events in a person's life ☐ Focuses on events the way the author remembers them ☐ Includes the author's thoughts and feelings about the events ☐ Includes story elements such as plot, setting, and character development ☐ Often includes an ending that makes readers think
Personal Narratives	Realistic Fiction
☐ Focuses on one particular incident in the author's life ☐ Includes specific details about the time, place, and people involved ☐ Includes dialogue ☐ Includes the author's thoughts and feelings as well as the actual events	☐ Story takes place in an authentic setting ☐ At least one character deals with a conflict ☐ Story is told from a first- or third-person point of view ☐ The characters are like people you might meet in real life
Science Fiction	Mystery
☐ Imagines the effect of science and technology on people and society ☐ Has an element that is based on scientific fact ☐ Can have a realistic or fantastic, futuristic setting ☐ Frequent themes include aliens, parallel universes, space and time travel, and inventions that go out of control ☐ Often makes a point about how we live today ☐ Tone is more often dark than light	☐ Plot revolves around solving a crime ☐ An amateur or professional detective is the main character ☐ The detective uses analytic skills to solve the crime ☐ The detective uses previous knowledge to solve the crime ☐ There is a feeling of suspense ☐ The story may include a "red herring" ☐ The setting can be any time, any place ☐ The detective reveals the culprit at the end of the story

Draft Genre Texts Features of Persuasive Genres

Book Review	Persuasive Essay
☐ Gives the title and information about the author ☐ Includes a summary of the book ☐ Analyzes the characters, plot, and ideas ☐ Evaluates the characters, plot, and ideas ☐ Identifies the strengths and weaknesses ☐ Identifies the intended audience	☐ Has a strong position or point of view ☐ Uses facts and evidence to make a case ☐ Suggests solutions or actions and may include a counterargument ☐ Uses powerful words to influence the reader ☐ Has a specific audience in mind
Persuasive Letter	
☐ Has strong position or point of view ☐ Suggests solutions or actions ☐ Uses powerful words to influence readers ☐ Uses facts and evidence to make a case ☐ Has a specific audience in mind	

Process Writing Steps

 **I** Informational Texts
N Narrative Texts
P Persuasive Texts

Revise for Voice

Good writers reread and revise their drafts to make their voice stronger and more effective.

▶ **Goal Oriented**

I I need to sound like the expert in this report. I will look for ways to do that as I revise.

N My personality is not coming through enough in my narrative. I'm going to look for ways to add my own voice.
N I don't feel I'm making enough of a connection with my readers. I'll look for ways to do that as I revise.

P I am not showing my strong feelings. I'm going to work on that.
P I want to talk to my readers directly so they pay attention to my arguments. I'm going to look for places where I can do that.

▶ **Directive and Corrective Feedback**

I You are using "I" throughout your report. Go back and revise your sentences so that the voice is not so personal. Remember, in reports, you don't express opinions or feelings.

N How would you say that? Tell me in your own words.
N Try using dialogue here to establish [the character's] voice.

P You need to convince me. How can you get my attention in this [letter, review, essay]?
P Tell me in your own voice why I should read this book. Now go put that same enthusiasm into your review.

▶ **Self-Monitoring and Reflection**

I Show me how you connected to your audience in this report.
I Show me a part where you feel you came across as the expert.

N Show me where you put your own personality into the narrative.
N How could you give each character a different voice in the dialogue?

P In this paragraph you said ____. Does that sound like a fact or an opinion?
P Tell me what you did to make your voice persuasive. What strategies worked for you? What was your biggest challenge?

▶ **Validating and Confirming**

I I notice how you kept your own thoughts, feelings, and opinions out of the report and just told the facts.

N I really hear [your, your character's] voice in this paragraph.
N I notice you used [the idiom, figurative language, etc.] _____ in your dialogue. That really helped me hear your character's voice.

P You used [sarcasm, direct questions, etc.] when you said _____. That was a very effective way to make a connection with your readers.
P You spoke directly to me when you said _____. That got my attention.

Revise for Voice

Text Type	Ways to Add Your Voice
Informational Text	• Establish a tone of authority and confidence • Establish yourself as the expert (with limited use of the first person) • Include a storyline within the text
Narrative Text	• Differentiate characters' voices through dialogue • Interject your analysis • Interject your thoughts and feelings • Write it the way you would say it • Use the first-person point of view • Ask the reader a question
Persuasive Text	• Use formal and informal language to connect with your audience • Use "we" to form a bond with your reader • Use sarcasm to downplay the value of the opposing argument • Interject your thoughts and feelings about the issue • Interject comments that assume the audience feels the way you do • Ask the reader a question

I Informational Texts
N Narrative Texts
P Persuasive Texts

Revise for Word Choice

Good writers reread and revise their drafts to use words more effectively.

▶ Goal Oriented

I I am going to reread and look for places where I could make my writing more precise by using appropriate terminology.

I I am going to choose some better descriptive words. I want my readers to see pictures in their minds.

N I will reread to look for words I have overused. Varying my word choice will make my [story, narrative, memoir] more interesting to my readers.

P I need to find some stronger emotion words to persuade my readers.

▶ Directive and Corrective Feedback

I In a report, you want to use correct terms for your topic. How could you be more precise here? Go back to your sources and look for the correct terminology.

N Notice the [action words, descriptive words] in your [story, narrative]. How can you make them stronger?

N Let's read this paragraph. Are these the words this character would use? Tell me how [he/she] would say this.

P How do you want readers to feel about this topic? Now find some words to use that will make them feel that way.

P Think about the [plot, character, writing style] of this book. What words describe your opinion about it? Use those words in your review.

▶ Self-Monitoring and Reflection

I What are some ways you can improve your word choice when you go back to revise?

I Show me a part of your report where you feel you used [precise, technical] words really well. Show me a part where you could still improve your word choice.

N Show me where you revised some words to make your character's [personality, actions] clearer. How did your revision help?

N What words did you use to make your readers care about your issue?

P What quotes from the book did you use in your review to show your point of view?

▶ Validating and Confirming

I You used the term ____ to talk about ____. That word choice helped you sound like an expert in this report.

N Great adjectives in this paragraph! I really see what's happening.

N When your character said "____," [his/her] personality really came through on the page.

P The words ____ and ____ are very effective emotion words in this [letter, essay, review]. You're thinking about how to be persuasive.

Revise for Word Choice

Text Type	Ways to Strengthen Word Choice
Informational Text	• Use technical or academic terms • Select accurate, or precise, words to describe your subject • Ask yourself, "Will the reader understand what I am trying to say?" • Avoid repetition of the same word • Consult a thesaurus to find different words
Narrative Text	• Choose words that describe places and events • Choose words that describe characters' emotions • Choose words that describe characters' traits • Use dialogue to establish characters' traits • Use strong verbs • Use idiomatic expressions • Use figurative language to create sensory images • Use interjections • Avoid repetition of the same word • Consult a thesaurus to find different words • Think about how your character would say it • Show instead of tell the action
Persuasive Text	• Use formal and informal language to connect with your audience • Use "we" to form a bond with your reader • Use sarcasm to downplay the value of the opposing argument • Use strong verbs • Use subjective language rather than manipulative language • Use emotionally charged words to explain the problem and your position • Interject your thoughts and feelings about the issue • Ask the reader a question

Process Writing Steps

Informational Texts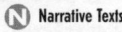
Narrative Texts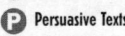
Persuasive Texts

Revise for Sentence Structure

Good writers reread and revise their drafts to improve their sentence structure.

▶ Goal Oriented

- **I** I am going to revise this part about _____ to vary my sentences. I know I won't hold readers' interest with so much repetition.
- **I** I started too many sentences with _____. I'm going to work on that part of my report.

- **N** I want to build some suspense in this scene. I'm going to use a series of short sentences to build excitement.
- **N** My sequence of events is a little confusing here. I'm going to go back and add some signal language to make the order of events clearer.

- **P** I like the argument I'm making here, but my sentences are too choppy. I'm going to combine these sentences about _____.

▶ Directive and Corrective Feedback

- **I** Look at this sentence. That's a run-on sentence. Think about how you can fix that.
- **I** Ask yourself, "Are these instructions easy to follow?" Try to make them more direct by starting with commands.

- **N** I got confused about the sequence when _____. Take another look at your verb tenses. Make sure they are consistent.
- **N** You can be creative with your sentences in a story. What could you do here to add [tension, suspense, excitement] about _____?

- **P** You could make a stronger case when you say _____. Try adding more information to that sentence.
- **P** I notice that many of your sentences start with _____. Your review will be more interesting if you vary those sentences. What could you change?

▶ Self-Monitoring and Reflection

- **I** What did you do to make your sentences varied and interesting?
- **I** Look at this paragraph. Tell me what you did here to make the steps clear.

- **N** Show me a part where you think your sentences could be better. What do you think you could do to improve them?
- **N** Show me some sentences that flow well. Why do you think they are successful?

- **P** Tell me how you revised words to make your arguments stronger.

▶ Validating and Confirming

- **I** I really enjoyed reading the information in this paragraph. The sentences were clear, varied, and easy to understand.
- **N** The phrase _____ gave a nice transition between _____ and _____.
- **N** You used short and long sentences really effectively in this paragraph.

- **P** I noticed how you talked about the past, the present situation, and what is going to happen in the future if things don't change. You used multiple tenses very effectively.
- **P** You included a fragment here on purpose, and it works really well.

Revise for Sentence Structure

Ways to Improve or Vary Sentence Structure

- Begin sentences with different words or phrases
- Use both short and long sentences
- Use dependent clauses in sentences
- Pay attention to verb tenses
- Use transitional words and phrases
- Break sentence structure rules for effect
- Combine sentences to form compound sentences
- Add more detail to elaborate
- Include questions to drive the text
- Avoid run-on sentences
- Begin sentences with command words
- Use multiple short sentences to build anticipation

Edit for Grammar and Conventions

Good writers edit their work to correct errors in grammar, punctuation, and spelling.

▶ Goal Oriented

- I I'm not sure I spelled this word ____ correctly. I am going to look back at my source and check the spelling.
- I I will read through my whole report and make sure that I have capitalized each sentence as well as the proper nouns I've used.
- N I notice I didn't put a comma after this sequence phrase. I'm going to add one right how.
- N I used a lot of dialogue in my [story, narrative]. I'm going to pay careful attention to how I punctuated those sentences.
- P I notice that I wrote some very emphatic sentences but I didn't use any exclamation points. I'm going to look carefully at my end punctuation.

▶ Directive and Corrective Feedback

- I Look at the word ____ in that sentence. Check your spelling in the dictionary.
- I I notice that your report includes many proper nouns. What do we need to do with proper nouns? That's right. They should be capitalized. Read through and find the proper nouns you haven't capitalized yet.
- N You started many sentences with dependent clauses. What is missing after each clause?
- N Look at this paragraph where ____ says ____. What's missing?
- P Read that sentence again. Does it sound right to you? Your noun and verb don't agree. How should you edit that?
- P When you write a book title, what do you need to do?
- P You wrote, "Dear ____." What's missing after the name?

▶ Self-Monitoring and Reflection

- I Show me a paragraph you edited for grammar. How did you improve it?
- I Show me some [technical, academic, scientific] words you checked in the dictionary.
- N Show me a sentence where you changed the punctuation. How did you know it was wrong?
- N Show me a place where you used commas correctly. What rule of punctuation did you apply?
- P You gave many statistics to support your position. Look at how you used numbers in the text. Were you consistent?

▶ Validating and Confirming

- I You spelled many difficult words correctly. Nice editing for spelling!
- N Your [story, narrative] included many compound sentences and you remembered where the commas should go!
- P Your letter included many possessives. I notice you were very careful to check them.
- P You used m-dashes very effectively to draw attention to your point.

Editing Checklist

Grammar
- [ ] Subject/verb agreement
- [ ] Nouns
- [ ] Verbs (past tense, irregular past tense)
- [ ] Adjectives
- [ ] Pronouns

Punctuation
- [ ] Periods
- [ ] Question marks
- [ ] Exclamation points
- [ ] Contractions
- [ ] Commas (series, compound sentences)
- [ ] Abbreviations
- [ ] Quotation marks

Capitalization
- [ ] Beginning of sentences
- [ ] Proper nouns
- [ ] Pronoun "I" in sentences
- [ ] Titles

Spelling Conventions
- [ ] Sight words
- [ ] Word wall words
- [ ] Content words

Writing Conventions
- [ ] Skip lines
- [ ] Spaces between words
- [ ] Legibility
- [ ] Paragraphs

Publish and Share

I Informational Texts
N Narrative Texts
P Persuasive Texts

Good writers select their best work to take to publication.

▶ Goal Oriented

I I will publish this report, because I think it represents my best work.

I I am going to find some photographs to use in my published report.

N I will focus on my title today. My [narrative, story] isn't ready for publication until I have a good title.

N I'm going to create a "Meet the Characters" spread to give readers some background about them.

P I will publish my letter about _____. While I researched and wrote that letter, I realized how important ____ is to me.

▶ Directive and Corrective Feedback

I Where are your sources? Remember, when you publish, you will need a bibliography to show readers where you got your information.

I Go back and think about graphic features to support your information.

N You still need a title for your [story, narrative, memoir]. Reread your text and jot down words that seem important to the events. They might help you.

N You need an author biography for our class story collection. Tell me what you'll say about yourself. Now go write the bio.

P Reread each letter. Ask yourself, "Which of these am I most proud of? Which of these do I want to share with the world?"

▶ Self-Monitoring and Reflection

I Tell me some formats in which you could publish your report.

I Have your considered what images will support your text? What thoughts do you have?

N How did you decide on that title for your [narrative, story]?

N Show me what you did to get your story ready for publication.

P Where could you submit this letter for publication?

P Tell me why you chose this book review to share.

▶ Validating and Confirming

I Your word-processed report is well-formatted!

I Readers will appreciate the photos and captions you added to your [report, biography, procedural]!

N The drawings you used in to your narrative really add to the story.

N Your title helps me predict what the story is about, but it doesn't give everything away. Nice work!

P It was clever and effective to make your persuasive letter look like a letter in the newspaper.

Informational Text	• Create a PowerPoint slide show and present it to another class • Create a hallway bulletin board for informational reports • Submit your report to a children's magazine (like *Highlights* or *Ranger Rick*) • Create a nonfiction book of related informational reports
Narrative Text	• Submit your story for publication • Invite parents to a reading • Create a class anthology to be placed in the school's library • Enter your story in a school-wide contest
Persuasive Text	• Send a letter to the editor of your local newspaper • Create a bulletin board of book reviews or persuasive letters • Launch a book review website on your school's server • Submit your book review or essay to a children's magazine

Responsive **Conferring Prompts** to Support and Scaffold Writers

Mentor writers at every step of the writing process with conferring prompts that target their individual needs!

Steps in the Writing Process

Step	Definition
Brainstorm Ideas	Good writers use their knowledge, memories, experiences, and feelings to generate ideas for a text.
Narrow the Focus	Good writers ask questions to help them evaluate and choose the best idea for them to write about.
Research	Many texts—informational, persuasive, and narrative—require writers to research facts and details. Good writers gather information from a variety of sources (including books, magazines, newspapers, primary source documents, movies, websites, and interviews). They take notes and document their sources.
Organize Ideas	Good writers use many strategies and tools to organize their ideas before they draft. Some writers plan in their heads. Others rehearse orally. And many writers use graphic organizers.
Draft	Good writers use their research, their organizing charts, and their creativity to get ideas on paper.
Revise	Good writers reread and revise their drafts to strengthen the voice, word choice, sentence structure, and organization of the text.
Edit	Before a text is final, good writers review it to find and correct errors in spelling, grammar, and punctuation.
Publish and Share	Writers select certain texts to publish and share with their audience. Writers publish their works in a variety of formats.

Notes

Notes